Culture
@ the
Cutting Edge

Culture @ the Cutting Edge

Tracking Caribbean Popular Music

Curwen Best

University of the West Indies Press
Jamaica • Barbados • Trinidad and Tobago

University of the West Indies Press
1A Aqueduct Flats   Mona
Kingston 7   Jamaica
www.uwipress.com

08 07 06 05 04   5 4 3 2 1

CATALOGUING IN PUBLICATION DATA

Best, Curwen
Culture @ the cutting edge: tracking Caribbean popular music / Curwen Best
p. cm.
Includes bibliographical references.

ISBN: 976-640-124-1

1. Popular music – Caribbean, English-speaking – History and criticism.
2. Music and technology. 3. Electronic music. 4. Calypso (music) – Caribbean,
English-speaking – History and criticism. 5. Gospel music – Caribbean,
English-speaking – History and criticism. 6. Sex in music. I. Title.

ML3486.B37 2004   780.'9729

Book and cover design by Robert Harris.
Set in Sabon 10.5/14 x 24

Printed in the United States of America.

To my wife, Charmaine.
To my family.

Contents

Acknowledgements / *viii*

Track 1   Reading Culture as Multi-tracked / *1*

Track 2   Sounding Calypso's Muted Tracks, Past and Present: Barbados + St Lucia / *10*

Track 3   Towards a Caribbean Gospel Aesthetic / *54*

Track 4   Discourses on AIDS (+ Sex) in Caribbean Music / *91*

Track 5   Finding the New Hardcore in Caribbean Music / *115*

Track 6   Music Video to Web Streaming: Cultural Ventriloquism @ the Leading Edge / *148*

Track 7   The "Big Technology" Question / *183*

Notes / *222*

Bibliography / *237*

Discography / *245*

Index / *249*

Acknowledgements

To God for the strength and ability. To my dear wife, Charmaine, who constantly discussed aspects of this work with me, and without whom I could not have fashioned such a work. To my parents, Orville and Gladys, and the rest of the family, God bless you all the time. To the chosen ones at www.prayline.com for intercession and inspiration. A. Brian Gooding for much. The Babb family. The staff at the University of the West Indies Press. To all those artists, practitioners, academics and people in the industry who shared experiences and information with me, directly and indirectly. You are all too many to mention here! The fellas @ Durhams N.T.C.O.G. To my past and present students of literature and popular culture. Again, to my wife for holding me up.

1/24

CC SALES

7590.26

AE	287.71
DSC	332.80
MC/V	16425.76

17,046.27

RETURN THIS PORTION WITH YOUR PAYMENT
REMITTANCE

FOR ORDER INQUIRIES & RETURN AUTHORIZATIONS CALL:
CUSTOMER SERVICE DEPARTMENT AT
    Phone: 1-800-996-6987
    Fax: 1-212-995-3833
    Email: nyupress.orders@nyu.edu
REMIT PAYMENT TO:
    New York University Press
    P.O. Box 7247 7435
    Philadelphia, PA 19170-7435

Reading Culture as Multi-tracked

What This Book Is About

The end of the twentieth century and the beginning of the twenty-first ushered in a new era in the evolution of Caribbean society, an era in which Caribbean culture came under significant influences, both external and internal. This has been an era of significant change. And no other facet of Caribbean culture reflects the tensions, compromises and complexities of this era like the region's music.

Culture @ the Cutting Edge is about popular music, music culture and culture generally. It is about modes of expression. It is about singing, songwriting, chanting and performing, both live and recorded. It is about the media through which these expressions are disseminated, including radio, television and new technologies of cultural diffusion, particularly the Internet. This focus offers critical insight into the ways in which Caribbean culture is mediated today, in the early twenty-first century.

This book centres the popular music of the anglophone Caribbean, but it does not set out to uphold the once-traditional tendency of pinning down Caribbean music discourse to just two islands: Jamaica and Trinidad. Having said this, I do not intend to deny the significant contribution of these two territories – they have been and continue to be major forces in the creation and expression of the region's music and culture – but I want to broaden the scope of Caribbean music-culture analysis to include some other islands of the region.

Many of the issues that this work treats are the subject of heated debate and discussion throughout the Caribbean. Some of these are issues not yet properly analysed, however, in "formal" critical writings. Formal criticism indeed lags far behind the creation, performance, production and dissemination of Caribbean culture. There are endless strands within Caribbean culture that must be felt out, traced and discussed. The reasons for the lack of criticism on issues at the cutting edge of Caribbean culture are varied. At the level of publication and production, there has been a tendency by some publishing houses to privilege studies which treat as wide a geographical area as possible, partly to ensure wider sale. The results of this tendency are apparent: some of these works have had to sacrifice depth for breadth of coverage. Some critical texts on aspects of Caribbean music are primarily responses to the marketing thrust and imperatives of publishers and educational institutions. Not enough of them spring directly from the vibes of the islands themselves, or from the experience of being confronted and challenged by the issues that pervade society.

Culture @ the Cutting Edge begins with all of this in sight. It is a critical response to some of the issues, phenomena and debates which are or have been contentious sites in Caribbean music culture. As such, it also responds to the critical silences on these issues, attempting to cover some new ground in criticism. Within the academy and in the wider society, there is a yearning for critical discussion of contemporary issues. But even as cultural studies and popular culture become increasingly centred by governments and universities within the region, there is still a lingering mistrust of studies not rooted in the traditional disciplines which colonial experience has encoded as legitimate. Hence, studies which sit within the liminal space between and at the cutting edge of disciplines can be victims of their own ambition.

The reference to the "cutting edge" in this book's title is significant in many respects. The title speaks of the work's engagement with Caribbean music in various spheres of manifestation. The book focuses on aspects of reggae, calypso, soca, gospel and new emerging forms such as raggasoca and ringbang. But it is also concerned with media and communications phenomena such as radio, television, the record and compact disc and, to some extent, the World Wide Web and the Internet. Underlying all these discussions is a concern with Caribbean societies, the societies that nurture these musical phenomena: the music and the societies share a discursive relationship that begs to be interrogated for its interactive properties.

This book examines the critical boundary between a series of binary categories: lyrics and music, the recorded and the "live", sound and video, the religious and the secular, the past and the present or future, tradition and innovation, production and dissemination, the real and the virtual. It is also critically aware of the relationship between Caribbean music and the music industry abroad, so that, for example, it examines the developments in Caribbean gospel in light of influences from Europe and the United States. And an entire chapter compares the alternative-rock music video with the dancehall music video. Some of the thematic debates dealt with include AIDS and homophobia, gospel culture, television culture, cyberculture, women and calypso, culture and exploitation, the labelling of musical styles, transnational companies and local culture, the reconfiguring of Caribbean culture, and technology and power.

The theoretical orientation of many sections of this text is not fixed in any one critical school or in its accompanying methodology or politics. In fact, I do not feel compelled to align this text neatly. My critical impetus is derived largely from an imperative to contextualize, to assess, to explicate and ultimately to stimulate debate. In this way, the work is useful to the uninitiated as well as to the connoisseur. It is necessary to relate to a variety of individuals and issues precisely because this new era of cultural development is one in which all of us are implicated. Society is therefore challenged to confront more rigorously the ways in which cutting-edge phenomena and technology have already begun to affect and help fashion this thing that we call Caribbean culture.

The region does not as yet have a substantial body of "formal" criticism which foregrounds a technology-sensitive reading of Caribbean culture. Let me demonstrate what I mean. Gordon Rohlehr, writing on Trinidad calypso, has focused on historical/social dynamics, which he fuses with incisive close readings of lyrics.[1] Carolyn Cooper, writing on Jamaican dancehall, privileges the "transgressive" through discussions of sexual politics rooted in a social, lyrical, paradigmatic critical practice.[2] Other recent writings on contemporary Caribbean music, by Peter Manuel and colleagues, Peter Van Koningsbruggen and John Cowley, are not concerned with going beneath the surface of the finished recorded product in order to interrogate the process of technical construction; their emphases lie elsewhere.[3] Indeed, all of these critics' emphases are vital. Caribbean critique is all the better because of these works. But you begin to sense that new ground begs to be broken. In addition to these foundational works, there is space for other kinds of discussions. The growing presence and power of leading-edge technology points the way towards future cultural criticism. So in this book, I perform what I call "multi-track readings", offering it as one path to follow.

The Internet and Caribbean Cyberculture

By the first decade of the twenty-first century, Caribbean culture was being experienced through new media and was being reshaped in the process. Caribbean cultural critique struggled to keep pace. Caribbean culture was in many respects high-tech, but cultural critique remained predominantly low-tech, rooted either in traditional practice or in early post-1980s praxis, paying reverence to poststructuralism, post-colonialism, feminism, nationalism, deconstruction or some other dominant Western mode of discourse. These modes were fine, but since so much of criticism proceeded on the premise of working out a theoretical and methodological approach, criticism staggered in dealing with new cultural developments and innovation.

The advent of the Internet and the popularization of the World Wide Web in the Caribbean raised fundamental questions relating to Caribbean culture. In recent history, Caribbean society was preoccupied with working towards national and regional community. These concepts of community have been at play among politicians and technocrats throughout the past two decades. The expansion of the Internet has brought into sharp focus the additional challenge of defining and harnessing the community of people who share in this regional identity and passion by way of real and virtual connection. Since 2000, many people outside the region have taken some active part in the experiences of Caribbean people. Those individuals are virtual participants in regional activity – reading regional newspapers online, following the fortunes of regional teams through streaming audio and video, supporting the region's initiatives on several fronts. The Internet has therefore challenged physical, temporal and spatial categories. Its presence and impact has opened up the domain of Caribbean experience to a potentially limitless number of participants. Some critical perspectives will embrace this reality, since it seems to open a door to unlimited possibilities. They will also point to the democratic and liberating experience of such cultural developments, as does John Perry Barlow of the Electronic Frontier Foundation.[4]

Caribbean criticism cannot avoid these issues. It must confront the new frontiers marked by the World Wide Web. The Web's near limitless portals, its lateral and vertical connectivity, anticipate a theoretical and cultural model that celebrates this complexity and apparent open-endedness. But approaches to the Internet must be aware of its attendant politics. Over the years communications and entertainment developments have worked to privilege some categories of people; the Internet is no less inscribed. It is not without its built-in systems. Hardware and software are the creation, property and preserve of specific groups of people. The World Wide Web does not operate independent of extant global corporations and interests – indeed, in many respects it functions to support more traditional corporations and institutions. This relationship is being altered from time to time. It is not always easy to discern how the alliances and power struggles are being formulated and contested. Caribbean cultural expression on show on the Internet is therefore always implicated in some way in the Web's "democratic" expression.

Regional expression is also enacted in the context of real and virtual culture wars. The Internet has its origin in military strategy. But the World Wide Web, which was launched in 1989, gave support to the non-military ambitions of the Internet. Questions of access to technology, the digital divide, privacy and intellectual property are now central to discussions that seek to formulate an understanding of Caribbean culture in the context of new technologies of this kind.

An innocent search for the concept "Caribbean culture" on any leading search engine reveals a hierarchical ranking of sites, which raises the question of the method by which this ranking is achieved. The realization that some companies engage in tech-spamming to achieve higher ranking than others points to the fact that the Internet cannot be taken at face value as a transparent, innocent, apolitical innovation. Caribbean people who participate in cyberculture are implicated in cyberculture's structure, systems, protocols and functioning. Caribbean society (like others) has yet to make sense of what the cyberworld is all about. Many academic and non-academic books have already been published about the Internet and other societies.[5] But relatively little has appeared that concentrates on the Caribbean. To that extent, there is the potential for unfair access, competition and exploitation on a number of fronts. It is possibly too early in the development of Caribbean cybertheory to make definitive conclusions, but it is evident that many youths have turned to the

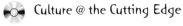

computer as a source of information, education and entertainment. Caribbean society can no longer ignore this phenomenon.

The Value of Reading Multi-tracked: Monophony, Polyphony and Multi-timbrality

This book recognizes that Caribbean music has increasingly come into contact with technology. In the 1980s, music technology began to affect Caribbean music like never before. Many of the new styles, such as dancehall, raggamuffin and, later, raggasoca and ringbang, have owed their developments to new "big technology". The effect of digital technology on Caribbean music in the last two decades of the twentieth century was indeed unprecedented. Musicians and laypeople have stood in awe and ignorance of this impressive leading-edge technology. This book therefore seeks to give a greater-than-usual presence to more technical issues, especially those relating to song and sound construction. *Culture @ the Cutting Edge* begins to assess the role of cutting-edge technology in Caribbean popular culture discourse. The final "track" (chapter) in this book is more direct, discussing the music technology itself. This is not, however, a book which foregrounds technology at the expense of other emphases; rather, it assesses the technological by way of amplifying more conventional readings of Caribbean music and culture.

My concept of a multi-track reading practice is based on the construction and production technology of music, sound and film. It considers the ways in which technology constructs and produces its finished products for consumption.[6] It recognizes that these products (such as a recorded song) are made up of a series of separate though related parts which have been fine-tuned and streamlined during the process of construction. In the recording studio, the music engineer sits before a state-of-the-art sound-mixing console,[7] receiving and controlling individual parts of a song on independent channels.[8] Each part is treated to an unlimited amount of technological processing before it is combined with the others in the final mix-down, for consumption.[9]

A multi-tracked reading is aware of this process and seeks to engage cultural phenomena by reading them backwards, if you will, interrogating the production process, de-scribing, unmixing the cultural product. It therefore concerns itself with analysing individual tracks of cultural data to come to terms with the ideology which is built into the production process. Thus, a multi-tracked reading can slow down the moving picture or break down a recorded song to analyse minute technological practices, which can then open up perception to radical ways of understanding cultural products and phenomena.

The practice of unmixing is not, however, a process of playful indulgence. Rather, it represents an act of constructing fuller knowledge about cultural tracks or data. Again, this method is firmly rooted in the production practices of the 1980s and later. It was only then, in the 1980s, that this technology came into wide use. Later in this book, I perform a close multi-track reading of innovative hardcore soca in order to demonstrate how Caribbean music was being reconfigured by technology in the 1980s – indeed, how Caribbean culture is presently being co-constructed by technology.

Multi-track reading practices are sensitive to the technological, musical, lyrical and performance components of texts. Such analyses engage with the "multi-timbral" constituents of cultural phenomena.[10] Whereas some criticism is satisfied to treat a song as a homogenous entity or text, the reality is that there is much interplay between the several instruments and constituents which go into the make-up of a song. This reality is even more striking today, with the popularity of multi-track sequencing and recording, which we shall look at in the final chapter.

In the mid-1980s, Caribbean music began to be predominantly technology based and technology driven. Soca, dancehall and ragga as recorded texts increasingly relied on drum machines, synthesizers, sequencers, samplers and multi-track layering. In the multi-track domain of the studio, each song is built on an endless array of parallel instruments that can be played individually (that is, track by track). When tracks are played together, simultaneously, they construct what we consider to be a "song". In my conceptualization, therefore, every cultural item is potentially multi-tracked.

How, then, is this notion of a multi-track reading different from those readings which acknowledge the multilayered nature of texts, and which therefore speak of "polyphonous" texts? For one thing, many of those readings do not proceed predominantly from the perspective of technology. Furthermore, the notion of multi-track reading – while acknowledging that polyphony (multiplicity of voices) is an advancement on the older notion of monophony (the singular voice) – is very aware that polyphony as a technological phenomenon has been superseded by the development of multi-timbrality:[11] whereas polyphony might be considered to be the existence of two or more "voices" that are usually similar to each other, multi-timbrality has to do with the existence of two or more similar or contrasting voices *and* their ability to be sounded simultaneously. Whereas polyphony has to do with the capacity to simultaneously play more than one internal note on an instrument, multi-timbrality has to do with the capacity of that one instrument to play the voices of other, different instruments simultaneously. Multi-timbral instruments are defined by the capacity to process and transmit internally as well as externally created voices. In contemporary practice where instruments function in the environment of interface, they are expected to process internal as well as external data. For example, when multi-timbral synthesizers are connected to other instruments, the synthesisers are expected to receive and transmit the varied data on account of being multi-timbral. Because of its capacity, a multi-timbral instrument can produce the sound of sixteen or more different instruments simultaneously. Multi-timbral instruments are therefore more expressive and have greater operational capabilities built into them. As a result, they offer the user greater control over the processes of creation, editing and dissemination.[12]

Because of this technological constructedness (make-up) it seems necessary to invoke a techno-driven reading in order to reconstitute textual meaning – that is, a critical approach which dismantles and "re-mantles" the sound (and cultural) text. As listeners and hearers, we receive songs (and other similar texts) at the post-production stage, that is, after the mix-down. This is when we experience them, either as two-track constructions in stereo mode or as two- through one-track constructions in mono.

As songs pass through a number of stages in the process of construction, they become increasingly ideologically and politically encoded. Beneath the artificial coating of the final mix-down, there reside a number of independent tracks to which the average listener is oblivious or about which he or she does not care. In the field of the dissemination and reception of popular music, this is a site of much hidden politics. This kind of rereading, which affords the reader or hearer the functionalities of the digital track recorder or sequencer, can be done. Such functions as isolating distinct tracks and punching in and out (of) the discourse offer unlimited possibilities in terms of performing close technical analysis.[13]

Throughout this book I engage in aspects of this practice – in analysing the hardcore styles of the 1990s and beyond, in assessing the music video, in interrogating specific components of selected songs as recorded productions. The average listener often takes for granted the multi-layeredness of cultural products. But a reading which is willing to deal with cultural forms as multi-track constructions – and is capable of doing so – can begin to observe things about these forms which are not readily apparent in other kinds of readings. The advent of the new robust technological era demands a shift both in the subject matter that is foregrounded and in the critical tools used in the study of Caribbean popular culture.

This study itself acts as a multi-tracked construction: it is multilayered; its sections can be extracted and treated separately, or they can be treated as constituting a total work. But in the same way that multi-track technology anticipates a situation of infinite track-building, this study also, because of itself, sits anxiously at the edge of other expectant discourses.

Sounding Calypso's Muted Tracks, Past and Present
Barbados + St Lucia

Discursive Sound and Silence

In the 1980s and 1990s, Barbados and St Lucia emerged as important islands in the practice of calypso. While before this time Trinidad stood out singularly in the Caribbean in its consistent production of high-quality calypso, after 1980 other territories began to come to the fore. Yet in spite of the advancements made in other countries throughout the late twentieth century, there has been relative critical silence in academic writing about crucial aspects of their development.

Nonetheless, I do not want to belabour this point, for surely it must be acknowledged that non-academic sources, such as newspapers, magazines, public and commercial radio, and television programmes, have been important conductors of cultural discourse. It could be argued that popular culture, because of its very nature, invites a type of critical response which is best facilitated through less formal debates. If this is so, then it must be said that there has been no absence of critical response to recent developments in the calypso art forms of St Lucia, Barbados and other islands throughout the region. I would rather, then, begin from this perspective, and with this knowledge.

Greater respect must also be paid to oral as well as to non-academic sources. Indeed, these sources have sustained the critical debate on Caribbean culture, and they have done so in a way that academic writing cannot. This is not to set at odds the impact and value of these two kinds of discourse: they depend on one another. Academic and non-academic discourses are not mutually exclusive categories. Popular culture studies are distinguished from some other kinds of intellectual inquiry because popular culture evokes a response from all people. Cultural development is dependent on a range of inputs. When non-academic and academic discourse are allowed to play with each other, the fullest gain is derived. When this dialogue does not take place, culture undergoes a process of muting.

There are always issues within a culture that remain muted as a result of limited responses to them. The two major issues taken up by this chapter reflect subjects that have remained muted, in part because of the lack of sustained academic dialogue. Connoisseurs of Caribbean culture and casual observers have hardly lapsed; they have discussed these issues. The role of the academic in this process is to respond as well, and also to attempt to categorize and contextualize, theorize and forecast. This is not to be done for the sake of unearthing some new relic, but rather for the purpose of igniting further dialogue. When critical responses are raised, then the process of cultural awareness and of national and regional empowerment is sustained.

This chapter does not claim by any means to be the first such examination of the issues that it presents; rather, I want to contribute to the ongoing discussion about the music culture of two new emerging islands. Although many of the issues I treat here have been debated in less formal contexts, I want to use this chapter to formally explore paths of development in the calypso culture of St Lucia and Barbados.

Barbados can lay claim to having one of the fastest-growing calypso-oriented music festivals in the region in the 1990s. But the modern rebirth of Crop Over as a calypso-oriented festival has brought into sharper focus the imperative to define what is calypso and the need to trace selected routes of its development in the Barbadian context. The first sections of this chapter seek to address these two questions while creating an expanded discourse on calypso, an art form that has not been sufficiently formally critiqued outside of the Trinidadian experience. (Readers will note that the first sections of this chapter do not completely isolate Barbados. Some segments which deal with definitions draw examples from St Lucia as well, by way of better representing the concepts presented.)

By 1995, the St Lucian "commentary calypso" was in some respects on par with that coming out of Trinidad and Barbados. But, surprisingly, a very small volume of its material was being heard outside the island.

The result was that this quiet revolution took place without notice by many people. This chapter's second group of sections is concerned with assessing the nature of the St Lucian contribution to calypso, especially during the 1990s. It examines, among other things, the thematic and technical features of selected compositions, as well as focusing on gender, the soca-calypso hybrid, and related social and institutional issues. The chapter therefore looks backwards into the distant history of Barbadian calypso, then forwards to the contemporary St Lucian scene, in both instances charting hidden passages in the development of the calypso art form in the Caribbean. This is the chapter's thematic logic and structural rationale.

Trinidad and Tobago: Creating a Discourse

The twin island state of Trinidad and Tobago can, with much justification, lay claim to being the land of calypso. But, as with most popular art forms, there is some danger in claiming exclusive rights, since these art forms are practised in the accessible domain of social and cultural space, open to influences from several sources – open to change. Calypso has had lifelines of practice in many other countries of the Caribbean, of course. In his discussion on the history of calypso in St Lucia, for example, Kendel Hippolyte makes the pertinent point that calypso has had a unique history within that cultural area.[1] But it is precisely because of the varying experiences of calypso in the several islands that there is need to consider how it has developed in specific countries. This is indeed a crucial step towards a fuller understanding of the phenomenon that is calypso.

A pronounced weakness within the regionalist project to assert a Caribbean state is the critical void within individual islands. With the dawn of the new millennium, the imperative is even greater to unearth and discuss these underexamined areas. This is one of the biggest problems confronting the region, in light of contemporary attempts to forge a tighter union at the political and governmental level.

Around 1996, when there was much talk of the "Bajan invasion"[2] – referring to the tremendous impact of Barbadian calypsos within Trinidad – many individuals, including cultural planners, suggested that the Barbadian calypso had come of age. Some overenthusiastic commentators even suggested that the calypso of Barbados had surpassed that of Trinidad in terms of popularity, craft and aesthetic appeal. Although this conclusion was not necessarily sound, it was founded on the observation that the growth of and participation within the calypso-based festival of Barbados was astounding. The calypsos coming out of Barbados were effecting other markets in the region and abroad. Since the mid-1980s, this trend had developed, with artists such as Gabby ("Boots", "Cadavers", "One Day [Coming Soon]"), Spice ("In de Congaline"), Grynner ("We Want More Grynner"), Ras Iley ("Spring Garden on Fire"), Red Plastic Bag ("Can't Find Me Brother"), Speedy ("Hold Yuh Bam Bam") and Adonijah ("Bounce and Shack Out"). Around 1995, this steady stream of hits peaked. The number of Bajan songs that were reaching the top of the charts in Trinidad, St Lucia and St Vincent, and on selected radio networks in New York, Miami and London, was phenomenal. This trend led to the general impression that the culturescape of Barbados was booming, and that calypso was its main catalyst. The former impression was only that: an impression.

The Barbadian case was the most pronounced going into the 1990s. But while the nation celebrated its achievements, more and more it was thrown back upon itself, faced with questions concerning the route(s) by which contemporary calypso evolved. These questions were posed from time to time in public and in the press as well as to academics, connoisseurs and practitioners.

Before the 1980s, there was a noticeable tendency on the part of some commentators to underplay the presence of a viable, practised, indigenous culture and tradition within Barbados. The perceived absence of a distinctive and vibrant culture had earned Barbados the label "Little England", in reference to Barbados's very conservative nature. Barbados has therefore carried the stigma of being one of the most conservative societies in the Caribbean. Although the tag is somewhat justified, some critics have ignored the types of subversive "low-frequency" movements that have existed in Barbados over the centuries. These underground movements are radical, indigenous, mostly non-European cultural phenomena that have fermented within Barbadian culture over its history. Such institutions as the tuk band are examples of a resistant creative spirit which has grown with the nation.

Some critics of Barbadian arts are inclined simply to judge the island in comparison with other islands of the Caribbean, such as Jamaica and

Trinidad, whose cultural manifestations have tended to be much more visibly bold than those of Barbados.[3] Specifically in terms of music, these other islands are perceived to have claimed their cultural identity through the creation of their national music. For example, Jamaica has nurtured ska, rocksteady and reggae proper – important cultural markers that in the international world stand as symbols of "Jamaica", the nation. Similarly, what we know today as calypso comes out of a long tradition whose lifeline has been persistently and overtly sustained in Trinidad and Tobago. It is sometimes felt that Barbados – and, indeed, other islands of the Caribbean – cannot be said to have a legitimate culture until they can lay claim to having their own music. So, at present, the question being asked of Barbados and its music is, what contribution has the nation made towards the creation of its own indigenous readily identifiable music?

Barbados's boldest claims to an autonomous musical form were made in the late 1960s and early 1970s through the music of *spouge*. Spouge was brought to the fore by the Barbadian Jackie Opel who had been a leading vocalist in Jamaica during the ska era. Some observers have described spouge as reggae played backwards. Its defining qualities have been offbeat drums, prominent strumming of the rhythm guitar and well stated percussive cowbells. This musical form became popular throughout the eastern Caribbean by the middle of the 1970s, when it was believed to be competing for position as one of the eastern Caribbean's leading music forms. The spouge era reflected the capability and capacity of Barbados to project a symbol of indigenous national creativity. But the music form was not sustained. Spouge predated the developments of the 1980s and 1990s. Barbadian music did not first begin to make an impact on the Caribbean culturescape in the 1980s. The post-2000 impact of Barbadian music through the new stylings of tuk, ringbang and raggasoca can therefore be seen as the continuation of a process.

Components of a distinctly Bajan culture and music have existed for a long time, even before the 1970s. Throughout the history of Barbados there has been an alternative music culture. From the slave period to the present, this music has perpetuated, but it has also undergone many changes. This is not the music of the rulers, but the music of the average citizen. It is the music of the slaves on the plantation, the music of tenantry dwellers. It is the music of field workers, the music of festive outings, the music of the street corners, the music of roving songsters, the folk song, the rhythms of Pentecostal congregations, the music of the Landship, the music of the tuk band. But what is the relationship between the type of music that was played and performed in Barbados during the slave period and the music forms that are being practised today? Is there a thread of development? I will go on to consider these things, but first I want to make some foundational points about the art form called calypso.

What Is Calypso?

Inasmuch as I want to propose here that the music of the slave period formed the antecedent to what we today call *folk* and *calypso,* it is necessary to address what calypso is. The actual practice of the art form predates the label *calypso.* Even before they had a label, the types of songs that characterize this art form were already being performed. There is nothing uncharacteristic about this – many musical genres are created well before they are named. For example, long before the word *jazz* was commonly used in the 1920s to define a type of music, that type of music was being played by the likes of Jazbo Brown.[4] This is not to say, however, that the relationship between a music form and its name is an arbitrary one and so should not be considered as important in a discussion of music histories. In fact, investigating the origins of a music label opens up our understanding of the word and of the musical genre itself. Because of this investigation, we better appreciate the cultural, linguistic, political and historical forces that are at work within the creative process – and how societies seek to control and define their traditions.

Since the debates surrounding the origin of the word *calypso* began, the list of possible origins has expanded. But there has also been a narrowing of the ideological divide in contemporary music discourse. Recent debates have pitted the African proponents versus others who argue for a non-African, European-influenced origin.[5]

The word *calypso* is believed to have first appeared very early in the first decade of the twentieth century, meaning "the Trinidad carnival song".[6] But there is less consensus regarding the issue of the word's original derivation. The actual word *calypso* is believed to have derived from one or more of several sources:

1. *careso,* a topical song from the Virgin Islands
2. the Spanish *caliso,* a label also used for a type of popular song in St Lucia
3. the Carib *carieto,* "a merry song" (this word itself evolved into *cariso*)
4. the French patois *carrousseaux* or *caillisseaux*
5. the West African (Hausa) *kaiso* (a corruption of *kaito*), which is an expression of mirth, support similar to the shout of *encore* or *bravo*

Atilla the Hun (Raymond Quevedo), who was at the forefront of calypso performance in the twentieth century, was adamant, based on his own personal knowledge, that the music actually evolved through the label *kaiso* and *cariso* before it became known as *calypso.*[7] It is the fifth interpretation above that is favoured by most commentators on calypso. This view is preferred especially for its support of African transferrals and survivals in the Caribbean.

Similarly, there have been contentious debates surrounding the origin and development of the art form which today we call "calypso". There is the view that the forerunner to what we know as calypso can be traced to the first shantwell, Gros Jean, who served as master of kaiso around 1784 in Trinidad and Tobago. In Trinidad, calypso songs drew heavily from the string music of French estate owners and their masquerade balls, and from Venezuelan dance tunes called *pasillos.*

In a real sense, one cannot talk of the development of calypso in Trinidad without mentioning the carnival. In Trinidad, where formal slavery ended in the 1830s, dances and masquerades were held in the early nineteenth century primarily by the wealthy. After emancipation, these festivities were soon taken over by the working classes. The rapid expansion of these festivities led to the colonial authority's curbing of what they called "revelry". Around the year 1900, tents were set up to support the masquerade celebrations. These tents began to house those singers who were then adapting songs of ridicule and praise into English.

Raphael de Leon (Roaring Lion) believes that the art form of calypso actually derives from thirteenth-century France and is a form of French ballade, with a fixed structure regarding the number of lines per verse and of lines per chorus. According to this view, the calypso form was transferred to Trinidad during the time of the French involvement within Trinidad.[8] Yet another view says that the calypso evolved on the slave plantations, where, among themselves, the slaves sang their songs of

ridicule and of satire against "massa". Related to this view is the opinion
that the art form has its roots in some African songs: some commentators
on calypso see the African songster or roving singer (sometimes called the
"griot") as the forerunner of the modern-day calypsonian.[9]

This latter view is the most popular among academics in the field of
calypso studies and other commentators. The strength of this particular
reading of Caribbean cultural history resides in the similarities between
the African griot tradition and calypso. Such features of calypso as its
extemporaneous practice – that is, the creation of words and music on
the spot, spontaneously – are also common to the griot tradition. So,
according to this view of African transferral, when the slaves were forced
to the Caribbean they brought with them aspects of their culture, chief
among which was their songs, their music – and undoubtedly components
of the griot tradition.[10]

But the question still remains. What is calypso? What are its core
characteristic features? The *Dictionary of Caribbean English Usage*
defines calypso as "a popular satirical song in rhymed verse, now mostly
associated with Trinidad, commenting on any recognized figure(s) or
aspect(s) of Caribbean social life and more often performed by a male
singer with much body gesture and some extemporization directed at
anybody in the audience".[11] Gordon Rohlehr, the leading writer on the
calypso of Trinidad, conceptualizes the art form as "being rooted in the
history of urbanization, immigration and Black reconstruction in post-
Emancipation Trinidad".[12] Atilla the Hun, the legendary calypsonian,
sees it as "a particular form of folk song".[13] The Vincentian artist Beckett
views it as an evolving art form. Throughout the 1990s, he openly referred
to himself as a singer of calypso, in spite of the fact that his repertoire was
dominated by calypso's party variant, soca. His major hits include "Disco
Calypso" (1977) "Teaser" (1990), "Gal Ah Rush Me" (1990) and "Small
Pin" (1999). David Rudder, a calypso performer since the 1980s, often
gave the radical open-ended suggestion on Caribbean radio throughout
the 1990s that calypso was "the music of the day". Rudder's definition
deliberately avoids closure. It recognizes that the art form is difficult to
define and so it returns the question to the wider society.

One neglected source of information in all this discussion is those very
songs which tackle the subject themselves. It is not a coincidence that
calypsonians throughout the region have given their opinions by way of
carefully structured and well-argued songs. These songs include Rudder's

"Calypso Music" (1987), John King's "I Am a Calypso" (1987) and Robbie's "King of Hearts" (1995). In these songs, the artists present engaging expositions on the subject. It is perhaps here that future researchers could turn for more compelling and insightful concepts of what calypso comprises.

It is instructive that there are potentially as many definitions of calypso as there are commentators within the Caribbean. However, it is still possible to pin down the discussion on this issue by attempting to list some of the characteristic features of the oral musical performance genre called calypso. For most commentators, the calypso is characterized by the presence of

1. *Extemporaneous performance.* That is, the singer composes on the spot, during the actual performance. Given the centrality of this feature in "traditional" calypso, it might be suggested that contemporary calypso practice lacks spontaneity: calypso today tends to be a pre-packaged art form. Some St Lucian extempore singers are Tricky, Invader and Ezi, and from Barbados, Charmer, Lord Radio and Gabby. The full list is not much longer than this.

2. *Picong.* Picong is the trading of words between individuals in song. In "traditional" calypso performance, the trading of insults was done extemporaneously. The Trinidadians Atilla and Roaring Lion are legendary performers of this mode of discourse. Contemporary calypso continues to reflect the presence of this feature. In Barbados and St Lucia there are still calypsonians who trade words in song from year to year.

3. *Satire.* Satire tends to be associated with biting social and political commentary. It is employed in witty compositions which expose or attack someone or some issue within society. In the Barbadian calypso context, satire can be heard, for example in the 1985 song "Miss Barbados", which ridicules the choosing of a "Canadian girl" to represent Barbados in international beauty contests:

> Ms Barbados don't know nothing about
> Sea egg and that's no lie
> Ms Barbados is as Bajan as apple pie

The satire is contained in the juxtaposition of Bajanness with "otherness" or Canadianness. The seriousness of the contest is undermined through the description of its creating "a friendly invasion", as well as through the playful overemployment of rhymes in the composition. The St Lucian Pelay's 1995 song "Wrong Position" makes use of double entendre to satirize the failings of male sexual partners, but also, more critically, the shortcomings of St Lucian politicians and political appointees who have been placed in the "wrong position":

> Don't you know as director of national culture
> Mr Jacques Compton is in the wrong position

4. *Call and response*. There are countless examples of call and response in calypso, where a chorus responds to the lead singer. The St Lucian calypsonian Educator's 1989 road march "Calypso Tyson", which extols the power of the calypso singer, is a good example of this structure:

> *Soloist (call):* Calypso Tyson taking over this year
> *Chorus (response):* Knock them out, Educator knock them out

The Barbadian performer Red Plastic Bag's "Can't Find Me Brother" (1987) also offers a good example of this feature:

> *Soloist (call):* I search Bush Hall and Bank Hall and . . .
> *Chorus (response):* Caan't find me brother!!

Barbados: Early Signs of Calypso

It must be said that acceptance of certain versions of calypso's historical derivation depends upon acceptance of the theories of transferrals, particularly African transferrals within the Caribbean. I will not discuss the notion of transferral itself here; thinkers such as Orlando Patterson, Kamau Brathwaite, Mervyn Alleyne, Melville Herskovitz and others have dealt with it.[14] The Barbadian historian Trevor Marshall has built on the phenomenon of cultural transferral and concludes that since Barbados was a central and early point for the trans-shipment (transferral from ship to ship) of slaves within the "new world", then Barbados was undoubtedly an early recipient of "calypsonians".[15] In this regard, Marshall supports a reading of Caribbean culture as put forwards by Africanists.

In order to confidently assert that an art similar to what we know as calypso was being performed in Barbados from as early as the slave period, it is crucial to provide some documentation. Although some commentators on the history of Barbadian culture have tended to underplay the presence of a vibrant (African) slave culture, historical evidence supports the view that the slaves on Barbadian plantations were far from passive. They did not give up their cultures wholesale for a European way of life. But this is not an experience unique to Barbados. Similar examples can be found throughout the islands of the Caribbean. It is therefore much more acceptable to suggest that the kinds of early songs, practices and performances which have now evolved into "the calypso" had their beginnings throughout the Caribbean region not only in Barbados. For instance, St Lucian play songs reveal lyrical texts that employ verbal strategies, metaphors, innuendo and inference. These are strategies integral to calypso. No one territory can therefore claim exclusive ownership of calypso – popular culture always seems to evade claims of exclusive ownership.

The proof of the early practice of calypso in Barbados is in selected historical documents and in the letters of Europeans who travelled to or lived in the Caribbean. One such important source is Richard Ligon, who came to Barbados in 1647, only twenty years after Barbados's settlement by the British.[16] Ligon commented on aspects of slave life, music and culture in Barbados. In conjunction with other sources like Ligon, we can put together a better picture of music and culture in the slave period.

The holocaust of the Middle Passage did not represent a loss of culture for those slaves who were shipped to the Americas. The plantation should be seen as a place of confrontation and acculturation, where European and African, African and African, forged a number of unique cultural manifestations. It is clear that music played a crucial role in the lives of slaves. William Dickson, writing in the 1780s, calls attention to this importance.[17]

Another description from the late eighteenth century confirms slaves' wearing of masks and points to the persistence of African cultural practices: "On Sundays and holidays it is common to see many hundreds of negroes and mulattos dancing and making merry. . . . They enjoy the dance and the song on the plantations where I have seen very large companies of field people making merry, sometimes at late hours on Sunday and holiday evenings."[18]

The negative attitude of some Europeans to the music-related practices they saw does support to some degree the view that the rhythms played were on occasion African in derivation. To George Pinckard, the "noisy sounds" he heard required only "a slight aid from fancy to transport one to the savage wilds of Africa".[19] But there are even more specific documented European responses to the rhythms played in the eastern Caribbean during slavery. There are no extensive comments from these early sources on the instruments or on performance techniques, but it is clear that such African features as polyrhythms (multiple rhythms), improvisation, and call and response characterized the music of the slave period.[20] These features, one must remember, are also integral to the calypso.

Instruments

Of the instruments, rattles would seem to have been quite popularly used. These might have been constructed from dried-out calabash shells, which were then filled with small stones or seeds, attached to a stick and shaken as musical instruments. The log xylophone, an African instrument, was reported in Barbados in the seventeenth century. Pottery and earthen vessels were used as drums. Hand clapping, clapping of parts of the body and foot stomping were prevalent as well. The slaves also used and played single-headed hollow log drums; reports observed that the drum was played upon with a stick or the fingers. These hollow log drums were occasionally played horizontally rather than vertically, according to Pinckard.[21] Slaves were also in the habit of using and adapting European instruments, especially those of the stringed variety. They made use of the conch shell trumpet on various occasions as well.

Laws were passed in Barbados, as early as the 1660s, with the intention of curbing expressive and subversive features of the slaves' culture. Plantation owners were aware that slaves could communicate through the use of their instruments and in song. The Europeans seemed also to fear the revolutionary potential that was locked up within the music of the slaves. Hence, they attributed a nefarious and evil symbolism to that music. It is significant that after over three centuries, this symbolism still lingers in sections of Caribbean society.

In 1688, a code further warned slaves not to beat drums, blow horns or use loud instruments. But, in spite of these attempts to suppress their musical production, the slaves continued their craft in many guises. For example, Dickson, in the eighteenth century, alluding to the prohibition on beating the drum, mentions "the black musicians who, however, have substituted in its place, a common earthen jar . . . which . . . emits a hollow sound, resembling the more animating note of the drum".[22]

Slave festivities produced music and songs which satirized the owners of the plantations. These songs were cleverly crafted so that the slaves understood what was being sung but "massa" was ignorant of their full meaning. Important sources from the end of the eighteenth century describe more precisely the types of songs that the slaves performed:

> Their songs are commonly impromptu and there are among them individuals who resemble the extempore bards of Italy; but I cannot say much for their poetry. Their tunes in general are characteristic of their national manners; those of the Eboes being soft and languishing; of the Koromantyns heroic and martial.
>
> At their merry meetings and midnight festivals, they are not without ballads of another kind, adapted to such occasions; and here they give full scope to a talent of ridicule and derision, which is exercised not only against each other, but also, frequently, at the expense of their owner or employer.[23]

Tuk Band

There is a school of thought that the Bajan tuk band may owe its origin to the fife-and-drum marching bands of the eighteenth-century British regiments. That said, although it is possible that early tuk bands were influenced in some way by British marching bands, it does appear that there were earlier bands of Africans who used singers, drums and other percussive instruments, which all came together on occasions of festivities. The presence of these bands does, therefore, signal an earlier history for the tuk band. These bands eventually used European drums, adapting them to their own rhythmic and metrical styling. Such bands survived the slave period, and in the post-emancipation period continued to serve their social function as institutions of entertainment and cultural continuity. But these were also subversive groupings, which held the potential to ignite upheaval and bring about social or cultural transformation. The rulership knew this and therefore tried to mute the tuk band.

It is important to understand that the tuk band was a carrier of the culture of the African Barbadian. Tuk bands were partly responsible for the passing on of songs from one generation to another. In addition to playing music at events and activities, such as Sunday and holiday dances, they were the support bases for passing on a number of songs and sayings. The tuk band was not and is not always exclusively an instrumental band; it has sometimes used vocalists.

Although instruments may have been played on a solo basis – that is, by single individuals in the solace of their own company and for their own personal enjoyment or therapy – it does seem that music in plantation and post-emancipation Barbados was widely enjoyed as a shared activity. Early sources refer to the sense of "community" which the music of this period seemed to bring about. The types of bands described by Europeans like George Pinckard were small bands of some four musicians resembling to some degree the modern tuk band. But Pinckard also remarked how the sizes of these bands would be increased by an additional number "on great occasions",[24] suggesting the fluidity, flexibility and dynamic constitution of the band. This point is significant since it points to the adaptable nature of the bands. Over the centuries, these bands were forced on many occasions to undergo changes.

It is reasonable to suggest that tuk bands served an active function in playing and disseminating the popular songs of the slaves, particularly after emancipation. Folk songs such as "Lick and Lock Up Done With" from the 1830s and "King JaJa" from the late nineteenth century were accompanied by the music of the tuk band. These popular songs now categorized as "folk" represented the feeling of the masses and hence served a purpose similar to that of the calypso. The folk song shares a dynamic relationship with later phenomena. Barbadian calypso discourse must therefore acknowledge the input of folk melodies and aesthetics. But there must also be recognition that popular African Barbadian song was not parochial in its reference. It should be recognised that songs such as the two above were inspired by larger political issues and were local responses to them. Traditional Barbadian popular song cannot therefore be categorized as inward-looking only; it has tended to look both inwards and outwards upon the world.

Banja

In December 1912, Columbia Records made two recordings featuring a singer called Lionel Licorish, who presumably was a Barbadian. The two songs were "Baijan Girl" and "I Has the Blues for Thee Barbados". This is particularly worth noting given the misconception that Barbadian culture remained dormant prior to independence in 1966. This early recording by a major record company also points to a much earlier interface between Barbadian music culture and international interests than is generally acknowledged. Many people assume that this association first occurred in the late twentieth century, with artists such as Jackie Opel, Gabby, Charles D. Lewis, Jiggs Kirton, Red Plastic Bag and John King. It would seem that Columbia's recordings of Licorish were distributed throughout the islands of the Caribbean and were popular to some degree.

There was a significant movement of selected Barbadian calypsonians to Trinidad. Some of these artists gained greater visibility through Trinidad's much more vibrant and structured form of carnival and calypso. For example, a *Trinidad and Tobago Mirror* article dated 4 March 1908, refers to "a native of Little England". This Barbadian sang with a popular Trinidad band called the Golden Star Band, which was involved in a competition of bands in Trinidad. The 1908 article refers to the vocal and verbal skill of this Bajan singer, who was but one of many practitioners of the art of extempore. The *Mirror* further reports how "this son of Bimshire had more adjectives and adverbs at his disposal . . . no matter whether they were misused or not". It is also significant that the Golden Star Band won the singing competition on that occasion.

Bajan songs were also recorded by the popular Belasco band in Trinidad. In 1914, Belasco recorded piano solos of the songs "Buddy Abraham" and "Little Brown Boy", both of which came from Barbados. The Trinidad calypsonian Atilla the Hun called the latter song "He Is a Dude", and his version of it became popular. The folk song–cum–calypso "Murder in de Market" (from Barbados), which originated around the 1870s, was retitled "He Had It Coming" and popularized by the Trinidad calypsonian Houdini. The popularity of this song stretched even to the United States. Barbadian folk-calypsos also made it to other places abroad, such as Panama, where the song "Glandary High Wall" was widely heard and sung in the early twentieth century. The song "Payne Dead, Payne

Dead" is reported to have come from Barbados and to have enjoyed popularity in some other territories of the Caribbean, especially in Trinidad. This song was relayed throughout the Caribbean by sailors who travelled between the islands on small schooners. It was especially popular in the early twentieth century (around 1910) and is reported to have been sung in homes and on street corners.

In addition to the impact of Barbadian words and melodies on calypso-related art forms in the region, it appears as well that the distinctively Bajan rhythm of tuk influenced the music of the region. An article in the *Trinidad Guardian* on 17 February 1923 refers to the increasing influence on the Trinidad kaiso of what it terms "the familiar music of the reed and steel of the adjacent colony of Barbados", clearly a reference to the impact of the Barbadian tuk rhythm abroad.

Nonetheless, it does appear that many of the songs originating from Barbados, though prominent abroad, were not being readily taken up by calypso singers. This might have more to do with the peculiarities of the calypso art form and less to do with inter-island rivalry. When Houdini released "Payne Dead", for instance, he was quite heavily censured by some audiences. The question arises as to why these popular songs in the public domain were not taken up and sung by the calypso singers of Trinidad. Atilla puts forward one possible reason, which has to do with the perception that these Bajan songs were too stiff in rhythm and too correct, that there was "no room for ornamentation, speech lapse, dramatic build-up and verve".[25] But perhaps there existed some misgivings on the part of some calypsonians in Trinidad and Tobago who were not wholly accepting of songs from outside of their land, far less of songs coming out of "Little England". If this was so, it was not a Trinidadian condition only. The several islands of the Caribbean have exhibited varying levels of contact with and restriction of each other throughout history. In the early twenty-first century, this is still the situation.

But what surfaces here is that the Barbadian calypso was considered to be different from the Trinidad and Tobago calypso in a number of respects. According to Atilla, the Bajan kaiso suggested "a correctness of measurement, an immovable synchronization of words and music, a rather staid, pious and proper melodic structure unlike a much more exciting, lively and uneven structure in the calypso derived from Trinidad".[26] Although one would acknowledge that there were some distinctions between the calypsos of other territories and those of Trinidad in this period, the sense of total order and refinement which Atilla attributes to the Bajan and Jamaican calypsos of the early twentieth century is open to question. Perhaps Atilla's perception of other calypsos was effected by the general impression of calypso outside of Trinidad. But, then again, maybe he was correct. For when some calypsos were transferred to Trinidad by sailors and other migrants, they underwent some reinterpretation of melody, metre and rhythm. But this being said, there is still room for interrogating some of the observations made of these songs. To the extent that these songs were performed by solo musicians and freestyle-playing tuk bands in Barbados, there is considerable doubt that they were as regimented as some observers have remarked.

Whereas the Trinidad carnival first existed as an outlet for the play of stick-fighting (kalinda) bands and then as a medium for the performance of song, there is not all that long a tradition of structured performance in Barbados. In Trinidad, by the early 1920s, calypso tents were undergoing significant developments. There was a budding corps of singers who were giving support to the national tradition and the festival of Trinidad. In Barbados, there was no such structure for the performance and practice of calypso: the development of the calypso in Barbados was not supported by an organized base, as in Trinidad. Many official agencies in Barbados viewed calypso negatively, referring to it as "banja", a secular and evil music. Still, in the same way that Lord Melody of Trinidad (for example) performed regularly in village and town shops, so the majority of Barbadian kaiso singers performed as freelance artists. But whereas Lord Melody was singled out by another kaiso singer, Lord Invader, and contracted to sing in a more professional context, the Bajan kaiso singer at the corner shop did not have such a facility for advancement. The singers of folk songs and calypso in Barbados therefore depended largely on special contexts – festive occasions, holidays, weekend functions or other local events, events at which they could perform impromptu to patrons, who might pay them in some way, if they cared to. So Barbadian calypso singers had to creatively fashion the performance and the art form in order to maximize the impact and the rewards. This, then, was another telling difference between the Barbadian and the Trinidadian experience.

Barbadian performers were expected to extemporize at any moment. These calypsonians and folk artists had to be familiar with the art of picong, since this was a popular crowd-pleaser and was therefore highly valued. The importance of this kind of impromptu performance to Barbadian singers of calypso might account for the relative sparseness today of calypso songs which date back to the 1920s, 1930s and 1940s because these extempore songs might not have been memorized by performers or remembered as fixed text by audiences.

This is not to suggest that there are no recollections of Barbadian calypsos from the 1920s through to the 1950s. Shilling, one of the most popular performers of calypso in Barbados throughout this period, recalls his song "Too Late Corkie" as being a 1924 composition:

> Too late O Corky too late
> Too late O Corky too late
> Too late to contemplate five years isn't fourteen days

His skill was supplemented by his lively guitar work, with which he thrilled many audiences.[27]

Music technology has always embellished and mediated Caribbean music. It is therefore not surprising that late twentieth century performers relied heavily on current technology to project and perfect their craft. In spite of this unmistakable talent, performers like Shilling were not respected as legitimate artists. They were seen largely as drunkards, idle individuals who had nothing better to do. They were looked down upon by the establishment and scoffed at by some in society. To the prim and proper in Bajan society, the songs of these singers were lewd, distasteful and were summed up as "banja", worthless and sinful. Although Charmer, another such performer, did performances with Kitchener and Small Island Pride as a means of gaining greater acceptance, respectability and finance, this respectability was not readily forthcoming in Barbados. There performers like Shilling and Charmer were the highlight of events on festive occasions. These roving singers played an important function in entertaining and informing the wider society, whether performing by themselves or with tuk-styled bands. The highlight of their performances often took place at Christmas celebrations, especially on Christmas mornings when tuk bands came around from house to house to entertain, spread good cheer and solicit rewards for their performances.

Charmer has commented on the conditions of his practice as calypso singer during the early years. He has often talked about the attitude of Bajan society to the calypso singer in this period. He has made it known who were the supporters of calypso and the calypsonians: "I actually get my publicity from the man in the street, that's right. The man on the street, the people on the street. From rum shop to rum shop in those days I used to get a little penny here and a little four cents there . . . and I kept it up. . . . The people used to look out for me. It's the man on the street who kept me going where calypso is concerned."[28] Charmer often performed in the St Michael area, but also wherever an event led him. Dressed in long scarlet coat, he performed picong on the old Coleridge pasture in rural St Peter, much to the amazement and delight of patrons and other aspiring entertainers. But performers like Charmer did not earn enough in this way to support a comfortable living for themselves and their dependents. In 1948, Charmer gained greater recognition when he performed creditably and placed well in a competition in Trinidad and Tobago that also featured Mighty Killer, Mighty Terra and Small Island Pride.

Da Costa Allamby was also a composer of calypso in the late 1930s and 1940s in Barbados. Some of his more popular compositions over the years were "Gallon-o-Rum", "The Wedding" and "No More Bacalao". His song "Conrad", which was recorded by the Merrymen in their prolific 1960s period, is a late-1930s composition which recounts the events surrounding the presence of a "duppy", or ghost, in Barbados. This composition takes the form of a lengthy narrative, with no fewer than six verses. It is a testament to the existence of the structured ballad narrative form in Bajan calypso by the 1930s. Songs of this kind also reveal that by the 1930s the calypsonian in Barbados had internalized his or her role as chronicler and commentator on local events and phenomena. Although Allamby sang calypsos for rum and cigarettes on Saturday nights around shops, his greatest love was for "sentimentals" (love ballads). Because of this desire, he worked out a deal with the Merrymen whereby he would record his sentimentals through their facilities, and they would get his calypsos. That said, though, Allamby insisted that the only song he actually "gave" to the Merrymen was "Conrad".

Around the late 1950s and for some time after that, the Trinidad calypso was heard selectively on cable radio. A popular feeling among Barbadians was that the style of calypso from Trinidad was a better variety – true calypso. This quite understandably derived from the acknowledgement of a much more vibrant tradition in Trinidad. But one feels that this also reflected the latent belief within Barbadian society that Barbados was not yet capable of sustaining a credible indigenous tradition that was based on African-Caribbean aesthetics. Barbadians would not believe this until much later. A cultural reprogramming would only begin to alter the national perception around the 1980s. The hosting of the Caribbean Festival of Creative Arts (CARIFESTA) and the institutionalization of festivities through Crop Over would serve to encourage a new perception of indigenous culture.

Other islands, such as St Lucia and Grenada, had a structured format for calypso practice through competition earlier than did Barbados. A performer like Mighty Terra, from St Lucia, could rule as king of calypso in the 1950s. Lord Melody of Grenada was instrumental in holding up the tradition in Grenada around that time. At the end of that decade, in 1958, the Barbados Jaycees experimented with a type of carnival that was similar to Trinidad's. At first, this festival did not incorporate a calypso contest, but in 1960 one was added. Calypso was by no means the central feature of that festival, though; for the most part, it was "elitist" in orientation.

This first competition attracted five calypsonians. The small number can be taken as a comment on the state of calypso in Barbados, but it was also a reflection of the cultural divide between the white elite, who organized the festival, and their lower-class "others", for whose craft the elite seemingly held little regard. The history of Barbadian popular song is a history of contestation. It is a history fought along the frontiers of class and race as well as of genre. Barbados in the late 1950s had not yet divested itself of the social and psychological structures that had been inscribed by formal colonization. If the upper classes had the resources to mount a festival, then working-class artists had the talent to evoke the festive spirit of carnival. Since there had hardly been a dialogue among the races and among the classes, early attempts at carnival were tentative.

The number of competitors increased over the years to about twenty-two in 1964. The practice of structured competition facilitated some degree of fuller musical accompaniment for the performers. Some of them, who were largely accustomed to performing with a single instrument, such as the box guitar, could experience accompaniment that was closer to what was being heard on recordings from Trinidad. Recordings in Barbados from this period reveal wind instruments, keys, cellos and stringed acoustics.

At these competitions, each calypsonian performed one song, in contrast to the present practice of doing two. Mike Wilkinson won the

1960 competition with a song entitled "Ah Coming Up". This was a spirited song that celebrated the joys of festivities. It was in no way a hardcore social commentary. Many people will be surprised at this, since there is the perception that hardcore social commentary is a pervasive feature of all "traditional" competition calypso. Many of the competition calypsos of this period were not in the same vein as "Ah Coming Up", though. A large number were of the "purer" social commentary mode. Many of them possessed a favourable amount of wit, humour and a tinge of picong. This calypso of the early 1960s was the forerunner to what might be called the contemporary Barbadian calypso. Many 1970s calypsos were built on some of the features which the 1960s began to explore. The work of Sir Don as singer and Phil Brito as songwriter represents a dominant styling of mid-1970s Barbadian calypso.

In the 1970s, the government moved to establish a yearly festival to attract visitors to Barbados during the regular period of slow tourist arrivals. Crop Over was reborn. The new festival was a reworking of an old festival celebrated by slaves on Barbadian plantations. Whereas the earlier experiment by the Jaycees had proved problematic, this 1970s government initiative circumvented some of the tensions associated with class and race in Barbados. Since the state had recently secured independence from Britain in 1966, it was easier for calypsonians and artists to align their project with that of the state. The connection between the new Crop Over festival and slave culture caught the imagination of those artists who at the time were beginning to see their role as integral to the decolonization process. But perhaps the government's prime imperative – to lure tourists – pointed to a contradiction of purposes.

It is these very contradictions that remained within the festival over the years. Throughout the 1980s and 1990s, Crop Over and calypso developed in the shadows of controversy and paradox. In the late 1950s and 1960s, the Jaycees project had failed to sustain a meaningful practice, partly because of unexamined social, political, historical, cultural and philosophical fissures upon which a fragile tradition was being constructed. At the start of the twenty-first century, those cracks were still there. As late as 2004, the nation had not as yet come to this awareness. Government had not formulated meaningful culture policy by way of developing meaningful structures for cultural advancement. Artists were still for the most part disorganized. There were many cultural shows and festivities, but Barbadian music culture stood perilously on the fulcrum of carnival-styled festivities. The ruling political administration shrewdly masked its public relations project under the umbrella of culture. The nation seemed not to know this. There was much loose talk about cultural industries, but hardly any attempt to examine the history of popular and folk traditions in order to shore up the very fragile foundation that supports the facade of cultural growth in Barbados.

If there is a recurring motif or symbol within the history of Barbadian popular music, it is the tuk band. Calypso history in Barbados cannot be conceptualized apart from the development and impact of the tuk band. Indeed, a more accurate descriptive listing of the features of calypso music in Barbados should include the tuk band and its sound. Although some calypsonians over the years have made accusations about the appropriation of tuk rhythms, there has been little national recognition of the ongoing impact of the tuk phenomenon on fashioning a Barbadian sound and aesthetic. And now that new technology has found ways of sampling percussion instruments, there has been little in the way of a nationalist imperative to examine the implications for indigenous institutions (such as the tuk band) and national sound aesthetics.

St Lucian Calypso: Commentary, Party and Related Issues

While Barbadian calypso caught the attention of the Caribbean in the late 1980s because of the popularity of artists who were performing largely commercial music, developments in St Lucia in the 1990s (which were no less significant) went relatively unnoticed.[29] This was because St Lucia's greatest advances were taking place in the domain of social commentary calypso. The social commentary calypso does not attract the kind of broad-based and commercial popularity of the party calypso. Simply put, social commentary calypso deals with more "serious" social issues. Party calypso tends to be less concerned with serious social issues, instead featuring "lighter" lyrics and foregrounding driving rhythms.

Throughout the 1990s, St Lucian artists seemed to be experimenting with a hybrid form. They produced a number of songs which were commentaries in terms of lyrics but which were also very danceable and rhythmic. The rigid compartmentalization of the art form therefore into "serious" commentary calypso and dance calypso, or soca, was challenged significantly. This was not a phenomenon unique to St Lucia, though. For example, in St Kitts and Nevis, artists such as Ellie Matt were demonstrating quite similar tendencies. But it can be argued that developments in St Lucia contributed greatly to the intertextual play between calypso proper and soca in the 1990s. Since many of the songs that were combining these two styles were performed as calypso competition pieces, this tended in some way to limit their popularity beyond the island of St Lucia. Thus, these developments, though significant, stand the danger of existing as muted tracks of culture.

It is true that national calypso competitions that feature social commentary calypso generate a great deal of national excitement, but this excitement is closely confined to the performance moment of the calypso competitions. There is still no swell of regional interest in the various calypso competitions throughout the territories. Regional radio stations play very few social commentary calypsos from any place in the territories. On the other hand, there is much more interest in the party-type calypso. Radio stations throughout the region are more inclined to play the various road marches and dance calypsos from the several territories. This is not to say that St Lucia was not producing good party calypsos in the 1980s and 1990s; St Lucian artists certainly were. Invader's 1988 "Walk and Wine" and Jaunty's "Oh La Lay" and "We Shall Hop" from 1993 and 1995 respectively certainly made significant impressions throughout the region. But it is in the category of the social commentary that St Lucian artists demonstrated a consistently stimulating output. When the 1999 calypso monarch Bachelor performed in the regional King of Kings show and placed in the top ten, beating some competitors from Trinidad and Barbados, many seemed surprised. But in fact St Lucian calypsonians had for some time in the 1990s been writing and performing some of the most engaging calypsos to come from the region in that decade. The mid-1990s was, in fact, a pivotal moment in the advancement of contemporary St Lucian calypso.

During the early years of the twentieth century, St Lucia had its share of roving songsters. Performers such as Battle Axe, Small Island Pride, Scrubb, Mighty Cobra and Mighty Bake kept the art form alive during the 1940s and 1950s. The Mighty Terra is considered by many to be the godfather of St Lucian calypso. He dominated calypso competitions from 1957 to 1966. His phenomenal success hinged on his musical abilities and his having studied literature at St Lucia's prestigious St Mary's College. His period of domination was nearly matched by another calypsonian, Pelay, also from Vieux Fort in the south of the island. Pelay was supreme in the late 1960s and early 1970s. In the 1970s, Lord Carro and Lord Jackson also made significant contributions as singers and as calypso tent leaders. The 1980s gave birth to a new, fresh group of entertainers, many of whom remained active participants in the 1990s and beyond. Some of these are Invader, Mighty Pep, Ashanti, Herb Black, Madam Sequin, Robbie and Tricky. In the 1990s, women such as Cheryl, Mary G and Lady Leen competed fiercely in national competition.

The artists were ably supported by arrangers, sound engineers and other industry personnel. Two important arrangers who helped shape contemporary St Lucian calypso are Clarence Joseph and Ronald "Boo" Hinkson. Clarence Joseph began arranging in the early 1980s, and by the 1990s he was a major force. He played with the likes of Beckett, from St Vincent, and Trinidad's ace arranger Frankie McIntosh. For a period in the mid-1980s, he arranged a string of exciting songs for the Barbadian calypsonian Black Pawn. He has arranged for many of St Lucia's big names in calypso. Black Pawn's "America", recorded around 1986, was regarded by some calypsonians as one of the "sweetest" arrangements of that year. Joseph's arrangements have been marked by rich horn passages and well-stated bass lines. And although he has arranged many traditional sounding calypsos, his oeuvre consists of many more innovative compositions.

Boo Hinkson is one of the most influential musicians in St Lucia. His now-legendary band, the Tru Tones, was extremely popular in the eastern and wider Caribbean throughout the 1970s. Although he began writing songs in the late 1960s, it was really in 1979, with the song "Foreign Journalists", penned for the Tru Tones, that Hinkson began to give greater attention to his skills as a writer of calypso. His musical skills have also extended beyond the art form of calypso; he has played and arranged in the jazz and pop idioms as well. He has been featured at past St Lucia jazz festivals. His calypso melodic lines (written for others) are often fresh, although some calypso purists might raise an eyebrow at the pop and jazz inflections which sometimes weave their way in and out of his arrangements as in some songs done for the female group Colours, for Cheryl and for the mellifluous-sounding Mary G. As a calypso arranger Hinkson has done songs for major performers, but perhaps his most significant contribution to the St Lucian calypso is the work he continues to do in his recording studio.

The reality of Caribbean music in the 1990s was that many of its creators, sound engineers and producers worked in the solitude of the studio. From there they shaped the sound of calypso. The St Lucian calypso, like most other calypso outside Trinidad, has made considerable use of sound synthesis. One function of synthesized instruments was for the reproduction of brass tones. A survey of St Lucian calypsos produced throughout the 1990s and after 2000 reveals the use of heavy layers of synthesized brass. The studio recording of Cheryl's 1998 "Massav Tree" positions the synthesized brass up front in the mix. Although it employs layered brass samples, they are slaved to one another, or they sit upon each other, and hence they play in unison (or appear to). The recording does not attempt to reproduce the harmonic richness of the live rendition, but opts for a "fat" brass achieved through voice/tone layering on the synthesizer. Conversely, the performance of the song by the live band during the finals of 1998 revealed a clear separation of brass instruments. Trumpets and saxes and trombone are not slaved to one another; each carries its own melodic line and harmonic signature. This difference between recorded and live calypso is not unique to St Lucia; it is also found in Antigua, St Vincent, St Kitts, Grenada, Barbados and throughout the region.

In St Lucia, the studio recording of calypso began to mushroom in the 1990s. The use of synthesized brass on calypso recordings was as much an act of economic prudence as it was a reflection of the confidence of St Lucian arrangers and producers in the power of technology. The reality was that hiring a set of live horn players was rather costly. Since music technology had produced the self-contained synthesizer, referred to as the workstation, which could reproduce all the constituent instruments of a calypso combo band, artists and musicians had seen the practicality of employing this technology. But there is a certain "up-frontness" in the treatment of synthesized brass by St Lucian producers. This foregrounding of the synthesized instrument reflects an ambition for synthesis and an awareness of the power of virtual accompaniment. St Lucian producers like Boo Hinkson were aware that on the horizon were virtual modelling synthesizers, which would contest for position against actual live instruments. Hinkson was aware that back in the late 1980s, trained musicians could not differentiate between Kurzweil's legendary "stereo piano" tone and the sound of an actual live grand piano. Calypso and music connoisseurs in St Lucia were thus preoccupied, as were their colleagues in other territories, with the merits and demerits of live and synthesized sound. Although most commentators valorized live instruments, the reality was that synthesized instruments are unmatched in their frequency of use by and popularity among musicians and calypsonians in the recent evolution of St Lucian music.

This, however, was but one of many debates. There was also discussion about the distance and difference between calypso and its derivative, soca – a discussion which, like that on technology, still continues.

The Calypso Hybrid in St Lucia

There is a popular view in the region that the rise of soca music has seen the gradual demise of the calypso proper. This opinion seems to suggest a relationship between calypso and soca that is inversely proportionate, where the rise of one brings about the decline of the other. This seems a crude way to conceive of the relationship between related music genres, but it cannot be totally dismissed. Contemporary approaches to cultural critique are mistrusting of this kind of either/or binarism. Contemporary approaches tend to privilege much more dynamic relations between opposing entities. Rohlehr, in his article "We Getting the Kaiso We Deserve: Calypso and the World Music Market", explores some of the contentious issues within this dynamic.[30] But the point must be made that the suspicion about calypso and soca is not a senseless point to be totally dismissed or ignored. There is a rationale behind this way of thinking about Caribbean music.

When soca began to emerge as a thriving musical style in the late 1970s, calypso performers and enthusiasts reacted passionately to that development. For some, soca was not a legitimate style. They thought of it as a leeching appendage to an authentic, legitimately established tradition. Others felt more positively. But in all cases it was recognized that calypso and soca shared some relationship, even if it was a relationship of some tension. The contentious nature of this debate has affected the way these musical forms have evolved and the role they have played in Caribbean cultural expression.

Throughout the region there are, therefore, distinct competitions for the two genres (see table, pp. 37–38). There is the calypso monarch competition on the one hand and the soca/party monarch competition on the other. By the late 1980s, soca had established itself as an autonomous musical style. Indeed, it had surpassed calypso in terms of popularity and support among patrons. But although these two genres shared a relationship of tension, it was inevitable that performers would challenge their rigid compartmentalization. Performing artists are always less inclined to adhere to neat categories. St Lucian performers in particular were well aware of the passionate debates about calypso and soca which raged in the 1980s. They also knew that the calypso art form was characterized by innovation, intertextuality and hybrid experiments. They interpreted the contentious debates of the 1970s and 1980s as a continuation of this dynamic.

St Lucian calypsonians in the 1990s were aware of the shifting emphasis on party calypso among patrons. They were also aware of the tradition of calypso competition. They knew that entry into the national calypso competition required them to adhere to the demands of the judging criteria. It was not always clear what the judges wanted. Performers often found themselves trying to work this out. From year to year there were calypsonians who expressed their frustration at not unlocking the secret to the judges' hearts. Pelay expressed his frustration in the 2000 calypso season. Commenting on what was only his second omission after the semi-final stage, Pelay reflected on the competition problematic. He also noted the unstable nature of contemporary calypso.[31] Other artists in the 2000 finals included the women Lady Spice, Cheryl, Mary G and Lady Leen, as well as, notably, A. G. Simpson, who has often endured criticism for the soul-type phrasing which he brings to calypso. In the same interview in the *St Lucia Star*, Pelay saw his omission in terms of the debate surrounding the judges, the calypso criteria, the changing art form, and authenticity versus aberration. For him the issue was straightforward. He weighed two options and fell on the side of "true calypso":

> When we examine the facts, we find that we (those left out) had sung calypso in its true and genuine form, which is the most important criteria.
>
> Apparently, the art form needs to change to embrace some other forms of music, and the judges have looked at it from that point. As for me, I will continue to be like the late Lord Kitchener and Chalkdust, and ensure that I do not "Horn the Calypso".

Calypso Competition Winners

St Lucia		Barbados	
1957–63	Mighty Terra	1960	Mike Wilkinson
1964	No competition	1961	Little Baron
1965	No competition	1962	Producer
1966	Mighty Terra	1963	Sir Don
1967	Lord Zandolie	1964	Mighty Charmer
1968	Lord Zandolie	1965	Sir Don
1969	Mighty Pelay	1966–67	No competition
1970	Mighty Pelay	1968	Gabby
1971	Mighty Pelay	1969	Gabby
1972	Mighty Pelay	1970–72	No competition
1973	Mighty Desper	1973	Romeo
1974	Lord Carro	1974	Mighty Dragon
1975	Lord Carro	1975	Destroyer (Crop Over),
1976	Prophet Haggai		Sir Don (Independence)
1977	Mighty Prince	1976	Grynner (Crop Over),
1978	Mighty Pelay		Gabby (Independence)
1979	Mighty Barrie	1977	No competition
1980	Lord Jackson	1978	Destroyer
1981	Educator	1979	Liar
1982	Inferior	1980	Black Pawn
1983	De Professor	1981	Romeo
1984	De Controller	1982	Red Plastic Bag
1985	nvader	1983	No competition
1986	Invader	1984	Red Plastic Bag
1987	Mighty Pep	1985	Gabby
1988	Mighty Pep	1986	Johnny ma Boy
1989	Educator	1987	Bumba
1990	Ashanti	1988	Rita
1991	Ashanti	1989	Red Plastic Bag
1992	Mighty Pep	1990	Serenader
1993	Invader	1991	Kid Site
1994	Mighty Pep	1992	Invader #3
1995	Mighty Pep	1993	Serenader
1996	No competition	1994	John King
1997	Educator	1995	Edwin Yearwood

Table continues

Calypso Competition Winners (cont'd)

St Lucia (cont'd)		Barbados (cont'd)	
1988	Mighty Pep	1996	Red Plastic Bag
1989	Educator	1997	Gabby
1990	Ashanti	1998	Red Plastic Bag
1991	Ashanti	1999	Gabby
1992	Mighty Pep	2000	Gabby
1993	Invader	2001	Adrian Clarke
1994	Mighty Pep	2002	Red Plastic Bag
1995	Mighty Pep	2003	Red Plastic Bag
1996	No competition		
1997	Educator		
1998	Ashanti		
1999	Bachelor		
2000	Lady Spice		
2001	TC Brown		
2002	Mighty Pep		
2003	Pelay		

Note: See http://www.caribbeanedu.com/kewl/mix/mix05.asp and Trinidad Calypso Tent of the Air, http://www.kaiso.net/monarchs.html, for listings of other territories.

In the early 1990s, the St Lucian calypso was judged on its music, lyrics, performance and originality. In 1995, these four categories were reduced to three. Originality was taken out as an autonomous category and subsumed within the other three headings. The points system therefore apportioned 40 points to lyrics, 30 to music and 30 to performance. Of significance is the fact that since 1989, lyrics have been accorded the most points of the three categories. The awarding of the highest points to lyrics has meant that St Lucian calypsonians have been forced to concentrate more heavily on lyrical composition when creating their commentary calypsos. The 1995 calypso criteria sheet therefore contained the following categories and points allocation:

Lyrics (40 points)
Lyrical fit (10)
Theme expression/content (10)

Word craft (15)
Creativity (5)

Music (30 points)
Melody (15)
Arrangement (10)
Creativity (5)

Performance (30 points)
Rendition (15)
Presentation (10)
Demonstration (5)

But these were only part of the criteria. There were other, unofficial requirements. The audience set their own criteria. As in other islands, St Lucian audiences valued entertaining and rhythmically pleasing calypso. So, faced with demands for exciting, danceable compositions on the one hand and "serious" calypso commentary on the other, some St Lucian calypsonians undertook a series of experiments. They worked to help legitimize a hybrid music form.

De Professor, a calypso monarch from 1993, performed his song "Play Me Mass" (1995) in bold defiance of the calypso purists. His song's refrain makes it clear that he will "play de mass" in spite of what anyone says. The song was carefully structured. Each verse identifies a frustrating situation which confronts the performer's persona, and the chorus expresses his intention to throw away his frustrations. At a deeper level, the song was a rejoinder to all those who felt that serious competition calypso should be more laid-back, measured and laborious. De Professor performed his "Play Me Mass" with flair and abandon. The chorus declared,

> I having a fêting feeling
> A play me mass
> Give me room let me soca give me room let me pass
> all who I owe go check me Ash Wednesday
> A play me mass

The song's melody was infectious. It made use of minor inflections which served to create a near-haunting character to the musical composition. The bass line was both rhythmic and melodic, creating a danceable groove. The heavily lyrical piece was counterbalanced by extended passages of band chorus. All in all, it was an engaging and catchy experiment. Although the tempo was not quick, De Professor's song nonetheless situated itself within the "party" mode by virtue of its music and the lyric's insistence on the imperative of fête. This makes the song a pivotal text in the assessment of how St Lucian calypso gestured towards "party". Its composition and performance highlighted the complex relationship between lyrics and music proper in constituting genres of Caribbean music.

"Play Me Mass" is systematically constructed to critique a wide range of issues. Each verse, therefore, confronts a set of separate issues. In the first verse, the speaker traces his ambition of becoming a successful artist from the days of "greasing pan" until he records "up by KK", but after he toils and sweats to put his music on cassette, he discovers that "before I could sell one, me fans done get". So what can a struggling artist do in the midst of artistic and cultural repression? "I playin me mass. . . ." The second verse sees the speaker diversifying his activity to planting bananas, and after his local purchasers and international markets squeeze him out, he throws his hands up in frustration and release – but not before he promises to "trade with Castro, Saddam and Gadaffi". The third verse continues to present his encounter with dishonest contractors who exploit him and then stop him on carnival day "to discuss the matter". In the final verse, the speaker returns to the question of the artist's struggles. He laments the lack of airplay for music, the unfair distribution of moneys by calypso tents and the injustices of calypso competitions that stifle the artist. But, significantly, this verse sees the persona conducting a discourse with his fans as he vows to them to "come out for me party". The song therefore provides a telling critique of Caribbean society while pretending to apotheosize party and playing mass. In the same way, then, that mass playing is also role playing, this song performs a veiled and deceptive rendition of its theme.

The Mighty Pep is another St Lucian calypsonian who has found this hybrid style functional. Although many of his calypso lyrics have been written by his associate Rowan Seon, Pep has always played a key role in constructing the product from conception to the finished song. His 1995 song "Crime Wave" is a good example of his manipulation of the calypso hybrid. The song laments the wave of crime sweeping not only St Lucia, but also the entire Caribbean. His approach to the subject matter is creative, thought-provoking and bound to gain popular response. But to better appreciate his song, you should first understand how the "jump-

and-wave" syndrome spread throughout soca culture in the Caribbean and abroad.

In the early 1990s, Trinidadian soca artists such as Superblue, Iwer George and Frankie McIntosh popularized a performance style wherein the soca singer urged audiences to jump and wave something while they performed. This performance practice, akin to call and response, grew in the early 1990s, reaching its zenith around 1995, when Pep's song was performed. Another song of this period, Robbie's "King of Hearts", a very "serious" commentary, paradoxically also incited the audience to "wave your hands to the king of hearts / two shots for the king of hearts". These were the antics of the party performance, which Robbie also enlisted to draw support for his radical stance against all forms of corruption and compromise. In "Crime Wave", Pep playfully uses the waving syndrome as a starting point for his suggestion that a new type of wave was hitting the land – not the jump-and-wave syndrome, but a crime wave. It is significant to note that inasmuch as the song begins by referring to the jump-and-wave party syndrome in its lyrics, this gave Pep the legitimacy to use a musical style usually associated with jump-and-wave party music. This competition calypso therefore, with justification, made liberal use of soca motifs.

> Now there is a change in culture in the Caribbean
> Watch the wave *(repeat)*
> All Trinidad and Bajans have the same intention
> Watch the wave *(repeat)*
> Superblue and John King spread the word around
> In Trini parties and the Bajan towns
> But now it reach St Lucia like we change the line
> From jam and fête and jump and wine to
>
> *Chorus:*
> Crime wave sweeping the land social disruption
> Crime wave crooks in control
> Robberies big and bold
> The country is rocking on this crime wave
> It's like we knocking on we own grave
> The country jumping in the wrong wave
> Do something to change the craze
> When the soca man say to misbehave
> What he means is to raise your hands

Wave your hands, wave wave wave
Not crime wave let's stop this crime wave

The song's first verse carefully and cunningly sets up the discursive field of play – that is, it provides the background. It suggests that there are new trends taking place in Caribbean music culture, and it suggests that the Trinidadians and Bajans are instigators of this. But as the verse ends and the chorus begins, it becomes obvious that Pep is no longer referring only to new trends in music culture, but to disturbing trends in criminal activity. The song craftily but strikingly segues from supposedly light-hearted concerns to a stinging criticism of the rise of violence in Caribbean society. The song's first verse therefore masks its ultimate intent.

The chorus unveils the deeper reasoning of its composer. But the musical accompaniment also serves a crucial function. It works in consort with the jump-and-wave/crime wave dialectic which the song projects. The spirited musical accompaniment conceals the composition's studied engagement with a grave subject. Some calypso purists might question the suitability of employing an uptempo rhythm for such a serious message. Calypso commentary with biting lyrics and clever wordplay has come to be thought of as requiring a more or less staid musical track. Pep's rendition of this song during the 1995 finals competition was at approximately 120 beats per minute. That is very fast – most traditional commentary calypsos are performed at less than 110 beats per minute. (Michael Jackson's popular hit "Remember the Time" plays at approximately 110 beats per minute, whereas Frankie Smith's "Double Dutch Bus" is 120 beats per minute.) Pep also allowed for extended bars of music during which he teased the crowd with his own double-edged repeating of "wave" and "crime wave". Through this and also the use of two hook lines in each verse, the singer was able to summon crowd support for his cause. This is the advantage that such compositions gain. Audiences react more visibly to the uptempo rhythm, so the performer in most instances works less hard to evoke response. Inasmuch as the calypso is an audience-oriented art form, there is significant value assigned to performances that evoke response.

Jaunty's role in establishing the calypso-soca hybrid in St Lucia must be noted. During the 1990s, Jaunty performed a string of soca dance hits. In 1993, he won the road march with "Oh La Lay", and again in 1995 with "We Shall Hop". In 1996, he performed what is arguably his most witty, biting and danceable composition, "Bobolist". The song came in a year when there was no calypso season in St Lucia. The National Calypso Association and some carnival bands boycotted the festival in protest over the minister of education's decision to continue the festival in the month of February contrary to the recommendations of a consultative report. Only five senior calypsonians released songs that year. By doing so, they opened themselves to a five-year ban by the association. Without doubt, Jaunty's "Bobolist" stood out that year, not only because there were few other songs to play on radio, but also because the song saw Jaunty making effective use of wit, innuendo, suggestion, the pun and infectious French Caribbean dance rhythms. Its popularity was built on equally strong lyrical and musical constituents.

The lyrical text of "Bobolist" presents the singer's persona's wish list for his prosperity. It insinuates that political and other leaders have created a list of cliques that share in the national rewards, while others, who are apart from this list, have to struggle. The song's chorus therefore repeats: "I want to be on the bobolist / somebody put me on the bobolist". It is deceptively playful.

The song's lyrical strategy is built upon its endless playing with the word "bobolist". The *Dictionary of Caribbean English Usage* defines the noun *bobol* as organized fraud and corruption. A *bobolist* is therefore a dishonest individual, someone who misappropriates public or corporate funds. Jaunty takes the second syllable, *bol*, and subjects it to a number of phonological and lexical variations and extensions. In one refrain, he urges St Lucians to "put your hand on your head and *bawl*". He also makes claims to being clairvoyant, professing, "man I looking in me crystal *ball*". At the end of the song he again repeats the names of interest groups which pass on their patronage, and he suggests the seemingly ludicrous idea that, like sportspeople, these interest groups are playing "basketball, volleyball, bobol". Jaunty's excursion into the realm of seeming absurdity is indeed a strength of the song. Beneath the facade of seeming puerile wordplay is an underlying satiric streak that jabs at the tendency to consolidate wealth among interest groups in Caribbean society. Another performer – say, Herb Black – might not deliver a song in this vein because of its apparent diffusion of its "serious" message. Herb Black's approach would be more direct, overtly confrontational; it is his particular strength. But Jaunty's vocal tone is bright and crisp, and suggests deliberate play. It therefore helps to shape this composition, in which his attitude mockingly exposes the scandalous behaviour of political and other leaders.

Two other artists working in this hybrid form at the same time as Jaunty were Educator and Tricky. Educator's "Bring Them In" is similar to Tricky's "Bad Bad Drugs" in some respects. Both are songs of warning against social ills, cautionary tracks. They are anthemlike in their treatment of music and in their lyrical construction. They therefore made use of choric melodic phrases and lyrical repetition. Both also made use of uptempo rhythms. Educator's "Bring Them In" was performed for the judges at a tempo of about 123 beats per minute. As a lyrical text it is a straightforward composition, not engaging in the type of veiling and unveiling evident in Pep's "Crime Wave" or Jaunty's "Bobolist". Both those songs are about the ills affecting the body social of St Lucia. But Educator's is different in its conceptualization and intent. If Pep's song deals with crime in its broadest manifestations, Educator's song wants to focus on a specific aspect of crime.

"Bring Them In" deals with firearms and shootings as a specific concern in St Lucia. Having therefore narrowed the discourse so sharply, the composition seeks to confront the problem of the proliferation of illegal firearms, and to do so with few impediments. The message of this song is not one for working out by way of riddles. The composer wanted a quick, direct, swift response. The uptempo style of the song's delivery conveys this urgency. The chorus's employment of call-and-response passages also embellishes the song's participatory intent.

> All around de town
> Mamma up and down
> Ah hearing de sound
> Of dem firearm
> Down in Wilton yard
> All on de boulevard
> Is like we gone mad
> You must admit that's sad
> But de time has come for us to save this land
> De future depends on we own contribution
> Three months amnesty
> To stop de shooting spree
> Bring your illegal gun to de nearest police station
>
> Bazooka　　　Mennen yo

Ratata   Mennen yo
Rocket launcher   Mennen yo
German luger   Mennen yo

Tricky's "Bad Bad Drugs" functioned in much the same way. Whereas Educator's song diagnosed the misuse of firearms as a social problem, Tricky identifies drugs as the most insidious social ill that has plagued the Caribbean in the 1980s and 1990s. Throughout the 1980s and 1990s, most major Caribbean artists had done an anti-drug song. Tricky's composition does not attempt to do anything radically new in terms of lyrics. Its lyrics are straight up, like Educator's. Tricky, too, wants to deliver a clear message. However, the song came in for some criticism from selected commentators who felt that the composer had blundered in the song's repeated refrain of "does he does or does he don't use it". When Tricky appeared on the Radio St Lucia 660 KHZ morning calypso talk show during the 1994 festival season, he asserted the rights of the artist, who has poetic licence to manipulate language to make it bear the burden of local experience.

The debate surrounding Tricky's song reflects the lingering tension between "nation language" and the standard variety in contemporary Caribbean cultural expression. But perhaps Tricky was right when he implied that calypso is not so much about rightness and wrongness as it is about the creative forging of new words and new rhythms for the greater purpose of causing a response. His song achieves this goal by transgressing the rules of Standard English grammar. But it also evokes response by subverting the rules of commentary calypso, by appropriating the lyrics of calypso and replacing them within the music of soca.

Say no to bad bad drugs   No no no
Say no to bad bad drugs   No no no

Again, the employment of the antiphonal (call-and-response) structure proves very effective in the formation of the song's anthemic slogan. This is a slogan that the singer belts out and thereby has his audience reaffirm their commitment to a drug-free St Lucia. In a further section of the song's refrain, Tricky introduces an alternative site of meaningful entrapment, when he encourages his captive audience to "say yes to the steel pan man". He therefore puts forward meaningful creative activity, such as singing calypso, as a binary opposite to entrapment by drugs.

In the final instance, of course, it is an exciting rhythm that captures the imagination of those who listen to the composition as a sound recording. The accompanying music is infectious and symbolizes the insidious flame that can engulf an unsuspecting user. Like De Professor's "Play Me Mass", the song also makes use of extended musical instrumentation.

I have been speaking about the hybrid as it relates to the ways in which St Lucian artists fused the conscious lyrics of calypso with the danceable rhythms of soca and post-soca styles. In some respects, this fusion reflects the way in which Caribbean artists have challenged the boundaries of the art forms they practise. Through these experiments, artists often create new subgenres. St Lucian culture, like other cultures of the Caribbean, was engaged in a process of self-analysis and critique. Many cultures of the region were reflecting in the 1990s on their achievements and creations over the previous twenty to twenty-five years. They were aware that a new century was approaching. They knew that the global economy had rendered many of their post-independence initiatives and protocols obsolete. The sense of an impending new arrangement had a tremendous impact on the way artists perceived their art form and its sustainability. Some artists returned to a more intimate practice of traditional forms. Other artists, mindful that creative industries held potential for commerce, challenged their art forms to expand. Still others responded to the immediate demands of local culture. But in all cases, regional culture experienced a set of dynamics whose effects were still being worked out well into the first decade of the twenty-first century.

St Lucian artists affirmed their ability to forge radical styles in the late twentieth century and the beginning of the twenty-first. But St Lucian calypso has faced the problem of its confinement to a limited market. It was especially difficult to access St Lucian music in retail stores throughout the region during the early and mid-1990s. This problem was not peculiar to St Lucia – it affected many other territories as well. But by the beginning of 2002, St Lucian artists began to more vigorously seek out markets and spread information about their products. Musical compilations played a significant part in this marketing drive. Through this method, artists were able to consolidate and concentrate their energies. Calypso tents played a critical role in this strategy of creating new bridges of opportunity. Whereas a popular tent like Trinidad's Spectakula expanded its base and that of its artists in the 1980s by holding shows in other islands, post-2000 conditions encouraged entities to market their wares by other methods.

Joint recordings and tent-compilation recordings were a popular route by which artists sought to access wider markets. Some of these compilations featured bona fide calypso as well as uptempo soca. They therefore represented hybrid products, pulling together a varied range of performers and performances. In the further drive to cross new boundaries, St Lucian artists interfaced with wider audiences by way of the Internet. By mid-2003, calypso entities such as the Ambassadors' tent had already turned to the Internet for virtual access to wider markets and to expand the parameters in which calypso was marketed. The Ambassadors' tent home page opens up to further links on the history of the tent, its members, the backing band and commercial tent recordings.[32] The recordings include *Ambassadors' Kalaloo 1995*, *Ambassadors' Kaiso Video 1998* and *Merry Christmas Our Way 2001*. The Web site's navigation is user-friendly. Its brown, beige and green textures of colour are appealing to the user. Although the site allows customers to order and purchase recordings, it seems equally intent on conveying information about the entity and its members. In this regard, it represents a departure from the all-out commercially oriented dedicated sites of other Caribbean musical outfits. This is not a problem for Ambassadors, since the motto that stands out on the Web site is "to enlighten, amuse and educate". The Web site therefore strives for a range of objectives. Like the music of St Lucia which it represents, it recognizes the tensions inherent within the drive to popularize an art form, and it moves to create a new space for its future development.

Women and Moral Conscience

Increasingly in the 1990s, Caribbean artists worked diligently to gain greater access to the national discursive space. This spectrum was becoming increasingly contested by a range of other entities. The culture of drugs and other social ills were being informally supported throughout the veins of society. There was fierce competition for the minds and bodies of many Caribbean youths. Some calypsonians saw themselves as active agents working against these negative forces. Indeed, the calypsonian has traditionally been viewed as the moral conscience of the society. So Robbie's "King of Hearts" (1995) vowed never to compromise the calypsonian's role as social commentator. Bachelor's 1999 monarch-winning "Hypocrites" called society to higher morals and values. Tricky took on the persona of Moses in 2003, warning society's pharaoh to "let my people go". In her 1998 calypso "Morality", Mary G put forward the view that society was in crisis. This song saw the calypsonian castigating the church, among other organizations, for not consistently upholding the standards of its faith:

> We talking casino church say that's a no no
> On a moral question they raising objection
> But bingo churches still playing
> And lotto is only half a sin
> This thing about morality all depend on who you be

St Lucia's problems were many during the 1990s. Like other Caribbean territories, St Lucia grappled with unemployment, crime, moral decay and economic pressures. The shift to more exciting compositions was therefore in some respects an attempt by the artists to maintain a position of visibility in the nation's communication space. At the same time, many St Lucian female calypsonians seemed more preoccupied with guarding the society against moral and social deterioration than with any other single issue. It was these women who were at the forefront of commenting on social issues during the 1990s.

The role of women in calypso in St Lucia is not unlike that in other countries of the region. Indeed, women have traditionally played a secondary role to male calypso performers. In the Trinidadian context, the 1980s and 1990s marked the era when female calypso performers seemed to come to the fore. For St Lucia, it was in the 1990s that its female calypsonians took on a leading role. Performers such as Lady Leen, Mary G, Cheryl and Colours, Akwa, Nadiege, Davis and Black Pearl competed steadfastly with the men. Outside of the competition context, their contribution was also being felt. Lady Leen, for instance, was given the Outstanding Achievement Award for International Women's Day in 1997. In 2001, she was honoured in Trinidad and Tobago for her outstanding contribution to the arts.

As in other territories of the region, many of the songs performed by women in St Lucia have been written by men. Whereas some commentators might draw attention to this to undermine the contribution of some female calypsonians, a careful examination of the relationship between these women and men reveals a more complex composer-performer dynamic. Cheryl, of the all-female group Colours, entered the calypso arena as a result of public pressure but refused to perform material by the musician-arranger Boo Hinkson if it did not meet a standard she considered to be worthy of her image. Indeed, Boo Hinkson has had to approach writing for Cheryl with an awareness of her ideology and interests.

In the final analysis, audiences have come to regard performers like Cheryl and Mary G as legitimate artists. The songs they perform are theirs, not the composers', in the minds of their audiences. They have therefore subverted the entire composition-performance process. This stroke of subversion is only possible when a performer takes command of his or her song and personalizes it. These performers have challenged the male composers to think and create in new ways, to produce a style and tone of calypso which otherwise, arguably, would not have been much produced in the Caribbean.

This is not a phenomenon that is unheard of in the wider realm of entertainment. Composition and performance are seen as specialist undertakings in the international music industry. Many major artists therefore perform songs written by dedicated songwriters or by other artists. The curious difference in the calypso domain has to do with a long-standing argument that distinguishes between a calypsonian and a calypso singer. Based on this argument, the "real" calypsonian is that individual who can both write and perform his or her material. The lesser calypso singer is the individual who performs but does not write his or her material. There is still a diehard core of calypso aficionados who privilege this argument, but, for the most part, calypso audiences pay less attention to this than to how an individual artist handles the material which he or she decides to perform. To some degree, it requires even greater skill to interpret another individual's composition than to do so with one's own. In effect, then, there is no straightforward, conclusive reading of the complex relationship between composer and performer.

In a real sense, calypsonians and audiences have not bogged themselves down with this dialectic. Just as the composer and performer have had to negotiate their relationship, so have audiences (though, arguably, with less thought or stress). St Lucian calypso went on in the 1990s unencumbered by this type of debate. For all intents and purposes, therefore, its female performers have not played secondary roles. Their performances are indeed perceived as bona fide contributions. Their points of view and politics have been privileged.

Many female calypsonians have established themselves as leading commentators on and gatekeepers of the standards of moral and social decency within St Lucia. At the end of the twentieth century, when Cheryl and Colours sang "Protect Lucian Women", it was interpreted as a feminist call to arms – and in part it was this. But at an even deeper level, it interrogates the biases within St Lucia's justice system. Through a compelling exposition, "Protect Lucian Women" sets up a dialogue between women's issues and an unsympathetic justice system. The song does not give up on the system of social and legal justice but advocates the need for a revamping of laws and procedures as they relate to rape, for example. It does not therefore present men as the opposition to female liberation and redress; instead, it calls the justice system into question. Indirectly, too, the male bias within the system is indicted, but, through a more subtle technique, "Protect Lucian Women" is able to rally people of both genders to confront the St Lucian legal system.

This is not to say that St Lucian female calypsonians have not concerned themselves with confronting men head on. They have and they do (as in Lady Strong's 1999 "De Ride"), but they have tended to do so in a much more furtive, persuasive and strategic way. Cheryl sings:

> What is de matter with men in St Lucia
> Assizes have rape case all the way, Lord don't let them beast get away
> Is too long this thing happening
> Like our women now frightening
> Police ain't able to protect we
> Join in hand we planning a strategy
> Cause rape does leave a trauma
> You never recover
> We tired with this due process of law
> We can't take disgrace no more
>
> *Chorus:*
> Women in de legal system
> Protect them Lucian women

Cheryl and Colours' 1998 calypso finals song, "Massav Tree", is arguably one of the most cleverly conceived, written and performed commentaries in the Caribbean in recent times. It is a statement on the range of issues that plagued St Lucia and the Caribbean in the late twentieth century and continue in the early twenty-first. Since there are so many such songs each year in calypso competitions throughout the region, calypsonians must find fresh angles from which to approach the familiar subject matter. This particular song by Cheryl stands out for its concentration on an actual tree, which the song treats metaphorically. The massav tree, which is situated in the capital city, Castries, becomes the point of departure from which the singer is able to branch outwards to identify the ills within society. Because the tree is centrally placed in the city and its roots spread throughout the town, it therefore seemed a suitable metaphor to employ. But the song also depends on a fictional "old man" who talks to the tree and puts his ear to hear what it says. Because there is some measure of senility or insanity about this old man, the singer therefore distances herself from the kinds of revelations that are voiced in the song. It is the massav tree and the old man that are totally responsible for any damaging inferences or revelations – a telling rhetorical device.

> This old man used to talk to the massav tree on the square
> Don't mind it name massav it know every thing going on here
> She roots deep in the ground spread right through the town
> And she branches cover the city eavesdropping on all of we
> So when the old man talk to the tree you wouldn't believe
> The things it reveal to he

Since the roots of the tree run under the police station, the tree therefore knows which police in Gros Islet allow people in custody to "just get up and walk away". Big lawyers, high-class drug pushers, people in cabinet, education administrators, the clergy, customs officers, diplomats – all are implicated in some way as contributing to the general social decay.

Cheryl's song "School Bag" is similarly clever in its conception. Many calypsos throughout the years have dealt with this issue of youth deviance. In "School Bag", Cheryl examines the current and future state of St Lucia. The song proposes that the clearest "crystal ball" for seeing into the future is the act of looking into the school bags of young people:

> It suddenly hit me
> That the turn of the century
> Is not far away as most people say

It's time to study what's in store for we country
I done know she history and culture
What I want to study is really she future
I thought I should get a crystal ball
I decide I don't need that at all
No the school bag could tell me
What's in store at the turn of the century

Like "Massav Tree", this song fixes on a simple object, which it uses to reveal profound yet hard truths about the state of the nation's children at the turn of the century. In many ways, the words of this song reflected a premonition felt by many within St Lucian society, particularly by women performers. Calypso has always dealt with the future, but, as Cheryl demonstrates in her song, the preoccupation with the future in St Lucian calypso reflects the particular uncertainty of Caribbean society in light of global and national pressures:

Chorus:
You finding knife and gun in the school bag
Packets of condom in the school bag
The future of we country ain't looking good to me
You finding blue movie in the school bag
Stolen jewellery in the school bag
At the turn of the century
Your country in jeopardy
I done see the whole of the future
Of my country St Lucia and it looking bad
I see the whole thing inside the school bag

Conclusions

If there is an underlying thread in the stories of Barbadian and St Lucian calypso, it is that Caribbean societies are still grappling with their realities, still very much in the process of working out how to go about creating images and visions of themselves through music. While creating in a context of instability, calypso artists of necessity interrogate these images. They wrestle with the visions they see through these (their very own) creations. The resultant is that cultures of the Caribbean are incessantly thrown back upon themselves. They must continually return to fundamental questions of self-fashioning and the politics that surround this. This is not a regressive process. On the contrary, it is progressive. The failure to recognize the value and power of this process could, however, render the whole exercise fruitless. This chapter has therefore intervened in the process, calling attention to the importance of a continuous, progressive cultural scrutiny. Although Barbadian and St Lucian cultures have made significant strides, a lingering reality is that they are still prone to falter. An ongoing engagement with the myriad issues presented through expressions of culture and the arts represents a sure strategy for ensuring a repositioning of the region in the coming years.

Towards a Caribbean Gospel Aesthetic

Gospel and Popular Expression

Caribbean gospel music holds a special yet peculiar place within the corpus of music in the region, hardly seen as a major category. Some would debate if there even is such a thing as Caribbean gospel. But few would question the contribution of a set of performers who have recorded and performed for the glory of God and to gain support for their ministry, their upkeep and the message of Jesus.

Nonetheless, given the marginal position of gospel among the various categories of Caribbean music, why then does this book – a book on popular music – centre gospel music culture? The reasons are many. For one thing, this book explores the borderlines of Caribbean music. And a careful assessment of gospel in the region would reveal the extent to which it has either participated in or affected core segments of the society. Gospel continues to have a sizeable following of people who actively participate in religious activities such as concerts and festivals as well as radio, television and film programmes.

Naturally, the category of music called "gospel" has never existed in a vacuum. In the late twentieth century, it interfaced with secular music culture to an unprecedented degree, and it continues to do so. Indeed, a significant number of "secular" artists turned in the 1990s to gospel music, which raised the issue of the relationship between gospel and other music categories. The post-2000 evolution of Caribbean gospel was also partly driven by the contribution of once-"secular" artists. The result of the influences the genre has subsumed has been that the category called "gospel" has both examined itself and been examined. Gospel today embodies the quality of other popular expressions, insofar as it appeals to a range of people. It is conservative but it is also radical. It often straddles the line between acceptability and unacceptability.

We will start with the general evolution of gospel music in the United States, because of the influence of that tradition on the Caribbean, and with the influence of Catholicism. This will provide a background for better understanding the development of the gospel genre in its wider context and in the Caribbean. We also need to acknowledge the challenges of identifying what "gospel" refers to in Caribbean usage. Part of this difficulty hinges on the multiple influences on gospel music in the Caribbean, part on the fact that the arena of Caribbean gospel and gospel music culture represents a relatively new site of debate in Caribbean cultural studies.

There are serious challenges of naming in the area of gospel music, and there are contentious debates in the global music industry, for example, surrounding religious music as a category in the Grammy Awards.[1] The music industry itself struggles to categorize Christian music, as is evident in the numerous awards categories at the prestigious Dove Awards – traditional gospel, contemporary gospel, urban recorded, inspirational recorded, alternative recorded, rap/hip hop/dance recorded. The point which must be made at this stage is that the term *gospel music* (as it is used in the Caribbean) does not carry the same meaning as it does in the American context. This is not a novel situation – there are always variations on cultural phenomena across geographical as well as temporal space. (Later in this book, for example, we'll look at the different names given to commercial reggae across the Caribbean.)

The Center for Black Music Research is clear in its definition. It considers gospel music to be "African-American Protestant vocal music that celebrates Christian doctrine in emotive, often dramatic ways".[2] This is a reasonable definition. In the Caribbean, though, the meaning of *gospel music* is not as fixed. Very often in the Caribbean the label "gospel music" is interchanged with "Christian music". Sometimes it refers to the dominant musical style of evangelical assemblies. At other times it is used to define a category of music that approximates the popular style of African-American religious music. Here I will treat the term *gospel* in a way that reflects its multiple uses in the region. I have, however, stopped short of concentrating on all forms of Christian music and have privileged the popular music often associated with evangelical assemblies.

Gospel music refers to that category which is now popularly performed on stage, at Christian and other cultural festivals. It is performed by choirs, chorales, soloists and bands. Central to the definition and description of gospel music must be the inclusion of that form of Christian music which makes use of modern musical styles and modern musical technologies. Its practitioners are mainly younger artists, although older people are also actively engaged in the tradition. A list of Caribbean gospel performers might therefore include such names as Reverend V. B. and the Flames, Sister Margreta Marshall, Harella Goodwin, the Regenerated Singers, the Grace Thrillers, Change, Jerry Lloyd, Judah Development, Shine the Light, Papa San, Sherwin Gardner, and Nicole Ballosingh-Holder.

The Caribbean is never alone; there are always cross-cultural and intertextual relations between Caribbean and other cultures. This chapter therefore considers several strands of influence on Caribbean "gospel" – the Euro-Catholic, African-American and African-Caribbean traditions. Of paramount importance, though, are the questions: Is there a legitimate phenomenon which can be termed "Caribbean gospel"? What are the necessary constituents of a Caribbean gospel aesthetic? What is the nature of the relationship between traditional gospel and "new wave" Caribbean gospel? What are the challenges posed to this category of music by internal as well as external forces? These questions will form the major thrust of this chapter.

Gospel in the United States and Christian Music in Caribbean Assemblies

The work of late-nineteenth-century American songwriters and singers such as Dwight Moody and Ira Sankey was significant. Their contribution to the gospel hymn genre cannot be overlooked in the development of religious music in the United States, particularly their innovation of "singing the gospel" in evangelical meetings in the United States and Great Britain, accompanying such preachers as Billy Sunday. Gospel hymn writers of the period borrowed from popular songs, including those of Tin Pan Alley. But after the Civil War, many religious denominations were branching off in new directions and exploring a variety of practices that reflected a greater awareness of African aesthetics through worship. By the late nineteenth century, the first compositions of a black gospel songwriter appeared: Charles Albert Tindley. Whereas Sankey's and Moody's songs suppressed emotional cries and passionate singing, black gospel took on its own character. Black writers and performers used conventional harmonies with diatonic scales and lucid vocal tones, but they implanted inflections and spontaneous rendition. As Eileen Southern states, "the song repertoires of folk churches might include . . . Protestant hymns . . . , spirituals and jubilee songs; and the Sunday-school or gospel hymns. But the way these songs were performed in folk churches was highly unorthodox."[3]

Black gospel writers and performers created and nurtured their tradition by adapting standards, but also by forging their own texts and styling. The National Baptist Convention's publication of *Gospel Pearls*, with more than 150 songs from black congregations, marked the development of a catalogue of old and newly composed songs.

This new tradition had grown in confidence. Some of its contributors were better known for blues, but it was clear that black gospel had established its signature. Many of these songs were performed to the lively antics of call and response, improvisation, hand-clapping and other African-inspired features. This practice has remained a trademark of black gospel practice to this day, and songs are performed with the particular styling of different congregations and individual artists. When many Caribbean black congregations took up the standard hymn books of their denominational centres in the United States and Europe, they were instrumental in subverting the notational prescriptions of songs like "Let the Lower Lights Be Burning", "The Old Rugged Cross" and "Since Jesus Came into my Heart".

In the earlier part of the twentieth century in the United States, musical instruments began to be used in some "folk" churches, instruments such as the rhythmic piano, the guitar and selected wind instruments. There was, by the 1920s, no real perceptible distinction between the sacred music sung and performed by blacks and the secular blues. Both frequently revolved around similar chord progressions. Thomas Dorsey, born in 1899, the famous composer of "Precious Lord Take My Hand", is credited with being the first individual to have used the term "gospel song" in reference to the songs of black churches. A great many of the songs composed by black writers in those early days featured clear, direct, vivid biblical images and references. These features have remained in gospel over the years, even as the music was exported to other societies in the United

States and the Caribbean by the medium of radio and by travelling singing ministers and performers.

Gospel quartets and the gospel female choir were popular institutions in the first half of the twentieth century in the United States. By the mid-1930s, there were gospel song and singing competitions which patrons paid to see. Mahalia Jackson was prominent in this era. This period also saw performances of gospel song in secular venues, such as the Cotton Club in Harlem, New York.

Gospel music became more sophisticated as it moved into urban settings and was disseminated abroad to other regions of the United States. This music was increasingly being performed to a much fuller accompaniment of instruments – strings, winds, percussion – and with much more complex chord and harmonic progressions. Improvisation and playing "by ear" were still common, as was the preference for a husky, aggressive and lavish vocal execution. These features have lived on. Particularly in the 1980s, Caribbean gospel acts, primarily choirs, aspired to this style of execution, but with mixed success.

In the 1960s and 1970s, black gospel acts in the United States began to pay much more attention to delivering "a show". Groups such as the Ward Sisters brought their own style, which seemed reminiscent of popular non-gospel artists. By 1963, gospel had its own television show. The music grew in popularity. Record sales were up, and the gospel music industry escalated. In the Caribbean, though, the impact of black gospel music would not really be felt that early. The main tremors would be felt only in the 1980s when performers such as Al Green, Andre Crouch, Jessie Dixon and Albertina Walker (who had been performing for a considerable time before then) were "reborn" in the Caribbean to a great many gospel choirs and chorales.

Interestingly, black gospel stylings were not widely popular in the Caribbean until this late in its development. Earlier (pre-1960s) transferral and popularizing were not affected, partly because of the absence of sustained connections between African-American headquarter churches and their local assemblies. There was a looser structure connecting some evangelical assemblies in the earlier days. Besides, the English religious traditions of ritual and worship lingered in many Caribbean societies long after emancipation. Black gospel stylings gained in popularity when regional gospel acts began to identify more closely with African-American performers whom they heard and saw with greater frequency via the media. An active endorsement of black gospel motifs was one method of freeing performers from a conservative religious music practice. The dominant motifs of African-American style offered a departure from Euro-Catholic practice but still symbolically maintained a degree of "high practice" and purity as a result of the foreign intonation and musical features of the American tradition. Therefore, some respectability associated with that tradition remained. However, the main external influence that affected gospel (and other religious music) when it was becoming an identifiable genre in the Caribbean was not the black tradition of the United States. It was the music of the established church and, a little later, religious songs sung to country and western musical accompaniment.

The music of the Catholic tradition has had a tremendous influence on forms of religious music performed in both Catholic and non-Catholic denominations. Islands such as St Lucia and Dominica have had a particularly strong Roman Catholic influence. Evangelical denominations in these territories have therefore had to operate in the shadow of this influence.[4] In the Caribbean, throughout the twentieth century, there was a marked distinction between the "big church" and the "small" or "little church".

In post-emancipation Caribbean society, established churches took on the role of education centres. The church leadership in many cases also perpetuated the social ordering and hierarchies that pervaded society. Many such orderings remained, even in the post-independence era. The European established churches were referred to as the "big churches", since they had a much longer history as institutions. In the Caribbean, these established church institutions had worked with the state and so became symbols and carriers of social status for many individuals in the pre- and post-emancipation eras. By the mid-twentieth century, the ritual, liturgy and music of the so-called big (Anglican and Roman Catholic) church lived on as symbols of a high culture – and a higher worship.

Although this was the case in islands such as Jamaica, Trinidad, St Lucia, St Vincent, Grenada and Barbados, there was still a growing participation in other, unofficial, rituals in the "little" churches. These were less well-organized groupings, which were very expressive and evangelical in orientation. The longer-established churches appealed to a sense of social mobility among the masses, so many individuals sought to establish a higher social standing through joining these predominantly Catholic denominations. However, it was in the growing number of evangelical denominations that many more people of African ancestry knew that they could actively participate with greater freedom.

In a manner of speaking, there existed, side by side, two types of music (and music practice) within the small church. First, there was the music performance of actual congregational worship, the much more spontaneous expression. Second, there was the less spontaneous musical performance of formal occasions, such as harvests and other special services. Pentecostal assemblies in the Caribbean around the 1950s and 1960s used a variety of standard church hymnals for song worship. But in many more cases, the words of songs and choruses were sung from memory, or shouted out during singing, in the old "lining-out" fashion, by the pastor or song leader. These songs were accompanied by hand-clapping, foot-stomping and the beating of benches and other implements. The playing of tambourines was a popular practice. Over time these instruments developed from two-shackle to multi-shackle instruments. The timpani, commonly called the "steel", was also popular. Some congregations also employed a pair of high-hat-type cymbals that were clashed together to add to the hypnotic rhythms of worship. There are also cases in the eastern Caribbean in which the conch shell was used integrally within congregational song services.

Important strokes of subversion were carried out through religious worship within the small church. The use of hymnal master texts originating in the United States and the United Kingdom was undermined by congregations that rearranged the songs to suit the rhythmic and performance peculiarities of their experience. Thus, many standard hymns from abroad were given a livelier interpretation. Melodies were altered. No fixed sense of beats per minute was upheld. Lyrics were added, deleted, contorted. Each performance created its own version of the work. This process resulted in several unstable versions. And the process itself served to cast doubts on the authority of the standard hymnal text. But it also resulted in competing versions and potentially conflicting renditions when different individuals performed together.

In contrast to this subversive practice, there was a tendency at formal occasions of worship to privilege the formulaic styling which was practised in the big church. Many local congregations are known to have adopted the styling of the Anglo-Catholic choir in particular. A stylized form therefore developed in the little church. There was no radical difference between these choirs and the choirs of the Catholic tradition. This type of formal choral practice therefore developed within both the big church and the little church, and it can still be seen in the performance of many Anglo-Catholic choirs and of some Pentecostal choirs with older memberships. This style of choral singing valorizes the four-part harmony in performance, the soprano and alto sections comprising female voices, and the tenor and bass sections featuring male voices.

The popular songs which belong to this tradition are sometimes called "anthems". (Sir William Leighton produced texts for some of these anthems in the sixteenth century as found in his *Tears or Lamentations of a Sorrowful Soul* [1614].) Among the list of songs which have been performed in this genre are Adger M. Pace's 1939 "I Can Tell You the Time" and J. W. and J. D. Vaughn's "Inside the Gate". These songs, in their harmonic construction, allow for much vocal interaction and counterpoint by the attendant voices. "I Can Tell You the Time", for example, provides an opportunity for interplay between the bass voice(s) on the one hand and the soprano, alto and tenor voices on the other. The performance of this genre is very regimented. It does not allow for much spontaneous improvisation, or for individual styling or embellishments. Since this type of singing valorizes a tight though formulaic harmony, much precision is sought after during practice sessions. The performance demands a faithful reproduction of what is practised.

In the Caribbean, this form of harmony has supported the old singing style called "sol-fa", where amateur sight-readers of music sing melodies of songs based on the association of the do-re-mi scale to notes on the musical staves. In this type of choir singing format, there has traditionally been a single choirmaster, who reads the music and interprets the four-part harmony for his choir beforehand. He teaches them, and they learn their parts through memory and reproduce them during performance. This type of singing has also been popular in the past at pseudo-religious events in selected Caribbean territories.[5]

Throughout the anglophone region, there are various interpretations of and variations on the style of European Catholic choirs. The impact of the European tradition has indeed been significant. There are few gospel artists of the 1980s and 1990s who do not acknowledge the effect of that tradition. In the Caribbean, when people refer to "gospel music", they mean that category of Christian music which partially borrows from the European, African-American and African-Caribbean traditions of religious music. This is indication of the complex evolution of gospel in the region.

In the 1950s and for most of the 1960s, the guitar was not yet a permanent fixture in most evangelical denominations in the Caribbean. But in the United States, instruments such as the electric organ, amplified guitar and drums were standard to many gospel ensembles. The Hammond organ became a central tonal tool of many gospel musicians long before its adoption by jazz practitioners. Although there were many individuals in the Caribbean who played the guitar, they tended to perform outside the context of the church. There was still a stigma attached by the church to certain instruments. In many instances, drums were also seen as being "the devil's instruments". It would only be during the 1970s and 1980s that significant numbers of regional churches would adopt a more worship-friendly attitude to such instruments. In the Salvation Army halls, the drums were accepted, as they were in keeping with the quasi-militarism of that organization, but even so, they were worn around the neck rather than positioned like a secular drum set.

The notion of a professional gospel artist was therefore going to be a much later development in the Caribbean than in the United States. This does not mean that there were no artists who devoted most of their time to performing "the gospel". In fact, some acts of the 1960s lay claim to some professionalism. But financial reward for personal upkeep was hard to achieve. No group of this period can claim to have lived comfortably, depending solely on the financial contribution of patrons. In the 1970s, some performers contemplated this possibility. Although there was an identifiable core of Caribbean professional gospel artists, the society at large cannot be said to have embraced this concept. Even in the twenty-first century, the idea of a professional gospel performer still raises some questions to do with the objectives of sharing the word of God and his son, Jesus. Others question the legitimacy of the professional gospel act because of the size of the market for gospel. Whereas there is a healthy audience for gospel music in the Caribbean, this has not translated into massive sales figures for gospel acts across the board. Many consumers have shown a preference for live performance over purchasing the recorded product. In the late twentieth century and the beginning of the twenty-first, gospel acts still lamented that piracy – music sharing through the Internet and more conventional media – was hampering their ability to be true professionals.

Constituting Caribbean Gospel

Gospel music has tended to be very popular in the Caribbean. It has always received the moral if not the financial support of its Caribbean listeners. Many people will acknowledge the impact of gospel music, but fewer are convinced about the authenticity and credibility of Caribbean gospel music. Is there such a thing?

Part of the challenge of gospel in the Caribbean is the perception that this category of music is not a bona fide entity. There are questions about its uniqueness. What does Caribbean gospel bring to the genre globally? These are vital questions. Direct responses to them could reveal a great deal about the viability of Caribbean gospel, about the state of Christian music and about the process of conceptualizing aspects of culture which are as contentious as Christian music. But another route of discovery is by way of proposing what *should* be the central features of Caribbean gospel and assessing the presence or absence of these features in the Caribbean tradition. This route allows for a closer scrutiny of different aspects of gospel music in the Caribbean. It permits a separate as well as a holistic study of the several layers of constituents that make up gospel music. But this process also of necessity raises another question: what set of criteria must the cultural critic bring to bear on an assessment of a special category like religious music?

The existence of a legitimate category called "Caribbean gospel" would require the presence of a number of distinctive features. I want to propose some of these features. For the purpose of this work, I will restrict them to three major features:

1. *Scripture, the Divine and Jesus.* The first component integral to the establishment of Caribbean gospel is that it focus on Christianity's central icon. Songs in this category should reflect a focus on "the Divine", on Jesus. Most Caribbean songs in the gospel domain do reflect this feature. If gospel in the Caribbean were to be judged based on the relative presence and absence of a focus on the Scriptures, on Jesus, on the Divine, then its practitioners would get high marks.

2. *Caribbean musical reference.* The second component necessary for creating a legitimate category called Caribbean gospel would be use of Caribbean musical reference. "Reference" here does not suggest a fleeting use of Caribbean music styles such as reggae and calypso.

Rather, it suggests the honest and imaginative use of Caribbean musical styles and the creation of engaging musical tracks through their use.

3. *Caribbean reality.* The third component essential to the establishment of Caribbean gospel must be the reflection of Caribbean reality – spiritual, social, political and so on – through its lyrics.

Gospel in the Caribbean has done very well in propagating the scriptures and the message of Christ. Let me restate here that, in many cases, the form of musical practice referred to as "gospel" springs predominantly from evangelical denominations. They tend to be oriented towards message dissemination. They also tend to be the most permissive in the use of modern forms of music, modern technologies and applications. Since evangelical churches have also tended to be scripture centred, the music which performers from their assemblies have produced has tended to reflect this strong influence. In *Barbadian Popular Music,* I explored the ramifications of this strong association between gospel artists and denominational bases.[6] Since Caribbean gospel artists are often inextricably linked to one or another denominational base, the timbre, tone, form and other constituents of Caribbean gospel have been fashioned by the denominational base. Many denominations in the Caribbean have their headquarters outside the region, including the Nazarene Church, the Church of God, the Wesleyan Holiness Church, the Seventh Day Adventists, the Christian Mission, the New Testament Church of God and the Salvation Army. When one considers the denominational base as being driven by built-in declarations of faith and accompanying ideology, then it becomes apparent that gospel in the Caribbean has for a long time been and is still hemmed in by the controlling directives of religious institutions.

A brief examination of one of the most popular solo gospel acts to come out of the eastern Caribbean, Joseph Niles, of Barbados, is instructive. Niles's background in gospel harks back to the moment of his conversion in 1955 within the evangelical tradition. A catalogue of his more than twenty albums and countless 45s would undoubtedly support my point about the lyrical emphasis in Caribbean gospel. In the mid-1980s, the gospel commentator/critic Emmanuel Joseph, commenting on Niles's repertoire, suggested that "ninety-eight percent . . . is not original material, most is a mere resurrection of old traditional church songs and choruses".[7] Niles's album titles are a testimony to this fact: *Gospel Ship, Let the*

Church Roll On, Royal Telephone and *Climbing up the Mountain.* This lyrical tendency is obvious, though, as a result of the ongoing immense debt which the emerging gospel act owes to the church, to its mission and to its ritual. For artists like Joseph Niles who were performing in the 1960s and 1970s, the church base was still the central point of influence for the construction of the gospel song. So it was only natural that the lyrics of these songs reflected the preferences and directives of the artist's congregational base. That said, Niles (and artists like him) cannot be categorized as conservative, because Niles has reworked standard hymns and spirituals in his own style. He has also confronted denominational rituals throughout his career. By the 1990s and after 2000, he had become less well known as an affiliate to a denomination. Indeed, because of his struggle and his longevity, he has rebuilt his image as a performer distinct from any single denomination. He has not, however, sought to reorient his reliance on existing conservative lyrical gospel standards.

The impact of standard hymnal texts on the lyrics of gospel songs in the Caribbean is a telling feature of gospel in the region. Some would argue that the retention of extant lyrical texts is also a notable feature of gospel music practice in other global contexts, such as in the African-American tradition. That is indeed the case. But even so, the development of Caribbean gospel has not thrown up a mixture of traditional (extant) and original compositions. In fact, whereas gospel in the United States has produced a consistent number of original lyrical texts, its Caribbean counterpart has been very much concerned with the dangers of veering too far from the prescribed words which such publications as *Songs of Joy and Gladness* have sanctioned as "all holy". Whereas gospel in the United States has legitimized a cadre of active songwriters, there is no such long-standing revered grouping in the Caribbean. This is not a result of a paucity of talent in the region; rather, within religious circles in the region the lyrical texts of "the Gospel" are considered to have been already written "in the Word".

Whereas the earlier singers of gospel songs in many Pentecostal denominations held on for formal occasions to a much more conservative performance, gospel performers of the late 1960s tended to interpret a set of Negro spirituals. However, these artists were not given the sanction of their pastors, congregations and audiences to engage in the much more subversive practice of composing their own lyrics. The rigid adherence to the hymnal master text stemmed largely from the oppositional hierarchical relationship between the Christian master and the uncivilized slave and from the imperative of upholding the principles of the institutionalized Christian faith. Christianity in the Caribbean has yet to be given an established indigenous signature. Contemporary artists of the 1980s, 1990s and beyond did begin to manipulate their art form to varying degrees, but for the most part they played it safe. The Regenerated Singers, the Gospel Comforters, Sister Marshall, the Grace Thrillers, Birthright, Papa San, Carlene Davis and Sherwin Gardner are all contemporary acts who still pay reverence to the lyrical style inscribed in "external" master works.

I might be seen here to be speaking with a double tongue, since initially I suggested that the existence of a genre called "Caribbean gospel" would require some substantial reference to its centre, to God and to Jesus, and I now seem not to be at ease with the ongoing tendency of Caribbean gospel performers to espouse the lyrical texts of existing religious standards, standards which are very scripture centred. But perhaps it should be said that the three main components set out in this chapter are not mutually exclusive. To my mind, there should be some degree of counterbalancing of these three components: the lyric of the scriptures, the musical influence of the Caribbean and a lyrical reference that also reflects the overall social reality of Caribbean society. So I have really been suggesting that many of the songs that have been chosen and performed by Caribbean gospel acts have tended to reveal an imbalance towards formulaic scriptural allusion. There is not enough effort given to an overall Caribbean experience in the gospel music genre in the Caribbean.

Music: Style and Performance

From as early as the 1960s, Caribbean performers of gospel music were beginning to accompany their songs with rhythms and stylings that reflected a Caribbean sensibility. As I suggested earlier, most Pentecostal congregations have tended in their worship to subvert the metrical, rhythmic and phrasing patters which were handed down in the musical scores of the songbooks from which they sang during worship.

In Jamaica, solo and group performers of gospel began to reinterpret a range of church songs to the styling of rocksteady. A record from a later period in the 1970s best exemplifies this method. Reverend V. B. and the Gospel Flames' *Let the Power* was an eight-track album that featured rock and roll, rocksteady and a heavy influence of soul. Reverend V. B.'s presence in old ska and rocksteady archives reflects the partial immersion of gospel within the sound of Caribbean secular music.[8]

In the same way that black gospel in the United States has been influenced by the secular forms of the day, it is reasonable to assume that gospel in the Caribbean has succumbed to the musical transformations and influences in Caribbean secular music. And it is true that the secular tradition in the Caribbean has influenced music trends in gospel in some respects. But I want to suggest that the extent of this influence has not been as pronounced as in the United States, where the division between the secular and the religious is not as marked as the gulf that has been created between religious and secular expression in the Caribbean. Again, this goes back to slavery and post-emancipation society and its construction of a range of binary oppositions: white versus black, good versus evil, Christianity versus "traditional" beliefs, the religious versus the secular. In the United States, post-emancipation developments allowed for the faster evolution of other systems of knowledge. In the Caribbean, the church continued to significantly influence and control social activity to a greater degree. Secularization as a process tended to take root in North America faster than it did throughout the Caribbean. The sharp division between the religious and the secular remained a feature of religious organizations and teachings in other spheres of Caribbean life. Gospel music is thus still considered by most gospel practitioners and the majority of their audiences to be an autonomous entity which does not have to borrow at all from secular styles.

Because of this deep-rooted attitude, gospel in the region has not as yet created an open, identifiably Caribbean identity. I am not suggesting that there needs to be a single, homogenous rhythm or styling which defines Caribbean gospel. Rather, I am suggesting that there has been no systematic trend of progressive engagement with indigenous Caribbean musical forms by Caribbean gospel acts over time. Many gospel performers have tended to be tentative in their employment of local Caribbean music forms.

On the other hand, the level of devotion that many live performances of the 1960s, 1970s and 1980s paid to the country and western aesthetic is significant. Arguably, groups such as the Chuck Wagon Gang as well as the Singing Rambos and soloists such as Skeeter Davis influenced

Caribbean gospel in the 1970s more than any other single phenomenon. The impact of country and western gospel is also reflected in the styling of contemporary performers. Samuel Ryan, previously known as King Styler, Montserrat's first calypso king, was influenced by the country and western tradition. His 2002 album *Turn Your Back on Satan* reflects aspects of this influence. Although Ryan experiments with Caribbean rhythms and with soul, there are clear inflections of country and western in his phrasing. The Nazarene Silvertones of Barbados included many country and western songs in their repertoire in the 1980s. During the 1990s they fought to shed this influence by performing contemporary stylings, progressive reggae and some original gospel calypso.

The 1970s also saw several musical experiments in the eastern Caribbean with well-known indigenous musical styles such as reggae and calypso. Spouge music also surfaced in selected gospel acts. When this style was at its most popular in the 1970s, and even after its waning in 1976, it was still being performed by gospel acts in the eastern Caribbean. Joseph Niles, the Redeemed Gospel Band and the Glory Landers, of Barbados, all flirted with this style. Up to the late 1980s, this style was still being performed by the Regenerated Singers, out of Tortola. But this did not have a lasting effect on Caribbean gospel.

Although there were earlier experiments in singing the gospel message to the inflections of reggae and calypso, significant achievements were achieved only in the 1980s. The 1980s and 1990s can be said to belong to two predominant stylings within Caribbean gospel. The first, and arguably the more strongly felt influence, was that of what is called "contemporary gospel". The second influence might be categorized as the self-conscious exploration of Caribbean rhythmic forms. Contemporary gospel was exported from the United States to the Caribbean via television, through the expansion of marketing initiatives by record companies, the staging of events and increased access by American acts to Caribbean communication networks. The major artists from abroad who were a part of this invasion included Al Green, Andre Crouch, Jesse Dixon, Albertina Walker and Larnelle Harris, and later, groups such as Commissioned, the Brooklyn Tabernacle Choir, and Kirk Franklin and the Family.

In the mid-1980s, contemporary gospel was a new thing in the minds of gospel artists and audiences. Leading in the Caribbean interpretation of these new musical stylings was a core of young acts throughout the region. In the eastern Caribbean, there was the band Promise, whose

1984 cassette *Safari Search* was met with both admiration and condemnation. It was an intriguing mixture of progressive reggae and funk, as on the title track. It also featured soulful pop, on "How Long Oh Lord", and easy-listening country rock, in "Jesus on My Mind". But, all in all, the album represented the hard edge of progressive gospel.

But the true claim to supremacy in contemporary gospel styling in Caribbean music belongs to the choirs and chorales whose performances in the late 1980s were responsible for an increased following for gospel throughout the region. Elsewhere I have talked about the impact of these chorales and their performance technique, especially in relation to audiences.[9] In the 1980s, the impact of contemporary North American styling was most evident on Caribbean chorales. Excessive vocal and musical embellishments became the order of the day. Almost as a reaction against this trend, a number of other Caribbean gospel acts, mostly bands, began to re-engage the indigenous rhythms of the Caribbean, this time with a greater technological emphasis. Their experiments ranged from fusions with funk, soft rock, and rhythm and blues to hardcore reggae, soca and zouk. Still, even by the late 1980s, North American styling remained dominant.

Although bands were at the forefront of responding to the performance formula of leading chorales, the group which would make the most visible impact performing Caribbean-influenced music was in fact a chorale group, the Grace Thrillers of Jamaica (especially before their late 2003 revamping of membership). This vocal-based group was in no way as progressive-sounding or as technologically inclined as many combo-based bands, but it combined simple musical arrangements with euphonious harmony to appeal to a wide range of people within Caribbean society.

While many groups began experimenting with Caribbean rhythms, in the early 1990s there still seemed to be something cosmetic about many productions. Some performers seemed afraid to invest more heavily in Caribbean aesthetics, at the level both of the music and of lyrical composition. Even the growing number of gospel acts which were beginning to employ Caribbean motifs by the 1990s did so apprehensively, still holding on to established lyrical and musical templates. In this way they secured a footing and a sense of grounding with the institutionalized tradition.

Project Band's 1990 album *Hallelujah Beat* is just one of several forward-looking productions from the early 1990s. It was an all-original cassette release, and its three Caribbean-styled compositions were disdainfully progressive. In a song like "So Divine", the musical tracks seemed wilfully created to seize the discourse from the voice, which has always claimed the dominant position in institutionalized gospel in the Caribbean. It is no surprise that Project Band was accused in Barbados of technological self-gratification, for they seemed to challenge the formula that had been established for gospel music in the Caribbean over the decades. Gospel music audiences in the early 1990s were not ready for the band's fusion of indigenous rhythms and their near attempts at socially conscious lyrics. Those groups that were smarter than Project Band took the middle ground and played around with the ratio of lyrical and musical properties to reflect a fifty-fifty or sixty-forty ratio of foreign and Caribbean influence.

The Jamaican group the Grace Thrillers are the best example of this clever crafting. They consistently produced a recorded package that reworked old gospel standards. Their musical styling has been formulaic, sticking to two or three main musical/rhythmic formulas. On an album like 1991's *We Give Thee Thanks,* for example, mento (near-calypso) inflections are the dominant rhythmic motif. But in contrast to uptempo mento-styled songs such as "Holy" and "I'm Yours Lord", the other rhythmic styling is a mixture of soul and pop, as on the tracks "Lead Me to Calvary" and "Around God's Throne". The lyrical texts are not originally exciting. These again are formulaic, as in the song "I'm Yours Lord":

> I'm yours, Lord
> Everything I've got
> Everything I am
> Everything I'm not

But although I seem to be critical of this type of formulaic gospel lyric, perhaps a more important consideration should be the measure of popularity which this group has attained throughout the Caribbean. The Grace Thrillers have done much better than most other contemporary gospel-performing groups because they have found and maintained their formula. In the same way that Jamaican dancehall artists can be said to have blazed the trail in secular music in the Caribbean, the Jamaican-based Thrillers have been leading the way in gospel – significantly, through an equally minimalist application of musical technology. Their featured tracks have continued to foreground mento-cum-dancehall rhythms over the years. This is a credit to their astounding vision.

The Grace Thrillers have also consistently produced cleaner audio recordings than most other gospel groups in the Caribbean, and their finished recorded product has tended to be more ambient than other contemporary releases in gospel. This is borne out by a short comparison with a mid-1990s production by the Wesleyan Chorale, of Barbados, entitled *The Victory Is Ours,* although it can be said that the latter recording is much more exciting in its musical interpretations, its selection of synthesized voices and in its forthright interaction between the performers and their perceived listener.

As evident in many gospel recordings from the late 1980s to the present, both the Grace Thrillers' and the Wesleyan Chorale's recordings make use of programmable music workstations which comprise synthesizers, drum machine and little else by way of musical (non-vocal) accompaniment, except maybe the rhythm guitar. In slower songs the Grace Thrillers have shown a tendency to privilege stringed and electric piano voices in order to achieve their rich textures to surround the heavily processed voices of the vocalists. Since the advent of the DX7 keyboard in the mid-1980s, Yamaha has offered up the textures of keyboard tones which are still sought after by gospel groups like the Grace Thrillers. Yamaha's SY series was therefore very popular throughout the 1990s. Only Roland synthesizers came close to the popularity of Yamaha in the Caribbean gospel arena throughout this period. The maverick company Ensoniq threatened this dynasty at intervals, by virtue of its competitive prices and explosive features on its synthesizers (such as Mirage and the SQ series), but, by and large, gospel musicians have shown a liking for the traditional rich textures of sound, preferring to stick closely to piano, digital piano and stringed tones.

The Grace Thrillers' use of the full stereophonic spectrum is a marked feature of their recordings. But what is also significant is that there is not much exciting building of tension and interest through manipulation of technology – say, for example, through manipulation of panning assignments to the left and right of the stereophonic mix. Their recordings tend to quickly establish and define the parameters of the musical spectrum within which each song will operate, and they hardly exceed the boundaries of this sound spectrum. In contrast, the radio edit of Project Band's 1995 song "Higher Higher" reveals frequent incursions into uncharted spaces of the musical spectrum. For example, the song begins with an acutely panned orchestral hit (sound samples of an orchestra playing a staccato note or chord) followed by a much more present and centrally placed brass cluster, giving way to a fuller range of instruments played together in the stereophonic spectrum. Throughout this song the lower sonic contours are altered considerably, when bass and sub-bass tones are introduced. As a result, the acoustic space is enlarged, perhaps uncomfortably so, when a digitally sampled congregation of voices invades the song's discursive parameter.

At the end of the millennium, the youthful four-woman (vocals) and five-man (musicians) group Shine the Light blazed the trail of popularity started by the Grace Thrillers. The St Croix, US Virgin Islands group, in similar manner to the Thrillers, built their fame around steady harmonies, clear diction, familiar melodies and predictable but highly infectious musical accompaniments. Their 1998 album *Arise Wake Up O Sleepers* reflects their compositional tendencies. The nine-track album features soca, reggae, middle-of-the-road pop and polite allusions to hardcore soca. Six of these tracks were written and arranged by the group. This was a commendable difference from the Grace Thrillers' method. *Arise Wake Up O Sleepers* was a carefully compiled album. It did not seek to break any new ground musically. Its most daring track (musically) was the adaptation of the song "Waiting Down Here". In this song, the drum track is raised higher than in other Shine the Light mixes. The high-tuned snare mirrors the tone and inflection found in many hardcore soca-oriented compositions. But even so, it is evident that synthesizer and drum-machine programming dictate a pre-assigned threshold of sound dynamics. The result is a composition that sits very comfortably within well-defined and clearly stated sound parameters. These kinds of mixes have a tendency to hold listeners, if not to excite them. These mixes can also make for "easy listening", which has translated into a favourable response from many audiences and buyers of gospel. This is also the Grace Thrillers' method, but Shine the Light arguably makes greater use of rhythmic constituents within their musical mixes. In the same song, for instance – as in their popular medley "Goodbye World" – they make use of a panned guitar, a panned strumming keyboard and panned string-cum-brass interjections. The resultant is a richly weighted praise, dance-based music propelled by an audibly present rhythm section. All of this enhances the solo voice, which is outstanding in these mixes, as are the accompanying harmonies rigidly panned full left and full right. This is the mixing strategy of the St Croix–based Backyard Studio, with Al Baptiste as engineer, mixer and co-producer.

Following on the success of their 1998 album, Shine the Light released *I'm Blessed* in 1999. Their method was clearly restated on this release. Its rhythmic styling fell within the same categories as defined their previous release, although there was more variety on the 1999 production. The tracks "Lord I Lift Your Name Up High" and "Wash Me" attempt to challenge the parameters of sound and rhythm as established on the earlier album. "Lord I Lift Your Name Up High", for instance, employs a dynamic synthesized orchestral hit and a rich, carefully sampled drum snare. Even so, these constituents struggle within the mix, seeming to anticipate an even fuller presence.

"Wash Me" is Shine the Light in a much more contemporary American gospel mode. This composition is a fusion of jazz, swing and reggae, and is even closer to new secular rhythm and blues than to gospel. This is a refreshing musical interpretation. The selection of instrument tones is a definite strength of the composition. The walking piano (fluid improvisation), understated organ, busy blues guitar, ambient drum samples and reggae references make this song one of the better-rendered and better-produced tracks on the album. However, these moments are not sustained on the recording – neither are they sufficiently exploited in Caribbean gospel.

Up to the mid-1990s, many gospel groups and producers in the Caribbean tended to be experimental yet cautious in their packaging of the sound (dynamics) of gospel. This is to say that gospel recordings generally have not been at the forefront of charting new spaces in the overall development of Caribbean music. It is easy to understand why this has been so. Since groups struggle to survive financially, the possibility of recording consistently has remained a dream for many. Other groups have resorted to manageable low-budget recordings. This has meant that quality is partially sacrificed. Many gospel performers have acted as producers of their own music. By the mid-1990s, with the advent of the home studio, some sound engineers took on several roles, as arranger, musician, engineer, producer and marketer. The dedicated professional gospel producer has therefore not had a long-established tradition in the region. Gospel music producers themselves were careful and measured in the fashioning of their products in the mid-1990s. For example, the production company Caribbean Christian Artistes Network hesitated to go beyond the fraternity of hand-picked artists on its label for some time. This had to do with limited personnel and finances, but also with a not-yet-accepted practice of embracing radical forms of gospel performance. Those artists who were prepared to go beyond the established conventions of composition and performance would have to wait until the late 1990s to gain greater acceptance.

Lyrics

By the mid-1990s, many more gospel artists were becoming fascinated with the possibility of writing their own songs. This increasing confidence in performing original material can be illustrated by comparing two albums, one produced in the mid-1980s, the other in the mid-1990s. In 1985, the Inter-School Christian Fellowship Graduate Ministries Choir, of Barbados, produced a nine-track release, *Mystery*, containing one original, the title track. The Trinidadian Reverend Peter Regis's 1994 *Confident and Strong* contained eight tracks, all original.

The increased interest in composing original gospel songs was supported by a number of phenomena. By the early to mid-1990s, Caribbean music had matured to a stage where it had begun to make some impact on the international music scene. In spite of its sometime fierce resistance to worldly influences, Caribbean gospel has always taken notice of other genres. Gospel artists began to recognize that cultural difference as inscribed in the music industry's 1980s "world music" category allowed scope for original composition. Secular acts were making some advances by way of original composition. Copyright ownership and intellectual property became additional concerns among selected gospel performers. The threat of globalization forced artists to consider their role in the new world order. They had to confront questions of the relationship between gospel music, ministry, culture, identity and geopolitics.

But gospel composers were not merely composing lyrics, and they were not writing them in isolation. They were also composing in full view of the musical experiments taking place. They were therefore composing mainly with strains of reggae, calypso and soca in their minds. In the early to mid-1990s, all the global and cultural phenomena listed above had not fully been internalized by the region's gospel composers. Although these external factors resonated throughout the nations of the region, the reality on the ground, in everyday practice, was still one in which composers had to confront questions of tradition, ritual, denominational control and the dangers of secularization. It is therefore not surprising that some gospel compositions of this period, though original and displaying traces of freshness, never strayed too far from conservatism.

The projection of Caribbean social reality through the lyrical text of gospel song would seem to be a necessity for this genre. This process of Caribbeanization cannot refer merely to the employment of specifically Caribbean terms or the use of Caribbean national languages. Though these features are essential, there are other requirements as well. Among these other requirements must be the reflection of a Caribbean sensibility through a song's use of allusion, metaphor, imagery and other literary and rhetorical devices, and an engagement with the particular issues which are current and problematic in Caribbean society. Caribbean gospel has not been built on such a tradition. Paradoxically, although it is evangelical preachers and spokespeople who have tended to be the most vocal in Caribbean society on moral and social issues, the creative arm of these denominations has not conducted this project through the creative arts. Gospel has therefore not worked hand in hand with the message of social and moral redress that has come from the pulpit.

Whereas the contemporary preacher who confronts social ills has antecedents, in that others have addressed local situations from the pulpit, the gospel artist has had to carefully create a culture of social critique in song. The gospel composer has therefore had to be careful with using musical, rhythmic and lyrical motifs that were considered for a long time to belong to "the world". The perception of this divide between gospel and its "other" has affected and continues to affect the development of regional music in no small way.[10] The earlier work *Roots to Popular Culture* suggests that denominational bases and their ideologically controlling centres are largely responsible for gospel's conservatism over the years, but it must also be acknowledged that historical and cultural conditioning have played their part in this dynamic.[11]

Caribbean social problems have not gone unnoticed in gospel. Most Caribbean gospel artists did an anti-drug song in the early 1990s. They have also tried their hand at AIDS-awareness compositions. But an overview of original compositions up to the mid-1990s would reveal the range of Caribbean social problems covered to be relatively limited. Unemployment, crime, violence, teenage pregnancy, generational dislocation, family breakdown, economic disenfranchisement, cultural penetration, materialism, secularization, the new world order and globalization are just some of the underexplored problems of contemporary Caribbean society. Caribbean gospel can hardly be said to have consistently engaged with and commented on these issues. There is still the perception that such issues are best left to the pulpit, to the preacher and even to the calypsonian. Gospel artists have not seen this dimension to be a direct concern for them. In theory it is said to be a concern; but in reality, it is the secular performers who lay claim to championing the cause of the underprivileged through the creation, performance and projection of socially committed lyrics. Gospel music composers have tended to remain true to formulaic lyrical tendencies. As part of this formula, they echo or reproduce old gospel standards, privilege scriptural allusion and deify overworked clichés. Their method tends therefore to be upfront, direct. They present the message of salvation – the hard sell. Lyrical subtlety, wordplay, wit, irony, double entendre, neologisms and other similar literary and rhetorical techniques are not traditionally valorized in gospel music writing in the Caribbean.

On Reverend Regis's album *Confident and Strong*, the overall message is clear. The album's persona propagates the necessity to be "close to Jesus". The chorus to the song "Never Let You Go", written by Audra, Julian and Tabia Rambally, epitomizes the lyrical message and method of the album:

> Everyday I thank and praise you for your mercy
> For you've been with me each step of the way
> I want to be a shining light to those who need you
> Be in your presence every moment of the day

The tone of this album, like many others in the Caribbean, is highly personal and almost devoid of social reference and context, save in the final track on side B, "Freedom", which tentatively introduces then discards its focus on social issues:

> The hungry is crying but they cannot be heard
> 'Cause everybody is thinking 'bout their own
> But there is an answer, Jesus Christ the King

The composers on *The Victory Is Ours*, Holbrook Taylor, Vasco Greaves and Karen Reeves, have also written in this mode. One of the Caribbean's best young composers of gospel, Vasco Greaves, of the band New Connections, presents this formula in the title song:

> The victory's ours for Jesus won the battle
> He broke the chains of death when he went to Calvary
> We have received it
> You can believe it
> The victory's ours not defeat

The employment of biblical imagery is a recurring feature, as in the song's use of the symbolism of the cross. Its chorus also makes use of the military scenario, which is a recurring motif of traditional hymns, such as "Hold the Fort" and "Onward Christian Soldiers". This kind of language and symbolism harkens back to scriptural references about the Christian walk as a battle. For example, the apostle Paul had constantly advised the Christian church to "fight the good fight of faith". The song is therefore well founded. Its theology is sound, and its tone serves to uplift the believer in the midst of contemporary battles. But although this particular song handles its scriptural references and symbolism well, there are other times when too much use of this method and kind of language can become hackneyed and cease to carry renewed impact.

Late 1990s lyrical compositions by Gloria C. Sexius Claxton, from Shine the Light, also fall into this vein. The 1999 release *If a Man Dies*, for instance, stays within the realm of traditional gospel discourse. It is concerned with the role of the Christian on the earth, and it reminds the Christian that death on this earth gives way to the victory of living with Christ in heaven:

> True believers in Christ we want the world to know
> you need not to fear death for God has a purpose for us
> when death comes it means the end of our earthly nation
> and the beginning of a greater life in Christ

The song "God Must Come First", written by Lynn Sexius-Kent, is built around the hook "God must come first / If you want your heart's desire, God must come first". This is interspersed with admonitions: "He'll supply your needs . . . Your heavenly father knows what you need."

I do recognize that my discussion here focuses on the printed word and does not engage with such issues as the motive for the construction of these songs and the primary medium for their dissemination. Arguably, these songs were composed with live performance in mind. When songs of this kind are performed on stage, they generally evoke positive response. Audiences are better able to appreciate and connect with familiar compositional strategies. In the performance context, compositions of this kind are better able to mask their lyrical banality because of the accompaniment of musical constituents. But at another level of reading and interpretation, it is possible that expected or predictable lyrical practice produces a programmed response. It is also possible that formulaic lyrical compositions do not necessarily result in meaningful connection with audiences. The persistent regurgitation of set phrases and allusions can also have the opposite effect: the immaturity of gospel music audiences cannot always be assumed. It is possible that gospel music has failed to capture the imagination of many more individuals and souls because of its own conservatism. The dynamics are not straightforward. It is evident there are a series of complex relations at work in gospel music culture and discourse. Maybe there are grounds for greater balance of traditional features and new strategies of composition.

It is possible to maintain aspects of traditional gospel formula while also employing non-traditional strategies, all to the benefit of ministry. Project Band's early 1990s release *Hallelujah Beat* illustrated one way of beginning to do this. They seem at the time to be working at a socio-historically conscious discourse in the title track. On "Hallelujah Beat", they appear to be partly concerned with the role of history and of some religious institutions in censuring expressive African-inspired Christian worship.

> In slavery they parodied
> This melody I said they crucified the beat
> Throw away my drums don't you know
> My heart still beats

Like the songs above, this one also makes use of biblical imagery in reference to crucifixion, but unlike some of the others, the act of crucifixion is not assigned to or inflicted on Christ alone; rather, it is perpetrated and perpetuated on a form of music and worship no less Christ-inspired. So the song begs the listener to consider the underlying scriptural references to Christ, the church and expressive worship. It does so by juxtaposing the imprisonment of Christ with attempts to confine African-inspired modes of expressive worship. In intent, this song anticipates the widely popular "Waving Ting" by Sean Daniel, which was released some twelve years afterwards.

Subtlety and wordplay were also distinguishing features of *Hallelujah Beat*. The speaker expresses the desire for his or her other in the composition "So Divine", which makes use of double entendre, somewhat in the mode of "old time" calypso. Here is a common theme in Caribbean gospel: love. In Caribbean gospel, the object of love is almost always God or Jesus. In "So Divine", this love is also being expressed between the speaker and his or her companion. Given that this song was also written for a departing band member who was going to New York to be married, further intrigue was added. In the following two verses, double entendre and lyrical playfulness are at work:

> I was searching in my heart for you
> When a certain dream of love came true
> The spirit and the fire
> All that I desired
> Don't you know it's so divine
> To be with you
>
> *Chorus*
> Be with you be with you be with you
> Don't you know it's so divine to be with you
>
> In the subway city
> It's amazing how crazed a maze can be
> No more underground emotions
> My love has left its station
> Its single destination
> To be with you

Not enough gospel composers in the Caribbean have exhibited this method of extended metaphor while exploring the intimacy that believers can share with the Divine. The extended metaphor is especially prominent in the second quoted stanza. The expression of love for God is no less potent here in this song than, say, in the 1990 composition by Karen Reeves and Julia Lowe, "The Name of Jesus":

> You are the rock, the rock of our Salvation
> Almighty God forever
> You are the way, you are the truth;

You are the life, we bless you.
Jesus, Jesus, Jesus, Jesus

By the late 1990s, more and more composers were writing original songs. The British-based Caribbean singer Judy Bailey had been composing radical gospel since the early 1990s, but by 1997, when she released *Between You and Me,* it was clear that she was traversing the border between gospel and what is sometimes called inspirational music. In the title track she sings,

I look at you you look at me
And there are differences indeed
But we must open up our minds
To see the similarities.

This move represented the opposite of those gospel acts who make repeated reference to the Scriptures in their lyrics. Bailey's lyrics make no direct mention of Jesus, and there are only three mentions of God on the entire album They also do not engage directly with pressing socio-economic and political issues. All in all, Bailey's method on this album was not different from the work of other major-label crossover gospel artists, such as Amy Grant. Near the end of the decade, artists were gaining in confidence. Ongoing developments in the region and abroad brought about some gradual change.

By early in the first decade of the twenty-first century, even conservative groups were more willing to explore. The Antiguan Adventist group Highest Praise, on their 2001 release *He Reigns,* exhibited a level of confidence not possible among radical groups ten years earlier. On the reggae track "It Must Be Love", they crooned,

I can't help the way I feel
It must be love
The things I feel are so real
It must be love

Signs of the Times

By the mid-1990s gospel popular culture was becoming an identifiable phenomenon and a powerful movement. Whereas in the early 1990s and before, there was a conservative core of performers and consumers of gospel material, by the late 1990s, gospel culture had become much more ostentatious.

Throughout the 1990s and at the turn of the new millennium, Caribbean gospel experienced the influx of a number of popular secular artists who converted to Christianity. Most of these recommitted themselves to singing gospel songs, including King Short Shirt and King Obstinate, from Antigua and Barbuda; Lil Man from Barbados, Carlene Davis, Papa San and Stitchie (formerly Lieutenant Stitchie), from Jamaica; and Chris "Tambu" Herbert and Singing Francine, from Trinidad and Tobago. Obstinate and Short Shirt continued to perform in the calypso idiom. Many of their compositions were calypso reworkings of traditional hymn standards, somewhat in the mode of Joseph Niles. Obstinate's rendition of "The Old Rugged Cross" and of "Wounded Soldier", made popular by Dolly Parton, increased his popularity within the region. These were uptempo calypso. They employed credible soca motifs, stopping short of being innovative. They also fit Obstinate's image; he had been performing in the calypso arena since the late 1950s, and his wit, humour and bitter criticism had shaped the art form and made an impact on Antiguan society over the decades. The lyrics of these songs, though not as controversial as his 1982 calypso "Coming Down to Talk to You", were effective. His rendering of them sustained some of the emotion and passion he managed to evoke throughout his career. Carlene Davis also reinterpreted traditional gospel songs, although her song "This Island" departed from that tendency and instead challenged the rulers of the islands, especially those in parliament, to commit their nation to God.

A more sustained radical response came from the former bad boys of dancehall. This period witnessed an upswell in popularity of a more militant hardcore presentation of the gospel. Papa San signed to Gospocentric, the label that also carried the radical American gospel act Kirk Franklin. Stitchie's "War" proclaimed fire and destruction on the gates of the enemy. Its driving bass and militant refrain were influenced by and in turn inspired other young gospel acts of the region. Trinidad and Tobago's Sean Daniel made a significant contribution in the late 1990s. He came to prominence in 1997 through Trinidad's "Scouting for Talent" programme. The following year he performed original compositions like "Pan in Heaven" and "Track Shoes". In 1999, he was a semi-finalist in Trinidad's National Calypso Competition. His entering the competition brought him much criticism, since he was foremost a gospel performer. Some people felt he was entering an unholy arena. But his strong lyrics and convincing rendition of calypso make him one of the most compelling innovators. His collaboration with people at the core of Trinidad's calypso industry contributed to a number of groundbreaking gospel tracks as found on the album *Divine Soca*. Another visible artist of the era who challenged the boundaries of conventional gospel was the Trinidadian Sherwin Gardner. Unlike Sean Daniel Gardner also employed heavy doses of dancehall musical and lyrical motifs. Around this time St Vincent's leading young band also began to proclaim this brand of delivery: "A new stylee / A new stylee / Jesus given me a new stylee . . ."

After 2000, youthful performers intensified their commitment to non-traditional performance. Although secular-turned-Christian artists made a considerable impact on Caribbean gospel in this period, their contribution was built on the steady war of attrition conducted by a range of gospel artists during the 1990s and prior. Caribbean gospel's evolution must be understood in these terms. Artists such as Grenada's Jerry Lloyd had challenged the established boundaries many years before. His mid-1980s "Jesus Is Sweeter", performed to embryonic dancehall rhythms, established him as an early radical. Trinidad's Noel "Professor" Richards established himself as king of "gospelypso" through his persistence. Whereas later acts such as Prodigal Son and Tiko and Gitta (Royal Priesthood) had the support of an identifiable growing tradition, gospel radicals of the 1980s had to negotiate their place at a time when Caribbean music was on the verge of technological reconfiguration.

Gospel acts after 2000 were inspired in no small way by external factors. The growth of the international gospel music industry has had a significant impact on Caribbean gospel.[12] In addition, many Caribbean denominations have come under increasing pressure to respond to the demands of a differently fashioned Caribbean youth population. This was a new generation of youths who grew up in the age of satellite television. They grew up in the shadow of Hollywood and of North American ideals and, to a lesser extent, in the era when Jamaican dancehall was gaining new international markets and when new hardcore styles in soca were gaining ground.

They also grew up in an era when Caribbean theology was coming under the increasing influence of North American televangelism, in the same way as, in earlier decades, Caribbean gospel music was inspired by North American contemporary styles. By the early 2000s, gospel networks such as Trinity Broadcasting Network (TBN) were having marked influence on the way some Caribbean believers conceived of God, worship and Christian doctrine. Preacher-minister-artists, such as TD Jakes and Creflo Dollar, and "word of faith" theology challenged the foundations on which much of pre-1990s Caribbean gospel theology had been founded. Christian culture came under the influence of a revived "praise and worship" movement.[13] This phenomenon echoed the Old Testament ritual of progressing from the outer court of the tabernacle to the inner court and then to the Holy of Holies, accompanied by music. It emphasized the importance of praise and worship as different manifestations of the worship process. Many Caribbean song services were renamed "praise and worship" sessions. They were characterized by the practice of elevating and releasing the intensity of worship through carefully chosen songs. But the praise and worship movement, which was popularized by route of North America, also served to create a new hierarchy of songs and artists. The leading ones were from outside the Caribbean.[14] Caribbean composers were not able to achieve the impact of the new creators of praise and worship music including Avalon, Ron Kenoly, Delirious, Kirk Franklin, Alvin Slaughter and Michael W. Smith. Ironically, regional congregations and composers had been exploring diverse forms of congregational worship long before the praise and worship craze, but the popularizing of the phenomenon through gospel popular culture legitimized and standardized a new set of rituals for many Caribbean denominations. By the mid-2000s there were few signs that Caribbean gospel culture would treat its very own expressions as legitimate. In the same way that secular players revered their northern alter egos, similarly, gospel participants knelt at the altar of North American traditions.

Caribbean gospel popular culture was systematically transformed soon after 2000. Satellite television was a major contributor. BET's blurring of the boundaries between black gospel artists and black secular artists further problematized the way Caribbean youths came to view religion and popular culture. Youths had therefore to reconcile their fascination with dancehall and hip hop in the face of traditional religious teaching, which held that secular music was just that – secular, non-religious. Gospel acts such as Kirk Franklin were interacting with secular artists.

Franklin's song "Revolution" was featured on the soundtrack of the profanity-ridden Warner Brothers film release *Any Given Sunday.* Yolanda Adams moved to Elektra, considered a secular label, on the roster with Missy Elliot and Tweet. Adams hosted the Soul Train Awards just weeks after doing the 2002 Stellar Gospel Music Awards.

Caribbean youths could hardly ignore the tremendous impact of dancehall, reflected in the early 1990s exploits of Shabba Ranks and Patra. Young people could not deny the control exerted over Caribbean music space by dancehall and other hardcore styles. Caribbean gospel of the late 1990s and early 2000s therefore reflected a response both to ongoing issues and to cultural phenomena which were at work almost a decade before. In the first years after 2000, a larger percentage of gospel acts began to experiment more openly and freely with Caribbean rhythms. They employed Caribbean national languages with some greater confidence. Careful analysis would reveal that a greater percentage of songs focused on contentious social issues, but that analysis would also confirm that gospel acts hardly sustained this focus. Even some of the more radical performers vacillated between songs of open protest and more traditional songs of praise and worship. Gospel culture could accommodate the all-out radical, but most acts recognized the importance of working at the tradition from within. They therefore carried out covert revolutions. They were also mindful of the politics of selling out. They were not willing in great numbers to challenge the historical and philosophical tenets of gospel. Nonetheless, gradually changes were being effected. Acts such as Sean Daniel, Sherwin Gardner, Prodigal Son, Nicole Ballosingh, Papa San, Judah Development, Chevelle Franklin, Monty G and Stitchie brought credible post-soca and post-dancehall beats to gospel. These were the beneficiaries of a changing social and cultural climate. The field was therefore much more ripe for harvest.

Stitchie's 2000 debut gospel album, *Real Power,* and the popular track "War" exemplified the tone, timbre and styling of this growing category of performance. The album claimed to rely on biblically sound lyrics. "War" was built on a popular Christian premise and explored the Christian struggle through the familiar metaphor of war. Stitchie chats in the chorus, "All Christian soldiers whether near or far / fully prepared – have no fear – Go tell the devil that we are ready for the war". Papa San's "God and I" from his sophomore album on the label Gospocentric, *God and I,* was not radically different in terms of its sphere of reference.

Not all songs by Stitchie, Papa San and Prodigal Son were equally reliant on scriptural imagery for their popularity and appeal. Papa San's album *Victory,* for instance, featured DJ Shabba Ranks on "Only Jah Mercy", a song that skirts the boundaries of bona fide gospel. Prodigal Son's song "I Wish" exemplifies a more direct approach to proclaiming the gospel: he espouses the message of salvation, but he does so by declaring his personal wish for Jamaica's secular DJs.

> I wish dem wudda done wid slackness
> and start to create some conscious lyrics . . .
> I wish to see Bounty Killer get saved . . .
> To see Beenie turn Christian . . .
> You know me a pray for Elephant Man

This song anticipates the all-out war on slackness and social decay waged by other performers, such as Royal Priesthood in their hard-hitting compositions such as "Green Man", "Rudiments" and "Sodom and Gomorrah":

> After dark in high heel shoes them ah step man
> You nah see them all ah infest Curepe?
> Come out ah road them talk bout fi catch man
> Best catch Jesus because that is the right man
> Take off your dress and gone look a wife man

After 2000, the new frontiers of Caribbean gospel were commodified in compilations such as 2002's *Soca Baptism* and *Dancehall Baptism*. Albums of this kind attracted the attention of a youthful listenership generally.

But while many of the new emerging radical acts fought to transform the methods by which they preached the gospel, there were others no less passionate and committed to the fight who struggled to walk the thin line between tradition and innovation. In Antigua, the gospel group Judah Development filmed a promotional video tracing the group's evolution and ongoing mission. The music video of their first release from the album *Movements*, the song "Modern World", aptly demonstrates the band's recognition that both the world and gospel music were changing. Their video therefore carefully traverses the thin line between traditional practice and trends of the future. It does so through its presentation of two young people faced with the choice between sex and abstinence. The music video is shot in a warehouse garage, where the rude boys hang out in ghetto music videos. But it ends with the boldly stated words of God, which warn a decaying godless society of the wages of rejecting Jesus and his word. Groups such as Judah Development are therefore more reflective of the direction of Caribbean gospel. Their challenge is to negotiate the future with a sense of vision and tradition.

Caribbean gospel acts have also begun to explore and interface with new global trends in communication technology, particularly the Internet. Although gospel acts did not move to gain a meaningful presence on the Internet until around the beginning of the twenty first century, it must also be noted that Caribbean society as a whole has not been swift in confronting the Internet. Whereas so-called First World societies eagerly embraced the Internet, societies in the Caribbean were encumbered first by lack of access, second by a generally more cautious approach to embracing en masse new phenomena like the Internet. In the gospel arena, artists slowly moved towards the Internet in the late 1990s in order to gain space and presence in cyberspace.

Some of the more visible artists on the Internet have been from among the more radical performers, those who have appealed more to youths. Lion of Zion Entertainment has a very loud presence in the cybergospel world. The 1999 label, founded by leader of the radical American reggae gospel act Christafari, prides itself in presenting a gateway to the wider world for Tiko and Gitta, Sherwin Gardner and the popular Bahamian Monty G. From the start, Lion of Zion used its Web site, http://www .lionofzion.com to present information about artists signed to the label. News on current gospel events was listed, as well as new releases. One of the site's most ambitious facilities was its providing of audio clips of selected songs using the MP3 format. Other acts were intent on also proving a palatable mix of information, hard- and soft-sell ministry, biography, online shopping and audio clips through their Web sites, including Paula Hinds, at http://www.paulahinds.com, and the Silver-tones, at http://www.silvertones.net. Not many groups offered video clips like the Grace Thrillers did. But the trends, embedded in cyberculture and strategies of circumventing traditional ways of gaining access to international audiences, also made an impact on Caribbean gospel. It was evident that some Caribbean gospel acts were engaged, if in limited ways, in employing the Internet in unconventional ways in order to gain access to other, wider audiences. Acts such as the Antiguan group Gospel in Motion can be accessed through the hugely popular free site the

Internet Underground Music Archive (IUMA, http://www.iuma.com).

Even conservative acts were committed to reaching wider audiences through new alliances, associations and media. Guyana's sweet-singing a cappella group the Dynamic Force produced their first album, *Liberation*, with the assistance of Grace, Kennedy Financial Services and Western Union. In turn, they performed the Western Union jingle at their Web page on IUMA, http://artists.iuma.com/IUMA/Bands/THE _DYNAMIC_FORCE/. The IUMA Web site provides photos and brief bios, but it is the group's renditions of "Lead Me to Calvary" and "Jesus Cares" that best convey their talent, which resides in vocal rendition.[15]

The Bahamian a cappella group Reconciled also made effective use of the Web for their album *Field of Souls*. Belize's Elaine Sutherland marketed *Sounds of Rejoicing* on the Web as Belize's first praise and worship album. It makes use of Garifuna drums and turtle shells. The marketing of this album on the Internet foregrounded the singer's nationality and her creative use of indigenous instruments. But the various sites on which it appeared provided a visual of the album cover which featured four individuals in praise, positioned in the clouds standing firmly on an open Bible – their magic carpet. Junior C of Bermuda also employed regional musical motifs for his debut solo album, *Faith*; through IUMA's facility for feedback on songs, Junior C received commendation from other dancehall gospel artists such as Jah Pickney.[16] Hence the Internet became a medium by which artists declared their endorsement of their fellow brethren. Other artists seized the opportunity to get their message across, like Kelisha Primus and Third Exodus Singers from Grenada, who posted their original songs and MP3 audio streams at the less well known gospel music site Messagemusic (http://www.messagemusic.org).

The Living Reality

The vitality of Caribbean gospel in the live performance context is not truly reflected and represented in the number of recordings which are accessible on the regional market. The Caribbean gospel music industry has tended to be unstructured as modern industries go. Tradition has left the impression that, like salvation, the music of gospel should be "full and free". This teaching has militated against attempts to introduce higher levels of professionalism within the gospel music arena.

This chapter has focused primarily on progressive gospel, but it must be remembered that there have been many Caribbean gospel artists who have seen their role solely in terms of ministry and service. Many performers have therefore preferred to operate in the live context. Others have had little concern with innovating since they feel satisfied carrying out the great commission in the way they feel best. These are some of the other real issues at work within the Caribbean gospel arena. Gospel artists know better than most how difficult it is to navigate a course through the complex realities of Caribbean society.

One problematic component of this nexus has always been in the area of dissemination of and access to traditional media. Caribbean radio has been one of the most crucial media in the dissemination of gospel music. Gospel artists have depended on the print media and on television, but pure sound has been valorized in Caribbean gospel music for a long time. This is an important observation, one which is still borne out by the preference to provide audio rather than video clips on the Internet. A closer, though brief, overview of selected Caribbean gospel programming can highlight the context in which many artists struggled to gain voice, particularly in the 1990s. Programme formats, perceptions about gospel, artist apathy, a dearth of requisite recordings and the absence of gospel lobbies have all contributed to the challenging times faced by gospel in the region.

A survey of Caribbean gospel radio of the mid-1990s gives a better picture of the reality. In Trinidad, the daily three-hour presentation *Family Focus* and, more so, the twice-weekly 10 p.m. to 5 a.m. gospel slots offered reasonable airtime for local and regional material. Radio 105's gospel countdown is another medium that has showcased national music there. In Barbados, programmes such as VOB 790 AM's countdown in the early 1990s were short on credibility. The countdown's charts needed to have broad-based criteria for compiling the top gospel tunes, and not all groups felt they were given fair airplay. In the early 2000s, Radio Guyana International provided limited gospel exposure on Sundays. NBC St Vincent's *Inspiration Time* was forthright and unpretentious, but, like CBC Barbados's afternoon gospel segment in the mid-1990s, it required greater depth in terms of presentation, analysis and focus. Grenada's Klassic Radio facilitated some gospel, but its emphasis was elsewhere, on soca, calypso, and rhythm and blues. Love 97.5, out of the Bahamas, provided a slot to include gospel and other inspirational music on Sundays between 6 p.m. and midnight.

Total gospel radio is an important component for facilitating the expression of regional gospel artists and for stimulating greater activity in music production. ZGBC Voice of Life Radio in Dominica is still one of the most popular gospel radio stations in terms of listenership and participation in the eastern Caribbean. This station hardly has mass appeal, but it has catered to a substantial number of mature (perhaps conservative) listeners throughout the region. Although it started to broadcast in 1975, Voice of Life is not regarded as a "progressive" station in terms of its programming. Its philosophy is not oriented towards indigenous creation, and this is reflected in its schedule. Although its earlier platform presence in the AM band did not endear it to younger listeners, what it lost by way of quality it gained in terms of wider regional coverage. It transmits to more than seven hundred thousand people across the south-eastern Caribbean with comparative quality. But it can also be accessed on the FM frequency. Grenada and Carriacou's Harbour Light of the Winwards' various frequencies, at 1400 AM, 94.5 FM and 92.3 FM, are effectively dedicated stations. St Kitts's Goodwill Radio 104.5 FM, which went on air in 1998, was message- and feature-oriented, with segments devoted to music. The Bajan station 102 FM, dubbed "Faith", is music oriented in its format. This is the kind of radio one would expect to capture a sizeable share of the listening market. But Faith has remained an automated jukebox which recycles unimaginative playlists of songs often categorized as contemporary Christian music. Among the artists still on heavy rotation are the Imperials, Sandi Patti and Amy Grant. Local and regional gospel compositions are all but outlawed on this station.

With the growing importance of the Internet as a medium of communication, advertising and discourse in the post-2000 era, Caribbean gospel also sought ways of entering into that domain. In the first years of the twenty-first century, many Caribbean radio stations began to facilitate Web radio. Radio networks such as Grenada's Redemption Radio provide audio streaming to Internet listeners. Caribbean Gospel Network also offers audio streaming, for a full twenty-four hours. Like Redemption Radio, CGN's site offers the bare essentials, with no colourful graphics or pop-up advertisements. These radio stations were more concerned with providing a window to the programmes they had on offer at pre-existing dedicated "land" sites. In June 2003, Main Street Music advertised on its Web site the imminent launch of "the first on-line Caribbean gospel music store".[17] It was not the first site to sound its interest in selling Caribbean gospel. The work of Caribbean gospel artists could be found at traditional Web sources such as (http://www.amazon.com) and (http://www.artistdirect.com) and on the less well known (http://www .cordiallyyoursgospelmusicshop.com) Sites dedicated to non-gospel artists and music were also important agents for the marketing and distribution of Caribbean gospel on the Internet. If dedicated Christian sites in the region were tentative in their exploitation of the Net's full potential, then extra-regional gospel sites such as (http://www.gospelcity.com) and regionally inspired secular sites such as (http://rudegal.com) demonstrated what was possible for gospel.

Conclusions

Caribbean gospel today needs to be invigorated. Gospel requires the continued infusion of a kind of artistic honesty that allows musicians to create and innovate for spiritual and cultural empowerment. Caribbean gospel may not be the only brand of gospel that gives up its interest in hard social issues in favour of songs of praise and worship, but given the history, development and future prognosis of Caribbean society, it is difficult to comprehend how a genre as centrally positioned as gospel can ignore its greater calling. In the final analysis, this points to the need for greater education and greater ideological and spiritual commitment on the part of gospel practitioners. It is possible that the relatively sparse critical writing on gospel music in the Caribbean is partly responsible for the absence of a sound formal discourse on the politics and ideology of Caribbean gospel; this is indeed a very real likelihood, given that some of the most relevant writings on this subject are highly descriptive.[18] Evidently there is need for theorizing and for much closer analysis. This chapter is but one part of that larger project. But in spite of this particular initiative, the greater reality may very well be that what gospel needs most is practitioners who will actually participate to help redefine Caribbean society.

track 2

Discourses on AIDS (+ Sex) in Caribbean Music

How Society Speaks

Popular music sees all and tells all. Popular music is a phenomenon of immense global significance. It is without doubt one of the most powerful expressions of a culture. Over time, Caribbean popular music has addressed a range of issues which have affected Caribbean culture and societies. Inasmuch as this is true, Caribbean cultural criticism faces the challenge of coming to terms with the volume and variety of materials that regional artists continue to produce. A major task for pop culture critics must be unravelling, interpreting and explaining cultural phenomena. Throughout the late 1980s – and, indeed, in the 1990s – Caribbean criticism became preoccupied increasingly with the imperatives of theory. Postmodernism, postcolonialism and poststructuralism have swayed criticism towards specific issues of race, gender, subjectivity, difference and indeterminacy, and away from confronting the raw material of cultural practice.

Acquired immune deficiency syndrome (AIDS) has had a tremendous impact on the region. Its far-reaching effects have only begun to be investigated in recent times. Cultural studies investigation into the social construction of the pandemic in the region has hardly gotten off the ground in any systematic way. This type of sustained investigation often results in many kinds of discoveries. Due to the relative absence of this type of investigation, the region also risks the danger of discursive silence. A protracted silence could be particularly threatening given that, outside sub-Saharan Africa, the region has the highest incidence of HIV/AIDS infection in the world. In the current global context, it is especially dangerous not to speak one's position. AIDS has surfaced as a worldwide phenomenon, with specific ideological debates which relate to the Caribbean in critical ways – debates that are fraught with tensions concerning race, sexuality, religion and other ideological considerations.

In the first years of the twenty-first century, Caribbean agencies and national governments moved to confront challenges posed to their economies by the AIDS pandemic. Regional and world agencies networked to share information and set out plans of action. In February 2001, a new pan-Caribbean partnership against AIDS was launched.[1]

Many of the scientific and technical documents dealing with AIDS, such as those in the bibliographic database of the Joint United Nations Programme on HIV/AIDS (UNAIDS), recognize that societal attitudes are also central to initiatives to combat HIV/AIDS.[2] Attitudes towards HIV/AIDS have gone through transformations throughout the years. International health and education agencies have played a significant role in shaping and revealing things about these attitudes. Attitudes towards AIDS globally have also been affected significantly by the Western media. In particular, Western popular culture has affected attitudes towards AIDS in a way that few other sectors can claim to have done. Popular arts and popular culture media are not only shapers of attitudes though; popular culture also reflects attitudes and trends within society. In the Caribbean as elsewhere, popular culture is a central site of experience. It is here that past, present and future trends are expressed more democratically than in any other domain. It is to this domain of culture that this chapter goes, in search of past and present tracks of knowledge about Caribbean society and HIV/AIDS.

Before definitive conclusions can be drawn about the region's attitude to issues that affect it, though, one must begin to understand the nature of Caribbean social expressions. An important reality about this society is that it comprises several institutional constituents. Formal agencies and informal agencies do not always share the same perspective on national or regional issues. One route by which some understanding of HIV/AIDS and Caribbean society can be had is through an examination of official governmental documentation, but other kinds of knowledge can be accessed through other media. And since Caribbean societies often speak more clearly and honestly through cultural and artistic media than through their politicians or formal institutions, it is sometimes more productive to engage with Caribbean cultural forms in order to discover hidden and other truths about social phenomena. An examination of expressions about HIV/AIDS in Caribbean society as reflected through popular music culture can, among other things, reveal many secrets and truths about this society.

Breaking Silences

On 5 June 1981, the Center for Disease Control in Atlanta, Georgia, published a report by Dr Michael Gottlieb about five gay male patients in Los Angeles who suffered weight loss, high fevers and lung infections. These were among the first individuals to suffer from AIDS. On 8 October 1989, the *New York Times* warned in a front-page headline that "AIDS Is Spreading in Teen-agers: A New Trend Alarming to Experts". But this trend was hardly new: adolescents have, since the beginning of the AIDS epidemic, accounted for an estimated 20 per cent of new infections. What the *Times* article did reveal was the slow reaction by societies worldwide to the impact of AIDS. Parents have been reluctant to admit that their children are engaging in certain lifestyles. Andy Humm and Frances Kunreuther have surmised that this reluctance on the part of "the system" to deal with youth and AIDS stems from the reality that addressing HIV infection means grappling with teenagers' habits, their sexuality and homosexuality, and their drug use – issues which such agencies have never dealt with adequately.[3]

Whereas studies of other cultures have begun to examine the relationship between AIDS and other phenomena as a way of better dealing with the epidemic in its social context, there is relatively little published in the Caribbean concerning AIDS and specific facets of popular culture, especially relating to youths. The intersection of AIDS, music and youth culture in the Caribbean represents a rich site for further enquiry. Although adolescents and youth constitute a high-risk group for AIDS, AIDS discourse in the Caribbean has not yet put into perspective the relationship between aspects of popular music culture and the epidemic. In that respect, this chapter, in its broadest application, facilitates a much-needed wider discourse on the issue. In particular, it should serve as a critical resource document on the Caribbean pandemic through its intervention into a domain of relative discursive silence.

Within the first decade of the discovery of AIDS there was uncertainty and fear in the region. The lack of information about and awareness of

AIDS globally left people to conclude that youths were particularly at risk of transmitting the disease through homosexual activity, unprotected sex and the sharing of needles for intravenous drug use. One opinion that is still rife in popular belief is that the music of youth culture supports the very practices that can lead to AIDS. This popular belief can be heard on radio call-in programmes, in the press and in everyday conversation. But to date "serious" cultural studies investigation has not sought to discuss the nature of the interface between music, music culture and HIV/AIDS. In this chapter, I want to present what amounts to a preliminary discussion of this interface. First, I will explore the shifting attitudes towards AIDS in Caribbean society over the past two decades as reflected through music and music culture. What will become evident is that as AIDS awareness has grown through education and a greater flow of information, there has been an accompanying shift in the attitude and tone of the message about AIDS in the music of popular culture. But in the first decade of the twenty-first century, there are still many issues and attitudes to confront. Caribbean popular music has itself had an impact on the AIDS phenomenon in many respects. This chapter will also, therefore, examine the exploitation of popular culture forms and icons in AIDS awareness programmes, and the apparent contradictions that arise from the use of these pop culture symbols. The relationship between the music, its message and the lifestyles of popular artists in the Caribbean is an area for substantial future debate.

The decade of the 1980s was a period of ignorance of and curiosity about AIDS in the Caribbean. AIDS has always been a mysterious and hence a mistrusted disease within Caribbean society. Although it was suggested by the medical profession that the disease could be spread only through the exchange of blood or semen, there still loomed a societal scepticism, which was based largely on the perception that researchers themselves, worldwide, had been unable to come to terms with the nature of the disease. Since it was initially propagated in the Caribbean that the AIDS virus was transmitted primarily by homosexual contact, AIDS was perceived to be a disease of homosexual men. Although this view is not as pervasive as it used to be, there is still the lingering suspicion in the region that it is this homosexual practice that was and is responsible for the widespread scourge of AIDS.

Like rock music, Caribbean music forms can be said to have reflected the tension of sexual anxiety throughout the 1980s, partly as a result of the emergence of AIDS. But if William Graebner is correct, that rock bands do not generally "sing explicitly of the dread possibilities posed by . . . AIDS", then Caribbean music is different.[4] The reaction to AIDS in the music of Caribbean popular culture has been significant. Artists addressed the topic from different angles. Reactions in the 1980s reflected in many respects larger societal fear of, ignorance of and scepticism about the disease. On his 1985/86 album *A Touch of Class,* in the song "Ah Fraid de AIDS", the Trinidad calypsonian the Mighty Sparrow treated the topic of AIDS. The song reflects both fear and mistrust of the disease. It espoused the view that the disease was started by homosexuals, and it reveals a fear that AIDS was endangering romance. The lyrics also refer to the impact of the disease on all and sundry, such as Rock Hudson, who in the song is deemed to be justly rewarded for his homosexual proclivity. Sparrow's song voices a number of concerns which were being felt within Caribbean society. His title, carefully chosen, conveyed the message of caution and trepidation towards this modern epidemic: "now a days you can't take a chance / dey 'fraid de AIDS".

Also in 1985, on the neighbouring island of Barbados, a fellow calypsonian, Viper, tackled the subject of AIDS. Unlike Sparrow's song, Viper's does not focus solely on the AIDS epidemic. The song "Jesus" (not recorded, but performed during Barbados's Crop Over festival in 1985) nonetheless analyses the body social, spiritual and politic of the Caribbean and concludes that the panacea for the deficiencies is Jesus. Viper's song sparked the most debate and controversy, after his compatriot Gabby's song "De List" (also 1985), on the AIDS question within the kaiso genre in the eastern Caribbean in the mid-1980s. Viper's composition began as a response to an earlier song by the Trinidadian Gypsy, who posed the question, "Where do we go from here?" Gypsy's question reflected the general lament over social degradation in the region. Crime, unemployment, deviance and the growing drug problem were major concerns of the time.

Arguably, there has been greater commentary on the Caribbean drug problem than there has been on AIDS. Whereas the drug problem has been viewed as an overt menace to society – as the central instigator of the range of ills in society – AIDS has been viewed as the "silent killer", since its transmission has been predominantly through sexual contact. AIDS was widely perceived in the 1980s as a domestic, "private" affair. To the extent that AIDS was viewed as resulting from immoral practices, there has been an unwillingness to own up to it. As a result, there has been a general reaction of fear, condemnation and silence, especially in the public domain. Caribbean popular song has always responded overtly to societal issues, whether through folk song, calypso, reggae or other forms. That is why Viper's song, "Jesus", is vital to the examination of AIDS in popular Caribbean music discourse.

Whereas, as part of an unofficial discourse, clerics in large numbers condemned promiscuous sexual activity and some criticized homosexual activity, few were as committed and overtly forthright as the speaker in Viper's song. The reference to religion is pertinent, since Viper's song proposed to enter the debate at that level. "Jesus" is still regarded as one of the most daring commentaries on sexual practices, AIDS and the eradication of AIDS within Caribbean society in the 1980s. It entered the discourse on religion, morality and AIDS at a time when Caribbean gospel music proper was still flirting with formulaic, thematically asocial, non-committal cover versions of North American contemporary gospel standards by Amy Grant, Petra, Sandi Patti and the Imperials. It entered the discourse some ten years before most gospel artists would dare touch the subject of AIDS, sex and morality. It is with this background and in this context, therefore, that Viper's song ignited some discussion about AIDS and socio-religious issues within Caribbean society.

The discomfort some felt about this song also had to do with its being performed like gospel, but in the calypso tent forum. Was it gospel? Was it calypso? Where was its place? This was another facet of this song's subversive qualities. But one sensed that the debates surrounding its genre was a diversion socially constructed to deflect much of the tension which the lyrics created through their unapologetic engagement with the Caribbean realities of AIDS:

> Dem homosexuals such undesirables that we have down in de city
> Contaminating and destabilizing all de youths with them philosophies
> Dem prostituting worse than the women
> So let we shun dem or better yet bun dem
> AIDS is a problem and we don't want them
> If yuh get de point help me clear de joint
> Cause we don't need prostitution we don't need cheap tricks
> Woman don't sell your body for no kind o' kicks
> We don't need blue movie we don't need sex show
> Woman respect your body don't do um no more

> Get Jesus he is de master
> Jesus he is de answer
> Jesus Jesus Jesus come to Jesus

In the controversial second verse (above), the speaker clearly associates the spread of HIV with homosexual activity and prostitution. A primary concern is with the effect of sexual practices (which it treats explicitly) on the bodies and minds of the young within society: a point which the mid-1980s furore ignored. When one examines the structure of the verse above, it is seen to be built on stating the problem, noting its effects and positing a solution: the solution of "shunning" homosexuals and their activity, or "better yet bun[ning]" them, is what drew the most comments. At the level of "high" national debate, this calypsonian's point of view was deemed to be distasteful. At the informal level, though, Viper's song represented the outlook of many other individuals. Its attitude was partly rooted in "local values" shaped by what has been called "a fundamentalist reading of Biblical scriptures".[5] But there is more to it than that.

In comparison with some other Western societies, large segments of Caribbean society are still very much rooted in a theology and philosophy which places God at the centre of man's livelihood. For example, natural phenomena such as hurricanes are seen as not all that "natural"; they are often viewed as representing, to some degree, God's inevitable power either to spare or to punish. This is not to suggest that there is an obsessive preoccupation with situating God in the middle of all eventualities; rather, it calls attention to the extent of this religious outlook. There is no consensus in Caribbean societies with respect to these phenomena. As John Fiske remarks, "the people" is not a stable sociological category.[6] Indeed, individuals are found to alter their perceptions with the severity of situations. They are more inclined to attribute a positive occurrence to God than they are some personally catastrophic event. But the reasoning given by Peter Manuel for attitudes to homosexuality is upfront and does not explore alternatives.[7] For one thing, it does not consider the ideological basis of the ongoing association of AIDS with homosexuality in the Caribbean. Since there has been an orchestrated attempt globally to deny the role of homosexuality in the proliferation of AIDS and to project the disease as originating in black society, whether in Africa or in Haiti, Caribbean peoples have been equally rigid in counteracting the ideology behind this hypothesis.[8] They have preferred to support the homosexuality hypothesis as a more credible rationale. They have also supported conspiracy theories about the origin of AIDS.

In a sense, there have been two disparate levels of discourse on AIDS within Caribbean society: one carried by the agencies of government and the medical fraternity, the other conveyed in public every day by individuals, supported in some sections of the press and expressed by artists and performers. It was only in the mid-1990s, through greater education in a number of forums, that there began to be some degree of synthesis between these two levels of discourse. For a long time, the unofficial discourse on AIDS, which is the "discourse of the people", sought to reflect *their* concerns, to pose their questions and to challenge the claims of official organizations within the Caribbean. Viper's song "Jesus" proposed to express the feelings of the wider populace. Although its message was not "politically correct", its dissemination brought more clearly into focus the existence of these discursive poles within Caribbean society.

Many 1980s "official" commentators on Gabby's song "De List" deemed it to also be in poor taste. It has been suggested that the song was ill conceived, and, just like the rumour on which it was built, the song has primarily been viewed as destructive. What many of these criticisms have not taken into consideration, though, is the temporal context – the period in which the song appeared, that is, in the years of almost total ignorance concerning AIDS. Calypso specialist critics saw "De List" as fitting into a category of calypso, and this was seen as its main value – it existed to belong to the category of historical documentation. It was hardly seen as a warning or as representing the cry of a helpless, susceptible populace, somewhat in the vein of Viper's "Jesus". Fewer individuals still have considered it to be a plea on behalf of the populace, a call for a much more candid and informed exposition of the problematic of AIDS by all agencies.

The song focuses on a widely rumoured list of male partners which an AIDS patient allegedly made before he died. The song claimed that the victim was a "young fellah":

> Nurse Babblelou say yuh won't believe it
> They try to keep de thing a secret
> But that don't suit Bajan character
> Dem know we mout' ain't have no cover
> Big names popular names

Make love to de boy at least that is what he claims
So now even married women saying they insist
De hospital show them all de names pun de list

Like Viper's song, "De List" locates the point of initial impact for the spreading of the disease in homosexual relations. The insistence on the part of married women that they see "de names on the list", however, is a foreshadowing of the eventual realization that the spread of AIDS is not restricted to any single form of sexual contact.

The futility that the song conveys surrounding the request to see "all" the names further emphasizes the clandestine constitution of the virus, dramatizing the early stages of an epidemic gone wild. Thus the cutting pains, "like razor blades", correspond with the lethal incisions within the body social of the Caribbean and the innate fear and suspicion that the insidious AIDS epidemic has created at the heart of Caribbean society. In retrospect, some nineteen years after the dissemination of this song, it must be assigned a reading of this kind, one that takes into consideration the development of discourses on AIDS in the music of popular Caribbean culture. The song's use of satire and its excursions into rumour only mask the underlying motive and serious message of the composition. This seriousness is latent, like the submerged mournful, portentous string samples which themselves lie hidden beneath the song's deceptively spirited musical arrangement. Politicians, doctors, cricketers, calypsonians – all are short-listed as having had relations with the dying victim. The song only hints at the curtailment of sexual activities. But it deliberately does not focus on the solution, as Sparrow's or Viper's songs might have. Instead, it employs the strategy of throwing the discourse unconcluded into the public domain. That is a strength of this song: its creator has made an insidious artistic incision. But his inability to take the song beyond the realm of rumour is also a failing. As a result, he was accused of trivializing a serious matter. "De List" was, however, a product of its time. No wonder it has hardly been played with any frequency in the decades that followed.

While some songs were direct and others made passing reference to AIDS, still others have continued to explore the nature of male-female relations in a business-as-usual fashion. To some extent, such songs deny the presence of HIV/AIDS as all-pervasive within Caribbean love relations. The Trinidadian "love man" Baron's "Somebody", from the 1989 album

Party Fusion, expresses the desire to have a woman for the night:

> If ah cyan find ah partner
> Simply have somebody home
> And get on bad bad bad bad bad bad bad

The song's erotic desire reveals a wish for companionship, one free from sexual and social repercussions. Such songs both reflect and play on the wishful thinking of society. But they also serve as ironic reminders that Caribbean society cannot ignore the harsh realities of its social, cultural and spiritual problems.

By the late 1980s, there began to be traces of change in the treatment of AIDS in some musical compositions. This was particularly evident in calypso. There began to be a shift away from the earlier association of AIDS with homosexuality towards a proliferation of songs which (if only in passing) carried a message of warning about AIDS. These tended not to point an accusatory finger; rather, they were beginning to address AIDS as another of the region's social problems. Thus, songs assigned a number of lines specifically to the AIDS debate as opposed to focusing solely on AIDS, as Gabby and Sparrow might have in the mid-1980s. So, by the late 1980s and early 1990s, AIDS was being integrated as another of the region's social ills. Songs such the Montserratian Arrow's "Death for Sale", on his 1991 *Zombi Soca* album, were therefore cryptically cautioning "don't buy death in sex", but going on to deal with other social problems such as drugs, unemployment and materialism.

Although one might read the calypso art form as having reflected this kind of shift in its commentary on AIDS, the point should be made that within its co-genre soca, there was not a similar shift. Soca has for the most part held closely to its stated imperative: party. In this regard, soca has always espoused the imperative of fête, which many of its detractors have reinterpreted to mean "slack" behaviour: sex and total abandon. A significant number of soca albums have featured scantily dressed women. It is a fact that soca music flourished throughout the 1980s and 1990s and that a major catalyst for its expansion has been its deification of reckless abandon. There are few soca artists who can claim to have stayed far away from issues relating to the play of male and female bodies. Metaphors of love-play and sex have characterized soca throughout its evolution. It is argued that calypso proper is defined by the crafty employment of such metaphors. Many soca acts have therefore relied on this explanation while celebrating activity of a sexually explicit nature. The better writers have been able to traverse the thin line between art and suggestiveness, but the worse cases have degenerated into unimaginative smut. A group such as Burning Flames from Antigua would argue that many of their dance songs have been more fun songs than anything else. They might suggest that their early 1990s song "If You Get What You Want" does not glorify sex-play at all but rather reinforces in the minds of partners that there are consequences to be borne for loose sexual encounters, hence the chorus: "If you get what yuh want tonight / will you remember me tomorrow". Beckett, from St Vincent, might also caution that his late-1990s suggestive "Small Pin" should not be held against him. The song employs the metaphor of a small pin to represent the phallus and provides a list of females who have been stuck by this "small pin". Like Burning Flames, Beckett would point to his use of the uptempo style to draw awareness to serious issues of loneliness, sex, deception and the destructive consequences of senseless play. His "Stranger Man" sits somewhere nervously between calypso proper and soca. This 1980s song offers a warning, but it is also a playfully suggestive composition:

> Windwards football and cricket
> I checking out de new picks
> Or when de West Indies come to town
> I does show de whole team around . . .
> Ask Irving Shillingford, Norbert Phillip
> Lockheart Sabastian or Tomas Kentish . . .
> Stranger man, watch that kind of man

Therefore, like their dancehall counterparts, many soca and post-soca artists would contend that although some of their compositions promote love-play and sex, much of the onus is on audiences to discriminate and to read deeper than what lies at the song's surface. But it is precisely because audiences are entrusted to interpret these songs that the issue has become so controversial. There are obviously, therefore, other readings of songs of this kind. Those readings tend to refer to the emphasis placed on the body and sexual pleasure by many soca and post-soca acts through performance and marketing. Throughout the development of soca, its emphasis and method have hardly altered significantly.

Soca's divas were no less provocative than their counterparts in dancehall. In mid-2003, the calypso stalwart Singing Francine acknowledged the contribution made to calypso by women. But she decried the damage being done to women and the art form by some soca performances, especially those by women. Destra, Alison Hinds, Denise Belfon and Faye-Ann Lyons set the pace and standard for soca in the post-2000 era. Lyons's "Focus" (2003) is reflective of the compositions sung by soca's women over the years. The lyrics, though not as explicit as those by dancehall acts such as Lady Saw, are nonetheless equally provocative. "Focus" extols the beauty and appeal of women. It encourages admiration of the female body. It playfully taunts all and sundry to "focus on me body / I want yuh focus how I sexy" but stops short of inviting any other sexual act. These teasing compositions have marked the method of soca over the years. Songs of this kind were very self-conscious in their creation, almost revelling in their own sensuality. Lyons therefore sings, "when I say hocus-pocus . . . all them man . . . have to watch me . . .". Many commentators, such as Francine, felt that soca's divas were inviting the objectification of women. But it was clear that such songs appealed to the market. They also caught the attention and sensibility of patrons, who supported many shows featuring female performers. Thus, like other popular styles, Caribbean music forged ahead in its exploration and exploitation of the body, of women, and of sex and sexuality.

The very popular and infectious song "Peepin" (2002), by Super P of Grenada, concerns itself with the voyeurism of Caribbean society. Its appeal springs partly from Super P's unique delivery but has more to do with the song's humorous treatment of a contemporary Caribbean preoccupation. The song lists a set of individuals, all engaged in the act of peeping, and it samples Rockwell's 1984 anthem "Somebody's Watching Me" (featuring Michael Jackson). Although this was done to enhance the theme of invasion of privacy in Caribbean society, the song's total effect emphasizes the extent to which privacy and intimacy have been breached:

> Even in the sea you bathin
> They passin with diving glass, they peepin
> Everybody peepin

Homophobia and After

Music has for some time come under scrutiny for its role in promoting promiscuity and sexual immorality. A 2003 study conducted out of Emory University, for instance, identified rap music as contributing to violence and promiscuity among segments of American society.[9] Caribbean music has been similarly branded. In the minds of some Caribbean people, dancehall has been much more notorious than any other contemporary Caribbean popular music form in terms of what is perceived to be its supporting of violence, "sexual looseness" and promiscuity.[10] Dancehall and slackness have been synonymously associated in mainstream perception. In Jamaica there has been an ongoing debate between opposing voices. There and elsewhere, dancehall (and other) acts have come under fire for performances at events such as Sumfest.[11] Dancehall is often regarded as the music of the "rude boy" and the "glamour girl".

This is not to say that dancehall is the only music form to come under criticism for its expression of vulgarity and slackness. Soca has also come under scrutiny. In July 1999, for instance, there was debate surrounding David Rudder's song "Down Dey". A leading AIDS researcher, Courtenay Bartholomew, echoing the views of many people on selected soca songs, cited Rudder's composition as advocating "sexual permissiveness".[12] In 2001, Joey Rivers, a founding member of the post-soca band Xtatik, questioned some of the lyrics Xtatik was performing.[13] Iwer George's 1997 song "Bottom in de Road" was deemed by some to be racist, sexist and perverted.[14] Jason Sifflet explored the association between soca, sin and promiscuity in an extended report in the *St Lucia Mirror* in 2002.[15] Throughout the region, calypso, soca and post-soca artists have had to defend themselves against charges of slackness and excess.

In 1995, the dancehall queen Patra was slated to perform in St Lucia. Her scheduled performance raised debates on radio, on the streets and among other artists. Radio call-in programmes reflected the dominant attitudes in society towards some dancehall artists and their composing and performing styles. The Patra controversy brought to the fore the extent to which acts like her have been branded as promoters of promiscuity, illicit sex and slackness. Patra was at the time the leading female dancehall act. She had been signed to Epic and was mashing up the airways and party venues. Debates raged in the theatres of the streets, but artists also took the discourse to the stage. The St Lucian calypsonian De Professor commented on Patra's scheduled show in St Lucia. In his 1995 song "Patra" (performed during the St Lucian carnival), he explored competing sides of the debate. His position was not obscured in the discussion.

> *Chorus*
> Patra they balling
> Patra all that I hearing
> She wears nothing under
> When yuh come over you show us
> Kingston Harbour
> The things that you do encouraging raper
> Show some decency anytime you come to this country
> If you want money employment here man ain't easy
> I work with sanitation and I cleaning
> The streets of corruption

An examination of the catalogue of songs by popular dancehall artists of the period might very well give some support to the perception De Professor expresses in his song. Artists such as the Jamaicans Shabba Ranks and Lieutenant Stitchie (before his late-1990s conversion to Christianity), who have both signed to major labels, had persistently described wanton sex-play between men and women. Their music videos are also replete with such images. A glance at the title alone of their most popular songs throws up many signs which a cursory reading of popular music culture might regard as marketing tools, but also as clear indicators of lyrical slackness: from Lieutenant Stitchie's *Rude Boy* album, "Rough Rider", "(I Need) Sexual Healing", "Ton-load a Fat" and "Mr Good Stuff"; from Shabba, "Twice My Age", "Love Punany Bad", "Girls Wine", "Kill Me Dead", "Wicked in Bed", "Mr Loverman" and "Hardcore Lovin' ".

Dancehall artists have premised their abhorrence of homosexuality on the religious teaching that it is sexual aberration. They contend that it is morally wrong. Ironically, the general mainstream perception of dancehall music and culture is that it too contributes to vulgarity and slackness, which are also inherently morally corrupting. But there has been quite clear differentiation of sexual desire and sexual play between heterosexual and homosexual parties.

Some leading dancehall artists have been particularly tough and homophobic when it comes to what they see as misplaced sexual proclivities. In a sense, these artists have maintained what has been loosely called a "fundamentalist" reading of homosexuality. Homosexuality is still perceived by many of these artists as being punishable by death and, as one way, through AIDS. Buju Banton's song "Boom Bye Bye" (1992) is emblematic of this attitude: "Boom bye bye in a batty boy head / Rude boy no promote nuh nasty man dem ha fe dead". The song has attracted many comments. In the international domain of the music business, the response has largely been critical. In the big league of large independents and major record companies, "political correctness" is the watchword. Large companies are very conscious of the power of gay and lesbian lobbies and know the influence these groups can exert on sales and returns. Protests began to dog Buju Banton's performances after the song was released. The Gay and Lesbian Alliance Against Defamation (GLAAD) targeted radio stations and record companies that supported the artist. The *New York Post* picked up on the story. This brought much pressure to bear on the then-young artist.

When Shabba Ranks appeared on international television, after his signing to Epic, in support of the point of view expressed by his countryman Buju Banton he too was threatened. His concerts began to attract even more activists and protests than Buju's, and some were cancelled. He was threatened with being taken off tour and was forced to retreat to a much more moderate, politically correct position on homosexuality and its consequences. He retracted his initial statements and agreed to promote freedom of sexual expression and preferences. Shabba subsequently went on to remain in the big league, although his era of greatest popularity was the early 1990s. By the mid- to late-1990s, he had lost much of his appeal throughout the Caribbean. Some people considered him to have sold out to Babylon. On the other hand, Buju was a rising star in the early- to mid-1990s, and he did not rescind his opposition to homosexuality. Whereas Shabba declined in popularity throughout the region, Buju remained much more popular throughout the 1990s. This might have little directly to do with their positions on homosexuality, but it certainly dramatizes the instability of Caribbean popular culture in the context of the transnational reconfiguration of the 1990s. Significantly, Buju has stayed relatively clear of this controversy. "Boom Bye Bye" has remained his most controversial offering on the subject.

Many post-1990 dancehall acts, such as Capleton, Sizzla, Anthony B and Bounty Killer, have continued to express their stance against homosexuality. Capleton has hardly let up. His verdict on such activity is "more fire". His song "Bun Out Di Chi Chi" (2002) and Beenie Man's "Badman Chi Chi Man" (2002) reflect their attitudes towards the subject. The Jamaican outfit T.O.K. song "Chi Chi Man" (2001), which was very popular among youths throughout the Caribbean, carries on the theme and tone which artists like Buju Banton had conveyed almost a decade before. In the song, T.O.K. chant,

> From dem a par inna chi chi man car
> Blaze di fire mek we bun dem!!!! (Bun dem!!!!)
> From dem a drink inna chi chi man bar
> Blaze di fire mek we dun dem!!!! (Dun dem!!!!)

In the realm of mainstream hip-hop music, there has been a similar onslaught by rap artists. Jay-Z's album *The Blueprint* (2001) played with variations of the word "fag". DMX's "Bloodline Anthem" (2001) made overt use of the word "faggot". There are countless other acts who have expressed similar sentiments; Dr Dre, Snoop Dogg, Ice Cube and Common are but a representative few. In spite of the advent of West Coast "homie-sexual" outfits such as Rainbow Flava and Deep Dickollective, East Coast clubs such as the Equinox, and gay rappers such as Caushun, mainstream hip hop maintained its macho heterosexual image well into the first decade of the twenty-first century.

By the mid-1990s, the British government was moving to put into law in its dependent Caribbean territories freedom of sexual orientation legislation; there was a swell of resistance from both church and other unofficial groupings.[16] The rejection of homosexuality expressed within popular music culture has been unwavering. In 2003, homosexuals and overt homosexual tendencies were still being widely decried through the music of youth popular culture in the Caribbean. Given the history of the region and the politics of AIDS, it is unlikely that Caribbean youth culture will in the foreseeable future readily accept homosexual relations in the way it has been embraced in some parts of Europe and the United States. In spite of the fact that many Caribbean musicians and citizens feign respect for individual sexual freedom, there is still a latent mistrust of the propaganda of transnational institutions. A survey at the end of the twentieth century would still reveal that most Caribbean citizens are averse to homosexuality and consider it to be the source of the AIDS epidemic. Indeed, in the dancehall domain a number of songs performed after 2000 trumpeted the unwavering stance of many artists to homosexuality and AIDS. Elephant Man's "Log On" (2001), done on the liquid rhythm (a popular rhythm/version track also used by other artists), was not a straight-up attack on homosexuals, but the central positioning of "chi chi man" in the chorus and the song's celebratory act of stepping "pon chi chi man" situated it as being in opposition to men who are not "straight":

> Log on and step pon chi chi man
> Log on from yuh know she sehh yu nuh ickie man
> Log on and step pon chi chi man
> Dance we a dance and a bun out a freaky man

But it was T.O.K.'s 2001 "Chi Chi Man" which caught the most attention. It was interpreted at several levels within Caribbean society – including the political. Whereas the group maintained it had no party political agenda, it was not in a hurry to curb other readings of the song. The song crossed over to North American urban radio and somehow did not gather the same kind of scrutiny and rebuke as had Buju Banton's "Boom Bye Bye". This was partly due to the heavier jargon on the T.O.K. track, but also, in some respects, T.O.K.'s gangsta iconography situated them closer to hip hop and provided them a position of some support in the hip hop discourse of homosexuality and disease.

Although resentment might well be the overriding sentiment of Caribbean youths as expressed through their forms of popular music, there have been subtle shifts and changes in the broader societal outlook on sexual preference. By the mid-1990s, Caribbean music revealed some changes in its treatment of and attitude towards the AIDS epidemic. Although major elements of roots reggae and dancehall held fast to the earlier outlook and attitude, at sporadic moments Caribbean music tended to demonstrate alternative viewpoints. These intermittent interventions stemmed partly from the kind of politics that guided the international entertainment industry. It was this overt kind of politics that hemmed in Shabba Ranks. But there was also another, less conspicuous covert politics that made an impact on Caribbean society. The role of international television and radio cannot be discounted as having greatly affected attitudes towards AIDS at the end of the twentieth century.

Western popular and institutional culture have been instrumental in subtly eroding the opposition between heterosexuality and homosexuality in perceptions of gender intercourse. In April 1997, the actress Ellen DeGeneres admitted to being a lesbian. Her sitcom *Ellen* became the first programme of its kind to focus on the life of a lesbian character. Significantly, the producers of the programme cast the hugely influential black talk-show host Oprah Winfrey as Ellen's sanctioning psychologist. The intentions were clear: this would bring about wider acceptance. Other progammes, such as *Melrose Place* and *Beverley Hills 90210,* have aided in reconfiguring traditional Caribbean notions of sexual orthodoxy.

In comparison with the earlier years of the AIDS epidemic, the end of the 1990s witnessed a mellowing of tone in respect to AIDS and homosexuality. Although there were no signs that dancehall and soca culture would ever embrace homosexual practice, it must be said that some dancehall acts have reflected alternative ways of viewing AIDS. It is not always viewed as a direct offshoot of homosexuality. Indeed, there are many songs that treat the problematic of AIDS separately from the issue of homosexuality. Anthony B's 2002 "Don't Wanna Be (an HIV Victim)" is an example of this.

By 2003, there was a more vocal lobby throughout the region decrying hate lyrics in selected Caribbean popular music. During the 2003 Trinidad carnival, the Antiguan soca act Wanskie came under immense pressure because of the song "More Gyul". The song's declaration of excluding "chi chi man" from a carnival band led to heated debate on Trinidad's 102FM talk shows. An organized lobby against the song led to the artist's being dropped from a major Republic Bank fête.

Comparatively, a greater number of songs were beginning to reflect the thrust towards AIDS education. Songs were therefore promoting caution, awareness and "safe sex". Even within gospel, the Caribbean's most conservative music genre, a group such the Ambassadors, out of Jamaica, was beginning to at least consider the issue. On their *circa* 1995 album, in the song "Pray AIDS and Drugs Away", they sang, with some detachment,

> We don't want no more Aids in this world
> We don't want no more Aids in this world
> It is taking the lives of the young and the old
> Let's join hands and pray Aids away
>
> God knows its an awful situation
> Sin of man has caused this condition

A more convincing treatment of AIDS by a gospel act was Sean Daniel's "One a Day", which employed secular and religious metaphors to dramatize the serious threat of the pandemic. Songs of this kind gestured to changing attitudes.

One of the compositions which best exemplifies this new attitudinal orientation was the catchy "A Sex World" by the band Touch, out of St Vincent and the Grenadines:

> Sex education make it a part of our productive school curriculum
> And this one it should be planned
> School's where they meeting there's where they courting
> There is where most dating begins among other things
> Teachers likewise parents have a role to play
> In preparing the children for the cruel world out there
> This knowledge is vital all the way
>
> Not knowing the facts they likely to get in trouble
> On this road of life you are responsible
> You'll feel the more they know the more they'll want to experiment
> Hey, they'll find out some how don't keep them ignorant
> No, no

This song offers a notable contrast with Viper's earlier "Jesus", especially in terms of lyrical and performance tone. Viper's lyrics are reflective of some fear and revulsion; his speaker distances himself from the AIDS culture. Touch's song appears much more controlled, and its speaker situates himself as part of the culture which AIDS impacts: "*our* . . . curriculum", "a sex world . . . *we're* living in". Whereas Viper's attitude is almost tough and militant, Touch assumes the voice of reason. Unlike Viper's calypso, Touch's song does not express openly its views on homosexuality and AIDS; it is more concerned with promoting the wisdom of educating children and the society about late-twentieth-century sexual permissiveness.

In some respects, though, the seeming shift in emphasis towards prevention and caution was only a mask. Popular artists did not buy into the philosophy that AIDS *itself* was the scourge and culprit infecting society. Sexual perversion – homosexuality in particular – was seen as a manifest agent. Some artists were determined to hold their position. As a result, up to August 2002, the BBC was forced to remove links to songs deemed as offensive from its Web site promoting the BBC2 series *History of Reggae*. It was felt by gay campaigners that the series page promoted homophobic songs.[17] In Jamaica, the Jamaica Forum for Lesbians, All-Sexuals and Gays (J-FLAG) campaigned for a change to that country's constitution to provide for equal protection under the law, but the debates have gone on.[18] As of 2004, Caribbean music showed few real signs of embracing the politics of Western gay rights movements or of other regional bodies.

Prevention through Popular Culture

By the mid-1990s, regional artists were increasingly taking on the role as teachers and messengers in educating people about AIDS prevention. Dancehall artists were also taking on the persona of teacher and messenger in educating about the dangers of AIDS. In this period and thereafter, leading proponents of AIDS awareness and their agencies pointed to the positive role cultural forms could play in the fight. Guyana's president Bharrat Jagdeo spoke about the importance of this interface when he drew attention to the substantial national resources allocated to fight HIV/AIDS, as reflected in Guyana's Strategic Plan. St Lucian parliamentary secretary Michael Gaspard, speaking at the second Caribbean Conference on Parenting in St Lucia in June 2001, called attention to the critical role of music in sensitizing the public on social issues. Around the same time, the Youth Coalition quarterly *Watchdog* carried an article by a Canadian, Tanya Baker, espousing a similar perspective.[19] Although the article presented a simplistic overview of the island and its attitudes, Baker's recognition of the critical role music could play in the fight was significant. But even before these interventions, Caribbean artists had already been part of the process of education and critique. The list of performers engaged in the project of education grew steadily over the years. The Barbadian Peter Ram's "Dangerous Test", which cautioned to "use your condom", was representative of this trend. Although the singer was a product of rude-boy culture, the song's educational objective did not render him out of place. After all, the song did not call for sexual abstinence but for greater care in making sexual choices. It was a product of the 1990s inasmuch as it experimented with entertainment and message. The 1980s did not produce in numbers songs that had the confidence to balance the mix of entertainment and didacticism while talking about AIDS. But this song was, in some respects, still a product of the 1980s in its show of uncertainty, reflected by the distancing of the epidemic from the on-the-ground experience of the speaker:

> Home pun me yard sitting down one day
> Radio turn up and I pulling a ice cold beer
> But what shock me I had to draw near
> News flash coming over the air
> Magic Johnson the top notch brigadier
> That does tek basket ball and dribble it from here to there
> put it pun he finger and spin it from now to next year
> Talk bout style make every body stare
> But sorry nuh laud cud dear no more magic all o' dat disappear
>
> *Chorus:*
> What a dangerous thing that nah body can't test A-I-D-S
> Got de men and de women nowadays dem a fret A-I-D-S

While Super Sweet of St Lucia performed "Deadly Epidemic" in competition in 2002, other calypso competitions throughout the region produced similar songs. In 2003, Socrates of St Kitts and Nevis produced the impactful "You Ain't Giving Me AIDS", on his album titled *Thong*. It is not surprising that the music of the Caribbean began to reflect this new attitude. Global trends at the level of politics, international law, health and culture required changed attitudes as a prerequisite to engaging these issues beyond national boundaries. In the Caribbean, governments secured greater input by way of national programmes and initiatives. Media, information centres and schools facilitated lectures, discussions and debates leading to a heightened awareness about AIDS. Once societies were more at ease engaging with the realities of HIV/AIDS in the public domain, it became possible to take the fight against AIDS to another level.

In the international world of pop culture, there have been many significant interfaces between popular artists and anti-AIDS agencies. These have resulted in concerts in benefit of AIDS victims and research. Recent trends in the global domain relating to the pop-music industry and AIDS-awareness campaigns point to two major initiatives. Organizations such as the US-based LIFEbeat, a music-industry AIDS charity, have gone the route of raising funds through star-studded charity events such as cocktail parties. Some of LIFEbeat's initiatives have been events such as

UrbanAID and SkateAID. LIFEbeat has raised in excess of US$1 million each year since its founding in 1992.[20] These funds have been earmarked for AIDS research and prevention. The alternative approach of the Red Hot organization is based on what its founder, John Carlin, deems to be its objective of providing preventive education in the guise of popular culture. Red Hot has been producing a number of benefit compilations albums. Profits from these compilations have been divided 80 per cent for AIDS efforts, 20 per cent for overhead and administration. Red Hot has also highlighted the benefit of disseminating preventive messages by targeting specific youth audiences through rap, alternative music and dance.[21]

This critical interface within the international world has trickled down into the Caribbean. Major Caribbean artists were also enlisted to perform in conjunction with anti-AIDS agencies, to promote "safe sex" through the use of condoms. Bounty Killer was enlisted by UNICEF, and Red Rat performed in the Atlanta Charity Benefit for HIV/AIDS orphans in late 2002. Buju Banton fit into the role as advocate in 1996. His 1993 AIDS-awareness song "Operation Willy" became the slogan for major shows within the Caribbean region:

> Ragamuffin don't be silly
> Rubbers pun you willy
> AIDS a go round and we don't want catch it

In spite of the popularity of these shows (or rather, their stars) among youths throughout the Caribbean, there was still perceived to be a contradiction between the stated objective of such concerts and the underlying signification of some pop culture icons. The society and its youths understood that large agencies were major contributors to such AIDS-awareness drives. They knew that many of these programmes were primarily public relations exercises, and they understood that many artists were role players. They therefore responded with guarded optimism. AIDS was still for many a complex construct. The institutional drive to enlist the music of the region (and its complex politics) as a preventive strategy added to the complication.

Regional initiatives of this kind have followed the examples of Europe and particularly of the United States. This pattern of following suit is a reality of Caribbean life. These initiatives have emphasized the potential rewards of such programmes, but they have hardly assessed the contentious issues that arise because of these very programmes. There are indeed underlying tensions. These have manifested themselves openly, as happened at the 1999 UNAIDS Colours XII concert headed by Foxxy Brown. Her invitation to the crowd to say "F— that" drew the attention of police. Organizers tried to distance themselves from her act. It would seem that promotional initiatives of this kind must be more aware of the music and icons they employ. They must also show keener awareness of the global, historical, ideological and cultural dynamics of AIDS. The construction of the AIDS phenomenon worldwide and in Caribbean society has been fraught with quarrelsome debates. Many Caribbean artists have overtly or covertly countered the views propagated by Western agencies and have resisted the construction created by the media. Staged AIDS-awareness rallies have therefore served as public relations hype. They have not always stood for what they set out to represent. Away from these negotiated events, artists and the public live out their real experience with the cultural phenomenon called AIDS.

Another attempt in the guise of education through popular culture was the late-1990s initiative by a group of artists in Barbados who formed themselves into an organization called Artists Against AIDS. The first major project undertaken by this association was the composing and recording of the song "One World", which promoted the importance of the preservation of life. A music video accompanied the song's distribution. The video performance is not overtly pretentious, hence the message is foregrounded within the discursive space of image and lyrical text. The proceeds from the sale of the production were intended to be used to promote AIDS education. This initiative claimed to be driven by the artists themselves. It therefore represented a more "spontaneous" undertaking than other performances, such as "Operation Willy". Arguably, the artists involved in the 1999 initiative were more credible and hence appealed much more to the sensibilities of those who heard and saw them. But, having said all this, it is instructive that to date that single video represents the organization's most ambitiously visible project. In 2002, there was talk of revitalizing this entity, but there was less commitment and energy surrounding it. This case reveals a truth about many AIDS-awareness initiatives throughout the region: they are hardly sustained for substantial periods.

Faced with the prospect of AIDS cases reaching epidemic proportions, Caribbean societies were forced to find new and effective means of preparing society to cope with the threat. For a short period at the end of the 1990s, Caribbean cricketers were employed to record fifteen-second AIDS warnings. The scripts were prepared for them. They were appropriately laced with cricket metaphors such as "Don't be bowled over by AIDS". In May 2000, Cable and Wireless, the Guyana Ministry of Health, Guyana's National AIDS Programme and the Guyana Cricket Board embarked on an initiative that saw Cable and Wireless donating free tickets for placard-waving, T-shirt-wearing youths to the first test match between West Indies and Pakistan. Reon King and Ramnaresh Sarwan were two of the leading players who endorsed the initiative. The theme, "Don't be bowled out by AIDS, bat with a condom", reflected the objective of appealing to mass audiences in the context of international sport.

Play You Ain't Know

All that said, in the first decade of the twenty-first century, the dominant message across the region is to "condomize". Perhaps the region has ignored a less sophisticated strategy, a viable method rooted in religious practice: abstinence.

Conclusions

Attitudes towards AIDS in the Caribbean have changed over the years since the discovery of the disease, and the popular music of the Caribbean has been at the centre of these transitions. Popular music has both reflected and shaped the outlook on this modern epidemic. Since societies are still learning about AIDS – learning how to cope with it in the new millennium – one way of gaining greater insight into its workings within society might very well be through further analysis and understanding of popular phenomena which have themselves engaged with the epidemic. This is not a simplistic undertaking; this alone cannot save the region. But it can certainly open up new ways of beginning to understand our own reactions to and attitudes towards the problems that surface.

Caribbean popular music has been at the forefront of discourses on sex and AIDS. The music has in some instances led the way by opening up the discourse when more conservative agencies in society have committed themselves to virtual discursive silence.

Finding the New Hardcore in Caribbean Music

Who's Afraid of Technology?

At the end of the twentieth century, popular culture began to be seen as an important entry point for gaining a fuller understanding of Caribbean society. Like economic data, cultural data is similarly loaded with information that can reveal the present and future condition of the society. With this in mind, it is important to explore the frontiers of cultural expression.

Caribbean music has undergone phenomenal changes in the last twenty-five years, but some of the recent texts which engage the subject of calypso in the Caribbean hardly give sufficient focus to the dynamic musical and technological shifts in calypso's dance music form, soca, during the 1980s and 1990s. In fact, recent works have stayed away from the very important subject of calypso's present evolution into other hardcore styles such as ringbang. So, in effect, an important cultural indicator has not come in for sustained scrutiny, and this absence of critical analysis represents a gap in the region's knowledge about the transformation of its calypso culture. Critically important works which have advanced knowledge about various aspects of Caribbean music but which do not engage with post-soca developments (partly because they have other objectives) include Peter Manuel's *Caribbean Currents*, John Cowley's *Carnival, Canboulay and Calypso*, Peter von Koningsbruggen's *Trinidad Carnival*, Michael Erlewine et al.'s *All Music Guide*, Peter Mason's *Bacchanal* and Louis Regis's *The Political Calypso*.[1]

Mike Alleyne's 1996 doctoral dissertation, "The Transnationalization of Caribbean Music: Capitalism and Cultural Intertextuality", comes closest to a studied analysis of the music, culture and technological dynamics in Caribbean society during the 1980s and 1990s.[2] Alleyne argues that analyses of Caribbean culture at the end of the twentieth century must be carried out by engaging with the technologies that drive and in effect help to create Caribbean cultures. It is a fact that academic writing on Caribbean music tends to privilege a socio-historical focus, an emphasis on lyrics or a theory-ridden discourse. Relatively little academic writing on regional music engages the music at a deeper level. Few commentators approach it from the standpoint of production or within the arena of technology, that which drives the music. In this chapter, therefore, I will examine the contemporary evolution of soca and other hardcore styles while paying attention to the technological process.

Reggae's technological evolution into raggamuffin and dancehall is better covered in published literature than are similar kinds of developments within calypso. A number of scholars have attempted to demystify the evolution of reggae's subgenres or co-genres, dancehall and raggamuffin. Major work in this area has been done by Dick Hebdige in *Cut 'n' Mix*, Christian Habekost in *Verbal Riddim*, Carolyn Cooper in *Noises in the Blood*, Kwame Dawes in *Natural Mysticism* and *Wheel and Come Again*, Kevin Chang and Wayne Chen in *Reggae Routes* and the various contributors to *The Guinness Who's Who of Reggae Music*.[3] But there is still much to be considered, including the dynamics of reggae's current relationship with the international music industry, reggae's interface with other styles and the recent popularization of post-dancehall music. In this chapter and the next, we will look at some of these issues, as well as music videos and Web streaming.

Soca discourse lags further behind and has been sustained mostly in the informal and public domains and among "casual" observers. Media personnel, connoisseurs and other music fans have played a crucial role in stimulating debate about this genre. Other non-academic sources have also contributed to debate. The mid-1990s publication of the music magazine *Ringbang* sent a fresh wave of discussion throughout the music culture of the southern and eastern Caribbean. *Ringbang* discussed recent trends in calypso and reggae, presented articles on new Trinidadian stars and on the calypso-chutney interface, and examined new musical styles in Antigua, among other concerns (see volume 1, number 2, and volume 2, number 1, in particular). Like many other leading-edge projects, *Ringbang* magazine had a short life. Though its articles were journalistic in style and format, highly descriptive rather than analytical or theory-engaging, publications of this kind do also provide a clearer understanding of cultural developments. In fact, in some respects, such initiatives are more forward-looking than what is offered up in academic discourse. This is less a criticism of academic proclivity than a recognition that popular publications are much more flexible in their production and dissemination.

Much of what published scholastic work on mainstream traditional calypso there is has not made the transition to engaging newer, hardcore calypso styles. That reggae's evolution has attracted many more cultural critics and critiques might have to do with the higher profile of reggae worldwide, but it cannot be imputed that soca's developments in recent history are tame in comparison with reggae's dynamism. In fact, it can be argued that, like reggae, calypso has undergone many changes in the last twenty-five years, partly inspired by developments in music technology. It should be said that the same technological instruments and musical applications that affected reggae as it evolved into dancehall around the early 1980s also affected calypso. Programmable drums and synthesizers in particular have had an equally significant effect on calypso as they have had on reggae. Indeed, there were few recording artists in the Caribbean in the 1980s and 1990s whose works were not affected by new music technologies. The current wave of high-tech synthesizer-, bass- and drum-driven music that has taken over the calypso domain had its beginnings in the 1980s. The evolving styles of that time were shaped significantly with the new power of music technologies.

Whereas reggae's evolution has been acknowledged by the naming of its derivatives, calypso discourse has been more reluctant to identify and categorize calypso's derivatives. This chapter is built on my perception that calypso's co-genre, the dance music called soca, which was replacing calypso in popularity by the early 1980s, was itself being transformed by the mid-1980s. And by the mid-1990s, soca would begin to be replaced by yet newer hardcore styles, such as ringbang, which by then was the preferred musical style of most leading calypso dance artists, such as Touch, The Man C.P., and Fireman Hooper in St Vincent and the Grenadines, Machel Montano in Trinidad, Invader in St Lucia, Square One in Barbados, and Dread and the Baldhead in Antigua, Barbuda, as well as, to a lesser extent, Byron Lee and the Dragonaires in Jamaica. This chapter therefore is devoted to locating (in the 1980s) the roots of a new technology-driven (1990s) music style, to illustrating how and when

Caribbean music began to gesture to post-soca styles, and to tracing the evolution to current movements.

Because popular informal debates since 2000 recognize that there are major transformations in the musical stylings of calypso, it seems that much more important to discover and disclose the pattern of development of the new styles. This investigation, therefore, returns to the early years of the 1980s. Among other things, we will examine selected innovative tracks that began to redefine the boundaries of soca music in the early to mid-1980s, using the multi-track reading introduced in the first chapter.[4] This ties in with the desire to consider the technological side of music: much of the impetus for multi-tracked reading derives from sound engineering, recording and production, and it is also supported by specialist texts such as *The Musician's Home Recording Handbook* and other magazines of the production industry.[5]

In 1995 a major debate in Caribbean music surfaced surrounding the creation of a new musical phenomenon called ringbang. Although this phenomenon claimed to have surfaced by name in 1994, it was in 1995 during Barbados's Crop Over festival, and then in 1996 during Trinidad's Carnival when there was talk of a "Bajan invasion", as highlighted in the *Trinidad Express*.[6] There was much debate surrounding the autonomy and validity of new styles like ringbang.

In *Barbadian Popular Music,* I addressed a number of issues surrounding the ringbang phenomenon, considering the concepts and ideology which informed the creation of ringbang.[7] The book depended quite heavily on materials drawn from interviews with ringbang's creator, Eddy Grant, as well as on interviews in the media. *Barbadian Popular Music* discusses the viability of ringbang as a musical style by examining its relationships with other Caribbean music forms, such as soca and reggae. At that time, though, I made only passing reference to antecedent musical trends, trends which anticipated the creation of the full-blown hardcore musical style which would become known as ringbang.

Eddy Grant has repeatedly called attention to the late-1960s song "Black Skin Blue Eyed Boys" by the Equals as a central work in the discussion of soca's evolution. There is, however, still no agreed reading of soca's genesis. Lord Shorty (later Ras Shorty) has been credited by some as having inspired the new 1970s genre.[8] Calypso began to evolve into another style by the mid-1970s. By the early 1980s, soca had become entrenched as an accepted subgenre of calypso. Arrow's "Hot Hot Hot"

(1983) had made its great impact on the international music world by the mid-1980s. But even as soca was usurping calypso's popularity, there was already in existence the seeds of other new dance music.

As reggae's raggamuffin is differentiated from earlier styles of reggae by its greater use of music technology, so technology similarly marks off later musical styles from 1970s and 1980s soca. Although here we will focus more specifically on ringbang, this development also has implications for other hardcore styles of the 1990s, like raggasoca. There is a perception that this new style suddenly burst on to the scene, and for some it seems to have no cultural affinity through a shared experience with other traditions or other musical works or texts. I want to examine the roots of this "new" style and to trace one path of its development to the present as a means of positioning it within the matrix of Caribbean music culture.

The Hard-Edged Roots

What is "ringbang"? Although this question has partly been addressed by Grant in his 1998 foreword to *Barbadian Popular Music*, there have been new developments surrounding the phenomenon. These developments have played out in the press, on the stage and in selected publications. Grant has also made other pronouncements about ringbang.[9] But relatively few critics though have concentrated on this phenomenon head-on.[10]

Simply put, ringbang as a musical style is characterized by a greater emphasis on the rhythmic aspect of a composition. A ringbang recording therefore tends to highlight the drums and other percussive instruments. The centrality of the drums and percussions in ringbang gestures towards the functional and symbolic significance of these instruments within the musics of many African peoples, for whom rhythm plays a vital part in music construction.[11] In this way, ringbang wants to connect to what might be called a wider African aesthetics. Ringbang in its present manifestation tends therefore to produce songs in which the drums are upfront in the mix and the other harmonic constituents play a secondary role. This musical style came to prominence through its association with soca. So far, ringbang has been operating primarily within the domain of calypso and soca. It is problematic to identify ringbang as an autonomous rhythm with specific inflectional and metrical traits. Since ringbang seems to rely on extant rhythms for its own existence and sense of presence, it is perhaps better to speak of it as a style rather than as a rhythm. Some popular ringbang-styled songs are Superblue's "Jab Molassie", Gabby's "Doctor Cassandra", Machel Montano's "Torro Torro" and Jaunty's "Military Jam".

Although there are signs that the predominance of drums in post-soca and post-dancehall is being challenged by virtual analogue effects, there are still substantial features which can be traced back to the 1980s. The roots of the new style called ringbang can be found in a range of tracks recorded by Eddy Grant. Indeed, we might find hints of ringbang in some of Grant's pre-1980s recordings. This radical suggestion is made more plausible when one recalls the difficulties posed for critics over time when they have attempted to categorize Grant's music. It has been called "reggae", "soul", "pop", "world music", "progressive soca" and more. *The Guinness Who's Who of Reggae*, for example, describes Grant's music as "his own sound – part reggae, part funk, strong musical motifs, strong melodies – pop with credibility".[12] In this chapter, however, we will not go back as far as Grant's days with the Equals but will focus on the 1980s period and thereafter – particularly from about 1982, the year that marked the beginning of a new phase in recordings for Ice Records.

Ringbang surfaced as both a cultural imperative and a technological necessity. This is to say that Caribbean culture is never static; it has always been dynamic, and it is this innate dynamism that drives Caribbean music. But in addition to this internal process, there are also other kinds of influences. In the 1980s, radically new developments in music technology altered the way music was conceptualized, composed, recorded, produced and disseminated throughout the world, and the Caribbean was not excluded from this technological revolution. Throughout the 1980s, already fast-changing cultures of the Caribbean interfaced with the revolution in digitized music technology to produce a highly streamlined dance music.

When Eddy Grant recorded his first Barbadian calypsonians, Gabby and Grynner, in the early 1980s, this marked a moment of some transformation in the production process, especially in the eastern Caribbean. Grant was bringing to the finished musical text a higher quality of sound than was being achieved in most other studios in the region. When one compares Grant's recordings with other calypsos of the same period, one noticeable difference is a greater track-to-track clarity on the Ice Records productions. The Ice recordings of this period call greater attention to the process of their construction through their greatly enhanced recording quality. The power of multi-track recording was becoming much more foregrounded in Ice recordings. Some commentators on the music of the period were beginning to express admiration for Ice's quality, while others had doubts about the bold use of the drum machine, keyboard synthesized "voices" and "sampled" voices, which were not widely characteristic of the calypso idiom at that time.

The calypso "Jack" by Gabby, recorded with Ice, shows the beginning of the replacement of the centrality of horns. "Jack" features extended measures of the "band chorus" in which rhythmic keyboard strumming is upfront in the mix. Horns are not a major motif in the song's empty (open) vocal spaces. The recording also reflects an early tendency by Grant, and by Ice Records, to streamline the finished product. This is to say, as finished products their recordings tended to be carefully balanced in terms of both overall output level and the decibel levels of individual instruments. This carefully engineered finished product served to emphasize the technological process which gave birth to the song, almost in the same way that raggamuffin's first major release, Wayne Smith's "Under Me Sleng Teng" (1985), calls attention to the mechanized synthesizer technology upon which it is built.

"Under Me Sleng Teng" is said to have been created on an inexpensive home keyboard from the electronics company Casio. Since its entry into the domain of musical keyboards, Casio has tended to appeal to the lower end of the market in its pricing. The attractiveness of Casio's products was built not only on its very competitive prices, but also on the functionality and easy operation of its music-producing systems. Whereas prior to the early 1980s, programmable keyboards tended to be stationary, bulky instruments, heavy like the Hammond organ, Casio and other producers of programmable instruments began to produce and to mass-produce lighter keyboards. These instruments now contained built-in drums and accompanying bass patterns, which could be activated by simply touching a single note in the lower registers of the keyboard. But whereas raggamuffin's musical beginnings are traced to that technological moment, the early evolution of ringbang is rooted in the higher end of the music industry's technology. In the early 1980s, Eddy Grant and his studio had access to such instruments as New England Digital's Synclavier keyboard. Whereas a simple Casio factory programmed keyboard in the

MT series retailed for US$250 in 1982, the Synclavier was priced around US$50,000.

The technologies that were important catalysts in the construction of these two Caribbean music forms in the 1980s were at different ends of music technology's pricing scale but were offering quite similar functionalities: programmability and preset built-in drums accessible at the press of a button. It is intriguing that two Caribbean styles were born of this technological digitization which itself has its origins in engineering labs in distant lands, far removed from the cultural and social realities of Caribbean societies. Whereas most readings of Caribbean culture are inclined to locate the roots and routes of new Caribbean musics in cultural and social phenomena, I would suggest that musical technology has an equal claim to the birthing of these styles.

Such sound processing gadgets as reverb and delay modules, compressor/limiters, and expanders were tools of the revolution.[13] These apparatuses were essential in coating the production on tracks coming out of Ice in the early 1980s. One integral feature of Ice Records' process of streamlining the recording was the tendency to reduce complex chord progressions and musical ornamentals. This appeared to be a reaction against the then-current mainstream soca methods, which glorified horns and sacrificed some quality for energy.

In 1983, a new set of recording practices was being honed at Eddy Grant's Blue Wave Studios, practices that gave form to the new techno-driven style widely called ringbang. Many commentaries on the Bajan calypso tend to locate the beginning of the new era of Bajan music in 1982, the watershed year when Bajan calypso began to be played outside of the Crop Over season, when Red Plastic Bag brought a new, young body of listeners to the calypso art form. But most critics have not as yet considered how this period also marked the beginning of a totally new era of sound. Blue Wave Studios began to challenge various aspects of the recording and production process to set new standards of quality and imagination, especially within the domain of calypso and soca. Sound and recording engineers, musicians, and producers were forced to come to terms with a different texture of sound and with new approaches to the construction of the sound recording. By 1984, Blue Wave was creating the benchmark by which other soca sounds were assessed. But equally as significant was the impact that Blue Wave had through its several innovations and experimentations.

Contrary to popular perception, most of the early Blue Wave innovations were carried out not on Gabby's recordings, but on those of Grynner. In such tracks as "Mr T", "Stinging Bees" and "Gabby Controversy", Blue Wave began to alter musical features which by the early 1980s had become entrenched as formulaic components of soca music. You can hear in these Grynner tracks that the producer was uneasy operating within the perimeters of the calypso/soca genre. This condition of unease is not unheard of in the creative industries; it reflects in part the desire for fuller expression, and it highlights the limitations imposed by cultural categories. But this anxiety can also be ignited by social, cultural and technological forces which combine to challenge received ways of thinking and creating. Blue Wave Studios was caught up in a nexus of possibilities. Whereas many other production studios were still nationally or regionally focused, Blue Wave seemed differently oriented: it was a regional studio with extra-regional ambitions, attracting international stars like Mick Jagger and the Rolling Stones as well as Sting. Its early 1980s work therefore constituted an attempt to forge new kinds of productions. The result of this initiative would not become full-blown and given a label until the 1990s, when better sense could be made of technology's power. First, in the 1980s, great effort had to be expended in learning the technology – it had to be interrogated, studied, manipulated and mastered. It had to be subjected to the cultural requirements of the region and enabled to bear the burden of the region's experience. It became possible to attach an ideology to this robust technology only in the 1990s.

In the formative years of this technology, music creators and users were less conscious of its overarching potential. At face value, this new hardware was the final product of scientific and technical innovation. But beneath the solid-state exterior there were other challenges posed by the leading-edge technology. This realization came into play when it was "discovered" that technologies (such as the synthesizer and multi-tracking) were not necessarily neutral, and that the digital domain was also an arena of struggle. It was only in the 1990s that music users in greater numbers vigorously took up the challenge to control the ideologically charged digital domain. One way in which greater control was possible in the Caribbean was through greater access to, understanding of and manipulation of the technology.

In the 1980s, the global music industry's technology led the region, in many cases, blindly. The extent of this control is evident in the proliferation of unimaginative, formulaic musical compositions that surfaced during this period in the calypso, dancehall, soca and gospel genres. The minimalist application of the drum machine and sequencer in dancehall is a representative example of what can be called the technological loop within Caribbean music in this period. Simply put, a *sound* or *song loop* refers to the mechanized repetition of that sound or song. For some sound theorists, sound loops evolve into stock metaphors; that is, they become associated with very specific themes or imagery or events. Drum sound loops became stock metaphors of Caribbean popular music in the 1980s. Drums had always been important components of Caribbean popular music, but 1980s technology elaborated their presence. In the 1980s, it was possible for the first time to have a sequence of pre-programmed sounds repeat themselves endlessly with the simple press of a button. The dancehall phenomenon in the 1980s revolved around this sound-loop technology. Soca compositions were also stuck in this technological loop, most obviously in the application of drum, percussion and bass programming. Blue Wave was a pioneering studio in the Caribbean in the use of music technology. It was therefore also a part of the sequencing, programming and multi-track craze.

When Blue Wave began to experiment with the use of synthesized horns in a song like "Mr T", there was both consternation and derision. This movement towards heavy programming, which was led by the synthesizer, created for a time a popular trend in the soca domain. This trend, embraced by many musicians and producers throughout the region, sought to redefine the way mainstream soca was being constructed. These creators advocated the further reduction of "live" instrumentation in recordings. By the late 1980s, most producers of dance calypso followed this practice.

In the 1980s, Blue Wave Studios seemed to be more in control of the technology than most other production houses in the region. This had to do somewhat with the financial might of Ice Records. Because of its place in the industry, Ice was able to gain access to and manipulate the latest equipment. Not many smaller studios could afford to keep up. But Blue Wave's control of technology also hinged on its drive towards experimentation. Not all of these experiments featured Barbadian artists. In fact, many of the studio's innovative productions spotlighted artists from throughout the region. Blue Wave also recorded the likes of Carl and

Carol Jacobs on the 1987 album *We Wanna Live,* Machel Montano on 1986's *Too Young to Soca,* and the progressive Vincentian band Touch.

Blue Wave was actively engaged in the practice of altering drum patterns within the soca genre. Songs such as Gabby's "One Day Coming Soon" and Grynner's "Gabby Controversy" were presenting a drum pattern which was much closer to a techno-styled disco than to calypso proper. Bass patterns were also being altered from the normal beat around the tonic and dominant notes within a chord to much sparser bass patterns; in a song like "Gabby Controversy", staccato pulses are played primarily on the first beat at the beginning of each bar in 4/4 time signature. By the mid-1980s, other soca acts within the region were also using these innovations to some degree, including, in St Vincent, Beckett's "Stranger Man" on *10th Anniversary* (1985) and, in Trinidad, Gypsy's "Caribbean Spirit-Song of Me Land" on *Life* (1988) and Natasha's "De Mass in We" on *Introducing Ms Natasha Wilson* (1987). The compounding of all these alternative applications gestured towards the creation of a new style.

Upping the Drum Mix

The drums are regarded to be the most dominant motif within ringbang. The use and function of drums in 1980s early post-soca tracks can be examined from two perspectives: first, by tracing the gradual experimentation with drums themselves in key songs, suggesting antecedents to the drums of ringbang, and second, by locating the creation of "ringbang drums" within the context of the studio, that is, as having to do with mix and track levels. These ways of coming to ringbang are not radically divergent: they recognize that ringbang surfaced both as a gradual series of experiments and as a technological moment.

Blue Wave's 1983 tracks reveal the extent to which the studio was embarking on a programme of altering the sound of calypso. The stark realization of this experimentation is best evident in Gabby's 1984 "One Day Coming Soon", in which the producer further centralized the drums. This was done by removing other active polyrhythmic percussive and stringed instruments, counterposing the drums with a harsh piano, and looping conga patterns. This production looks forward to ringbang through its aggressive drum application, a treatment that became the stated attitude of drums in other Blue Wave mixes. The snare drum is militant, almost explosive in the mix. It is a mid-pitch snare, tightly tuned yet slightly gated (the wired snares at the bottom of the drum are set to allow for momentary vibration), to achieve explosive ends. The snare drum in "One Day Coming Soon" envelopes the entire mix in a way that other calypso and soca drum tracks of the time did not.

This point can be enhanced by making a simple yet representative comparison between this Blue Wave recording and Arrow's 1983 album *Heat*. Arrow's music is important to any discussion of 1980s leading-edge soca, serving as an important comparative source, especially because Arrow was a leader and innovator in the soca domain during the 1980s. He is rightly regarded as having brought soca to international attention. Albums such as *Soca Savage* (1984) and *Deadly* (1985), both arranged by the Trinidadian maestro Leston Paul, were pointing the way towards greater fusion of soca and funk and other urban street-music trends in rap. They also gestured to pop and rock. It is also significant that Eddy Grant and Arrow were careful to remain producers of their own creations. This political stroke represents their ongoing struggle to shape their recorded works and to situate them at the cutting edge of the creative hub. Although they have entered into alliances with Ras Records (Grant) and Mango (Arrow), they have aspired to control their works.

But these two creative entities are not similar in all respects. Arrow and Planet Sound Studios (a major recording base for Arrow) have never overtly contested the position of their music within the soca domain. Arrow has always accepted and promoted himself as being the soca king of the world. Grant and Blue Wave, on the other hand, have held an uneasy position with respect to soca. Grant has raised questions about the musical origin of soca,[14] but at the same time, his soca-oriented compositions have sat uneasily within that category. Arrow's avant-garde excursions into new territory (as in his 1984 song "Party Mix", which sings of and suggests musically "crossing over") are more often than not tempered by traditional soca (as in his 1985 "Hot Mix"). Overall, Blue Wave has been more blatantly experimental, daring and unapologetic in its recordings. Throughout the 1980s, the studio persisted with a series of experiments which they did not simply try and discard, but built upon. These can be traced through three stages: the subordination of horns, the foregrounding of (the) bass and experimentation with and foregrounding of drums.

Blue Wave was thus not the only facility engaged in experiments at this time in the early 1980s, and Grant was not the only producer who was trying new things with soca. Indeed, it is possible to theorize that the producers of soca and calypso have individually been embroiled in a four-way confrontation: they have had to wrestle with traditionalism, creativity, individual instrument proclivity and ideological politics. This is to say, the outlook of calypso producers in the Caribbean has been and continues to be defined by the degree and strength of commitment to calypso tradition, individual creativity, the instrument of first love and engagement in the politics of the international music industry. The face of Caribbean music today, especially in soca, is a reflection of these tensions. In their many divergences, soca and post-soca tracks signify and reflect the problems that confront producers of cultural products in the region.

The 1983 Arrow album *Heat* serves as a fitting comparison with Grant's productions of the time since it moves away from what was then the stated soca drum pattern. Although subtle transformations have also taken place with the high-hat cymbals, it is the foot drum and the snare drum that are at the heart of the drum set in soca, and it is the foot and snare drums that have been most altered in these experiments. In 4/4 time, the foot drum (*F*) and the snare drum (*S*) share the following type of relationship in conventional soca (rests are suggested for the snare wherever there are no notes along the four-beat timeline of each bar):

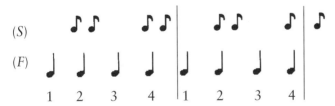

In many Blue Wave songs of the period, as also in Arrow's "Rush Hour", this treatment is altered and becomes less syncopated:

Herein is the similarity between some of Blue Wave and Planet Sound's early experiments with drum tracks.

But there were marked differences between Blue Wave's drum applications and those of other studios, including Planet Sound. Arrow's "Rush Hour" deals with the hassles of rush hour in the metropolis – good enough reason for employing a reference from the music of North America. His song begins with samples of street noises and sirens and with the pop-styled snare drum just referred to. In the song's chorus the inflectional character of the composition changes into a much more traditional soca groove before reverting to the initial pop-styled drum. Through these shifts, "Rush Hour" is at once experimental and rooted in its association with the soca genre. But there seems some kind of anxiety or uneasiness in the composition with its own transgressive practices. Of course, a counter-argument to all this might suggest that the song is seeking to establish its own sense of difference through this very intertextual method of rhythmic juxtaposition and referencing.

The Blue Wave productions of the period were equally self-conscious but seemed less apologetic of their transgressive applications. "One Day Coming Soon" begins with one and a half bars of outspoken drums. This pattern and its attitude are not altered throughout the entire production. The song's intensity, which Gabby creates through clear vocal diction and forthright aggression, is strongly supported by a recurring insistent drum pattern. The song's musical tension is created primarily by the interplay between its bass (the bass line) and the horns in the band chorus. This is released somewhat abruptly, deliberately but momentarily, at the beginnings of verses, when the horns and bass are "dropped out". But the song falls back on ever-explosive drums, which are laid on top of an aggressive piano. Indeed, it is this overall aggression in many early Blue Wave songs that later comes to characterize its hardcore music of the early 1990s.

The other major difference between the songs being compared here has to do with the very feature of aggression. The sustained explosive treatment of drum tracks is a distinctive signature of Blue Wave recordings in this period. Arrow's "Rush Hour" – or even his 1984 "Party Mix" – does not assign this same aggression to the drum mix. Indeed, one might say that the Arrow recordings reveal a greater balance among the range of instruments within the mix: horns, bass, guitars, keyboards, percussion and drums. Although the Ice recordings are good overall in their recording quality, they do not possess this same balance of individual recorded instruments. The Trinidadian Leston Paul, who began to co-arrange for Arrow in 1982, is arguably the foremost producer of this texture of balanced recordings. Ed Watson was the main arranger for Arrow in the 1970s, but Leston Paul took greater prominence from 1982. By the mid-1980s, Paul's method of arranging became the benchmark for arrangers-cum-producers aspiring to good soca. Ed Watson, Kenny Phillips, Pelham Goddard, Eddy Grant, Frankie McIntosh and Byron Lee, though producers of good horn recordings, are not as renowned for the kind of balance achieved in Leston Paul's recordings. Arrow has also been noted for his employment of two arrangers, one for the combo section and the other for brass. The Vincentian Frankie McIntosh has shared the arranging credits with Leston Paul on occasions; Jocelyne Guilbault's 1996 interview with Paul reveals the workings of that relationship.[15] Other arrangers who featured on Arrow's work in the late 1980s were Roland Richards, Kenny Phillips, Charlie Lagond and Arrow's brother Justin "Hero" Cassell. Within the Arrow mixes of the mid-1980s, the instruments seem to know their pre-assigned position and mix levels. They also seem to fit comfortably within the total sound (dynamic) spectrum.

This is not so, however, in the Gabby mix: there are a number of mixing indiscretions in Gabby's "One Day Coming Soon". This is to say, the recording reveals the presence of uncharacteristic mixing features, those not then common in soca. The drums sit unapologetically upfront in Gabby's song, calling attention to their presence, to their central position within the mix. They assume a new role of power, subordinating other characteristic components of soca such as horns, guitar and bass. They struggle to situate their decibel (db) reading in the mix as being level with the vocals.

This description of the play of instruments could give the impression that they are engaged in a struggle – and so they are. Or at least they begin to sound this way when one listens to the subversive Blue Wave soca tracks of the 1980s. I have already mentioned Blue Wave's apparent uneasiness with the limitations of soca, an uneasiness I characterized as that of the producer. But it is possible to take that conclusion even further. A more radical suggestion might be that Blue Wave was constantly engaged in a conflict with both art form and technology. Grant's contentious relationship with soca's mainstream was reflected in his alternative reading of what soca was all about, but a much more challenging confrontation preoccupied Blue Wave studios. Much effort was spent gazing at and wrestling with the unlimited potentialities of digital technology. Blue Wave's 1980s recordings reveal an almost rabid preoccupation with state-of-the-art mechanisms. This was not a sordid preoccupation, however; the deeper intentions were clear.

Blue Wave seemed intent on coming to terms with and gaining power over breakthrough technology. The struggle took place with both hardware and software applications. It surrounded many of the new instruments being produced for musicians and sound engineers. One site of concentration, energy and power was the mixing board. Since all recorded sound was being processed through the mixing board, its near unlimited multi-tracking and interface facilities came into prominence. It was through this ingenious state-of-the-art console, with more than thirty-two channels, that Blue Wave embarked on a series of experiments. On the one hand, this probing was a celebration of technology's power, but on another, the transgressive experiments highlighted the dialogic tensions of sound production in the Caribbean – that is, they highlighted the extent to which sound and sound production were critical concerns in the creation of cultural works. Sound is therefore loaded with attendant issues; its production is not an innocent exercise. When artists and musicians set about in the 1980s to challenge the conventions of sound production, they also called attention to sound's hidden politics. Whereas there was a perceived format for soca recordings, as demonstrated in the Arrow song "Rush Hour", with its complementary mixing and assigning of relatively equal status to a number of instruments, there now began to be an increasing "de-equalizing" of constituents in Blue Wave productions. Figure 5.1 illustrates the stereophonic soundscape of mainstream soca compared with that of Blue Wave's early post-soca experiments.

Gabby's "One Day Coming Soon" further reveals the nature of the struggle with technology. The drums in this song assume their enhanced position of power through significant readjustment of the drum tracks within the mix. First, the drum voices are carefully chosen. They appear to be laid down with methodical insistence and astuteness. The foot kick is very pronounced; it is punctuated and enhanced by the accompanying congas, which, when sounded together with it, give the kick a fuller presence. The kick therefore appears to have presence not only down-centre of the mix (as most kicks do), but also a pan-left and pan-right

Figure 5.1

Post-soca mix

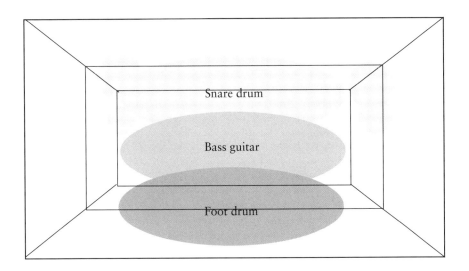

Conventional soca mix

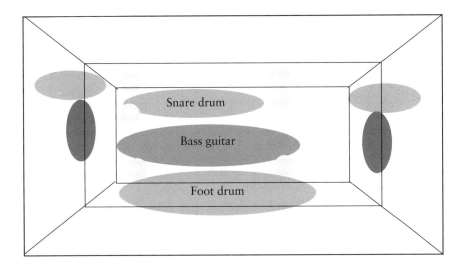

assignment. This effect is also created for the snare drum, which, even more than the kick drum, interacts with the congas. There are two congas, one panned left, the other panned right, and one tuned higher than the other. The congas are second only to the drums in the overall mix presence of the song. They have been passed through various effects, processes which create an enhanced ambience for them, the effect of a dry echo within the ambience of a large hall.

The snare drum operates within this enhanced highly effected domain. It resonates as a heavily gated snare which is carried pan-left and pan-right throughout the parameters of the stereophonic mix. The gated echo is not sustained for too long, but is cut off. It decays using what seems to be an inscribed compressor/limiter. The overall effect is an aggressive snare drum that leaps out of the mix and is sustained momentarily but abruptly fades before it is sounded again. In 1983, the calypso domain was not accustomed to this type of application of the drums, this type of aggression. This was more like the drum application in rock music.

The accompanying aggressive piano on "One Day Coming Soon" was also a subversive inclusion. Its only parallel might be found, again, outside of the calypso genre in rock, in a song like Survivor's 1982 "Eye of the Tiger". In "Eye of the Tiger", the piano plays next to Dave Bickler's high vocal register and creates a sustained interest of tension throughout those segments of the song when the rock guitar is absent. Gabby's "One Day Coming Soon" makes use of the piano as an understated though harshly present constituent which adds to the overall aggressive timbre of the sound.

It is this hardcore attitude and application which is the stuff of ringbang. This is not to deny all that has been said about ringbang's reliance on drums. Rather, it suggests that ringbang is identifiable not only in the "upfrontness" of the drums, but also in the types, timbre and attitude of instruments employed. This is also to suggest that vocal aggression marks this new hardcore style. The vocal aggression referred to here has its roots not in the calypso idiom, but in the chanting tradition of dub and dancehall. Indeed, ringbang as it evolved in the early 1990s made reference to a number of soca, tuk and dub or dancehall practices, and over the years of its subsequent evolution it has also gestured towards rock.

A careful listing of tracks which mark the evolution of drum applications must also include the 1986 re-recording of Machel Montano's "Too Young to Soca" on Ice Records. This recording gave the song a more commercial sound, closer to pop, through the reprogramming of the soca drum and bass parts. In addition, the drum track was much more aggressive than that on the original version. Carl and Carol Jacobs's songs "I Want to Live" and particularly "Savage" (both 1987) represent further excursions into the realm of experimentation. In "Savage", the drums threaten to take over the mix as they complement the song's engagement with the theme of mankind's savagery.

But the more explosive songs of that early post-soca, pre-hardcore era were other experiments with drums, percussion and bass coming out of the eastern Caribbean: Grynner's "Gabby Controversy", "Three G's" and "Bajan Yankees" and in Gabby's "De List", "Ms Barbados", "Cadavers", "Swim", "Ballroom", "Rambo: Gabbo Is Rambo" and "Jimmy Swaggart". Any attempt to locate seminal sound texts that prefigure the evolution of 1990s dance styles must contemplate these songs of the 1980s. Arguably, Gabby's album *One in the Eye* stands as the single most representative collection embodying early post-soca trends and anticipating 1990s features later to be termed ringbang.

1990s Evolution

The year 1994 was the watershed for this new hardcore style in Caribbean music. This was the year of Black Stalin's *Rebellion*, on Ice Records. It featured two singles which emphasize the word "ringbang": "All Saints Road" and "Black Woman Ringbang". This was also the year of the compilation *Fire in de Wave*, a more audacious post-soca production that sounded and defined the arrival of ringbang. *Fire in de Wave* includes songs such as Viking Tundah's "Ring-a-Ringbang", Gabby's "Dr Cassandra" and Square One's "Ruk-a-Tuk Party".

Superblue's widely popular album *Flag Party* was also released in 1994. Interestingly, *Flag Party* includes two remixes boldly titled "Flag Party Ringbang Dance Mix" and "Flag Party Ringbang Dub Mix". It also contains one of the more successful early ringbang standards, "Jab Molassie". This song was the point of some disagreement between Ice Records and the artist with respect to the final mix. Whereas Ice wanted to complete the song without horns, the artist himself was adamant that there should be horns. Had Ice gotten its way, "Jab Molassie" might have received the production treatment assigned to "Dr Cassandra".

The disagreement between artist and record label reflected the tension at play between mainstream soca and emerging styles such as ringbang. For mainstream soca artists, horns were essential constituents; ringbang advocated their subordination. The politics of sound rendered this situation as momentarily irreconcilable. In the end, Superblue took the tracks back to Trinidad and had horns added to the final mix. The released version builds up layers of sound from verse to verse, developing into a crescendo of instruments through the systematic layering of new instruments as the song develops. By the last verse, horns have been introduced as the final constituents, the final rite. Although it is the drums that empower the production, this climactic entry of horns serves as a reminder of soca's presence. Whereas ringbang unpacks a set of instruments to reveal the power of drums, soca stacks up well-defined layers of sound. The eventual form of "Jab Molassie" can be read as a celebration of soca's endurance. But the gradual building of sound instruments also served to emphasize the very clear demarcation being established between soca and ringbang. The process of track-building which the song illustrates also underlines technology's role as accomplice in the reconfiguration of Caribbean dance music.

In 1994, Ice Records also released a compilation, *A Taste of Soca*, on which then Ice Records president Michael Dolan alludes to "the show-casing" of "the next generation of East Caribbean talent" in New Generation's "Roll It", Square One's "Make Ah Wine" and Viking Tundah's "Ringbang Soldier". In the liner notes, Dolan also refers to what he calls the thriving "current dance style ringbang".

The year 1995 saw the release of the follow-up to the phenomenally popular *Fire in de Wave*, more audaciously called *Ringbang Rebel Dance*. When I spoke with Eddy Grant before the release of this record he was excited about the new ground to be broken. He saw it as a major release at the cutting edge in a new era of Caribbean music. Given the deliberate mapping out of strategy in the two compilations, *Fire in de Wave* and *Ringbang Rebel Dance*, it is reasonable to suggest that the progression of ringbang in the mid-1990s can be traced through these releases. These are not the only raw materials, but they represent major products that were carefully fashioned at Blue Wave.

Whereas *Fire in de Wave*'s title track was carried by the old stager Grynner, the follow-up compilation featured the robust Viking Tundah on the title track. This was not a totally surprising change given the immense popularity of Viking Tundah's song the previous year. But since Grynner had for very long been a central artist on Ice Records, the switch to Viking Tundah was a major turning point for the music of the eastern Caribbean. The hardcore had truly arrived, and it would be pioneered by a new breed of artists.

The similarities between the two compilations are noticeable. Seen together, these represent Grant's working out of the formula which he devised for the legitimization and dissemination of this techno-Caribbean style. There is continued emphasis on drums. Horns are not central to the overall sound, and remixes abound. The chanting-cum-singing-cum-screaming vocal rendition is also retained, as is experimentation with the soca-dancehall fusion, attempted on Viking's "Ringbang Soldier".

Fire in de Wave and *Ringbang Rebel Dance* were also different from each other in some respects. One of the most evident differences is the total absence of horns (that is, "live" horns) in the 1995 release *Ringbang Rebel Dance*. This one also features more explosive drum sounds. Much more work appears to have gone into this production at the post-recording stage. Vocal rendition is on a whole more aggressive. There are many more references to the rock aesthetic, through the use of distorted and over-driven electric guitars. But *Ringbang Rebel Dance* also sought to present a more credible version of "cool" ringbang, and therefore featured songs that sat somewhere between soca and dancehall.

This type of fusion was very similar to the growing subgenre called raggasoca, but it also sought to mark its difference in some respects. Whereas raggasoca was being founded on the perceived meshing of soca and ragga into a tightly knit unit of sound shaped and maintained from the beginning of a song to its end (for example, listen to RPB's "Ragga Ragga" and Atlantic's "All Aboard"), Ice's experiments were more self-conscious of the separate aesthetics of soca and ragga, and therefore seemed to represent a much cruder clash of sounds. Thus, a song like "Ringbang Soldier" was at once more soca-oriented than ragga and more ragga-oriented than soca. Whereas most raggasoca songs were tending to assume their identity in the pre-recorded stage (that is, where a "live" band performs the song cover to cover), some of Grant's experiments in this vein pointed to post-recorded editing and remixing (that is, when the engineer, like a disc jockey, mixes and edits two distinctive songs or sounds). The result is a cataclysmic fusion with a very hard musical edge and a menacing vocal attitude.

In the final analysis, however, there are few other real distinctions between Blue Wave's dancehall-soca fusions and that other subgenre now called raggasoca. These genres have now grown closer in terms of production and style. *Ringbang Rebel Dance* carries tracks which reveal the affinity between the two styles, such as "Believe in Love" by Adisa and "Ringbang is de Ting" by the female trio Legend. Further examples of fusion with soca, pop, and rhythm and blues were featured on Legend's ringbang cover of Whitney Houston's "Saving All My Love" on *Carnival Ringbang Special* (1997).

A number of cool ringbang tracks by Roaring Lion, who died in 1999, were also released on the two albums *Roaring Lion* (1993) and *Roaring Lion Viva le King* (1995). Eddy Grant has been careful to name his own slower version of ringbang "Säf",[16] or soft ringbang. Conversely, the label "raggasoca" is used more widely in the eastern Caribbean to define this style of soca-oriented music, even though the form's boundaries are not always clearly defined.[17]

Ringbang, Ideology and Music

The future evolution and viability of hardcore styles such as ringbang and raggasoca depends on their ideological commitment and their ability to sustain credible musical configuration. In *Barbadian Popular Music*, I raised the point that the early ringbang compilation *Fire in de Wave* appeared to lack sustained engagement with social or political issues.[18] Many would argue that the compilation album privileged "the party". Grant has made no secret of this; he has suggested (in personal interview with this writer) that within his vision for ringbang, the dance "must come first". For Grant, the imperative of the dance is located in an African-Caribbean artistic paradigm. According to Grant, in this paradigm the dance which accompanies the drums is an act of resistance, rebellion and power. When this is taken into account, it is evident that an assessment of ringbang's lyrical tracks in isolation is perhaps misguided. After all, ringbang does claim to be predominantly (and initially, at least) a dance style.

Although there is merit in Grant's reading of ringbang in the early stages – that the ideology of ringbang resides in the music itself and the dance which it instigates – it is still rewarding and revelatory to examine features of the lyrics of early ringbang releases. Square One's "Ruk-a-Tuk

Party", on *Fire in de Wave* expresses the philosophy that "ringbang raggasoca" has not come to "confuse de teenager"; rather, "ringbang come to educate" – though the song does not say how. The collection of songs on the compilation does not say how either. Neither are there liner notes that seek to explain, as on another Ice release, *A Taste of Soca*. The only other direct references to what might be called socio-ideological issues on *Fire in de Wave* are in Viking Tundah's two songs, "Ring-a-Ringbang" and "Ringbang Soldier", in which he bellows, "Viking got a new slang" and "who a de ringbang soldier who a go kill dem wid lingua". These lyrics promise that ringbang will go on to be subversive through language. The first ringbang compilation, then, contains only passing references to the lyrical potentialities of ringbang for engaging with socio-political concerns.

Another point which must be made here relates to what surely must be seen as the cultural value of songs such as "Dr Cassandra" and "Debra", which are built on wordplay. Since these songs thrive on their double-edged meanings, they gesture to that category of traditional calypso which is defined by the skilful use of double entendre. Surely, as well, Viking's listing of natural Caribbean aphrodisiacs – "linseed, saga . . ." – can be read as traces of lyrical and cultural potency, integrity, if not of socio-political engagement. These are some considerations which must be mentioned as a means of better understanding the presence or absence of "strong" lyrics in hardcore styles of the 1990s and beyond.

Fire in de Wave's sequel, *Ringbang Rebel Dance*, is much more socio-politically engaged in its lyrical tracks. The songs "Devils" and "Ringbang Rebel Dancing" engage in significant ways with "serious" issues situated in cultural, social and political experience. "Devils" is a commentary on marital cuckoldry, drug traffickers in schools and televangelistic trickery. "Low Blow" serves as a metaphor for the concealed lethal blows which African-Caribbean culture still packs, in disguise:

> De culture in history books – low blow
> We culture in how we cook – low blow
> In how we is wuk we waist – low blow
> An' bacchanal in de place – low blow
> It come back though massa try – low blow
> Exposing all he lies – low blow
> Don't care what nobody say – low blow
> We culture is here to stay – low blow

In this song, Adisa returns to the socio-political lyric that characterized his politics as a rhythm poet (as on his 1994 release entitled *Conscious*).

The song "Ringbang Rebel Dance" is ideologically charged, with its listing of Caribbean rebels and revolutionaries. Within the song's construction there is a potential lesson in Caribbean history as it places a series of colonial actions in binary opposition to anti-colonial agents. Massa's "big stick, cutlass, old wood, no good" are therefore countered by "Shaka, Butla, Toussa, Bussa" (all black revolutionaries). But the struggle the song dramatizes is also a contemporary one, as seen through references to twentieth-century black revolutionary icons, "Nakruma, Kenyata, Lumumba, Tundah" (Kwame Nkrumah of Ghana, Jomo Kenyata of Kenya, Patrice Lumumba of the Congo and Viking Tundah himself). The juxtaposition of this disparate body of revolutionaries amounts to near-magical realism. This method is reminiscent of Wilson Harris's fiction and Kamau Brathwaite's poetry, especially *X/Self,* in which Brathwaite's various historical personages all exist in one time frame. "Ringbang Rebel Dance" is a deceptively subversive work of art. It best epitomizes the revolutionary potential of which ringbang is capable in its lyrical manifestation. "Ringbang Rebel Dance" has its pop-rock equivalent in Billy Joel's "We Didn't Start the Fire" (1989), in which Joel recites the names of important global figures and phenomena as a means of accounting for and situating the then-turbulent state of world affairs within a wider historical context. Joel suggests that events of the present have their roots in the past. "Ringbang Rebel Dancing" does not address broad global issues, but it is without doubt a more subversive song than "We Didn't Start the Fire", if only because Viking's song is not given to the detached philosophizing and fatalism of Billy Joel's Grammy-nominated composition, which declares that global turmoil is destined to go "on and on and on and on". The message of political, economic and cultural revolution lies at the base of "Ringbang Rebel Dancing". If this message has not been detected by some individuals who danced to the song, then maybe it is the song's driving techno-cum-jungle/soca rhythms which have masked and obscured its serious lyrics.

On *Ringbang Rebel Dance,* Ice Records continued to assert the difference between calypso/soca and the new hardcore styles, primarily within the musical tracks of compositions. *Ringbang Rebel Dance* reveals almost total abandonment of "live" horns. Its uses of bass and bass voices are more diverse and emphatic than before. The bass tones on most of the songs are dissonant and weighted. Bass patterns are non-complex and allude increasingly to the dancehall aesthetic. The bass and drums seem to function as extensions of each other – that is, the bass instruments (bass guitar and synth bass) on some of the tracks tend to function as an embellishment of the drums and vice versa. Now, how is this intricate relationship suggested in the mixing of songs, and how is it possible? One way in which this can be explained is through reference to the frequency response level of the drums and bass instruments. Simply put, the foot drum and low drum toms operate at the same frequency level as the bass guitar. It is because of this closeness, within the 30 to 40 hertz frequency range (the bottom end of the range of the piano),[19] that a sound engineer or workstation arranger can manipulate the sound contours of either the drums or bass so that they become almost indistinguishable one from the other. Throughout *Ringbang Rebel Dance*, then, there is this constant conscious play between bass and drums at the tonal and sonic levels. The effect is to blur the boundaries between drums and bass.

Whereas in the 1980s Blue Wave's sparse bass-guitar patterns characterized the studio's method, by the late 1990s drum and bass instruments shared the same tonal, metrical and rhythmic capacities. Two of the most audacious examples of this process can be heard in the middle of the song "Low Blow" and on the title track by Viking, when all else stops and bass or low-tuned drums or both are played in the open spaces. Careful listening can reveal the distinctness of instruments, but it can also complicate their relationship.

The vocal intensity on successive Blue Wave albums has been heightened. It is this vocal aggression which continues to assert ringbang's difference. This same vocal aggression is even more prevalent in dancehall and alternative rock. Significantly, therefore, ringbang's vocal application seems to draw on those two musical genres. Before ringbang, the most aggressive vocal rendition and application in the soca domain was that of the likes of Superblue, Carl Jacobs, Machel Montano, Crazy, King Short Shirt and Obstinate. But the new hardcore movement of the 1990s introduced vocal attack as a feature of its performance. This became a signature trait by the mid-1990s. One way of distinguishing this new style from other, similar genres (such as soca) was to listen to its harder, harsher vocal treatment. Chanting, greater lyrical repetition and enhanced vocal intensity further defined the new hardcore styles. In songs such as

"Ringbang Pickney" and "Ringbang Rebel Dance", the attitude of the vocalists is menacing. The semiotic significance of this aggression hinges on the subversive, revolutionary motive that underlies ringbang.

This is a significant area for further discussion, especially considering how these vocals and other components of the music are assigned their character in the post-production and performance stages. That is to say, the early music that one began to hear as ringbang was heavily dependent on technological processes. Ringbang surfaced precisely as a recorded music: it was fashioned primarily in the domain of the recording studio. Inasmuch as it was inspired by progressive technology, the practices that arose as part of ringbang also posed challenges to the technology itself. Aggressive vocals placed demands on the recording process. The difficulty that this new vocal aggression posed to engineers was significant. Engineers were faced with the question, "How do I capture this vocal intensity and yet not produce a distorted record because of 'shouting' vocals?" One way of doing this was to distance the vocalist from the microphone while he or she vociferated. The major disadvantages of this method were the decay of articulation and the overextension of gain or volume levels at the mixing board, resulting in hiss and noise. Engineers therefore had to solve this dilemma of how to convey vocal intensity with a "close" microphone while diffusing the direct sound that causes distortion. They turned to extant technology: reverb, delay, compression and limiting. When a "dry" (that is, non-processed) instrument which distorts because of its loud signal is given reverberation, this reverberation can serve to diffuse the original direct sound, leading to a slight reduction in the direct sound-pressure level and a significant reduction of distortion. Engineers have had to manage direct sound. New electronic gadgetry assisted in this process. The increase in vocal and musical aggression has therefore been directly proportionate to the increase in the use of reverb, delays and flanges on recent productions.

This is the kind of technological necessity that the aggression of ringbang has engendered. Studios have therefore had to produce this music with expertise and creativity, to tread the thin line between aggression and distortion. It is technology that has helped to define the discursive space for Caribbean hardcore musical styles. This technology is the hidden component in discourses about cultural construction; it has diffused the boundaries of sound mixing and production. To the extent that ringbang is marked by the assigning of hot levels to various percussive instruments in the multi-track performance domain (at the mixing console), it could be argued that ringbang is a creation of the technological moment.

Significantly, the 1995 compilation *Ringbang Rebel Dance* begins with a sample borrowed from Grant's 1983 Billboard hit "Electric Avenue". It is the sound of a revved-up motorcycle, which creates a heightened atmosphere for the track "Ringbang Pickney". As the song develops, this sample diminishes within the mix until it is submerged, but the overall ambience of the mix is sustained by the strains of an aggressive alternative-rock guitar. The guitar is distorted, but "cleanly" so. That is, the guitar is not positioned upfront and centre as in most rock-oriented productions (for example, Tears for Fears' "Cold" places the rock guitar in this position, and hence does not disguise its presence; it is unabashedly noisy). However, Grant's use of the guitar diffuses its potentially obtrusive presence (in the Caribbean context) by assigning it an altered status in the mix. It is "put away" in the wider contours of the song's total projection. As a result, the rock guitar is experienced in "Ringbang Pickney" as being effected by reverberation and is given full-left and full-right panning assignments. All of this together has the effect of diffusing the direct, blaring sound of this instrument, whose overall gain level is carefully held back by the engineer to give just enough to coat the song with a layer of carefully disguised aggression. This method is stock in trade on many productions coming out of Blue Wave after the 1990s.

This application of rock aesthetics is different from the 1980s trend where, as on Arrow's "Rush Hour", the rock guitar was an instrument of curiosity and a thing to behold. In its 1980s soca application, the rock guitar was a peculiar motif, alien to Caribbean music construction. It was at times introduced selectively into songs and then audibly discarded from the mix. The guitar hardly settled down to being a legitimate constituent of 1980s Caribbean music. Grant's 1990s re-engagement with the guitar seemed to hinge on its tonal, textural and expcriential properties. By the 1990s, it was not a new instrument to soca, and it therefore came to play many roles. It assumed a latent presence throughout Square One's "Ruk-a-Tuk Party". In Grynner's "Who Make de Ringbang", it steps out to full-gain level and becomes a recurring wail. And in Calypso Rose's "Play Oh" and Gabby's "Hold On to the Ball", on 1994's *Taste of Soca,* it sits more comfortably with bass and other percussive voices. Given the disruptive aggression of 1990s hardcore music, the presence of rock motifs is understandable.

There were also generous infusions of blues and country music motifs in selected productions. Gabby's "Hold On to the Ball", Adisa's "Jooky Jooky", Gillo's "Boisbande" and DJ Grandmaster's "Devils" use the blues or country harmonica and the blues guitar as integral components of their construction. Their use is important given the history of rock music and misperceptions about its origins. The use of motifs from these two traditions harks back to the origins of rock and roll and to its relationship to both blues and country music. Through these conscious re-engagements with the motifs from those traditions, Grant seems to allude to the necessity of revisiting discussions of the politics of race, culture and music history. His musical references are therefore a reminder that his explorations in rock are not without legitimate cultural basis, in spite of a popular idea that rock is white people's music. Much in the same way that the 1950s was giving birth to a new genre, rock and roll – one which would increasingly address social issues – Caribbean music in the late 1990s was symbolically also on the verge of evolving into newer forms. And in the same way that rock and roll was born out of a necessity to confront issues in an era of change, the new hardcore styles which emerged in the Caribbean represented the artistic response to Caribbean society in transition.

Beyond 2000

At the end of the twentieth century, hardcore tendencies continued to dominate the music of dance calypso. The performance tendencies and applications discussed in this chapter represent the trends that define modern post-soca music all over the world. These styles could be heard at other calypso oriented festivals such as Labour Day in New York, Caribana in Canada, and Notting Hill in England. Their driving, often quick-paced rhythms fuelled festive events over the world. Raggasoca also emerged as a credible category. Most soca-oriented acts embraced a range of genres, including ringbang, rapso, raggasoca, chutney soca and bouyon. This cultural eclecticism deepened, and individual acts experimented with different styles from time to time. There were also many collaborations between artists of different territories and of different musical orientations. In the same way that reggae and dancehall compilations became centerpiece items in the market, many recording entities invested more effort in producing soca compilations. Dancehall's popularization of specific trademark rhythms (such as the "hurricane" and the "knight rider") influenced soca-based artists to follow suit. This came into vogue especially after soca-dancehall fusion took off in the mid-1900s. By 2000, most leading soca acts were creating their own trademark rhythms on which they and other collaborators rode.

Throughout the Caribbean, post-soca styling dominated the music of acts such as Machel Montano, Bunji Garlin, Sanell Dempster and Iwer George, of Trinidad; Jaunty and Invader, of St Lucia; Dread and the Baldhead and Burning Flames, of Antigua; Tallpree and Super P, of Grenada; Byron Lee and the Dragonaires, of Jamaica; the Explosion Band, of St Maarten; Fireman Hooper, of St Vincent; and King Ellie Matt, of St Kitts and Nevis. By 2001, Iwer George had invoked the wrath of soca purists with his "Let Me See Yuh Hand". The song's refrain, which is really a cry of "nah nah nah nah nah nah" brought on him many criticisms. Some felt he was singing foolishness, while others openly declared that his record was noisy. But all in all, he got a lot of airplay in the islands and on Caribbean stations outside the region. The reference to his song as "noisy" reflected the newer directions that the music was taking in the first decade of the new century. It also reflected the difference and distance between more traditional calypso and the new experiments. The criticism levelled at Iwer George was thus less a direct commentary on his music than a reflection of general feelings about the direction of Caribbean music.

Though there continued to be scepticism at home, the international world caught a taste of what these regional stylings were seeking to offer to world music development. In 2001, Miami DJ Peter Black played a remixed dance version of "Electric Avenue" during the Miami Winter Music Conference. The remix soon caught the attention of local radio and quickly spread on to mainstream. Grant endorsed the remix and entered into an arrangement with Black. The new version was marketed as "Electric Avenue: The Ringbang Remix". It differed from the original, especially in terms of its dance appeal. The ringbang mix made use of overdubbed layers of drums. The popularity of this song catapulted Grant back into the international media limelight. It also represented a major opportunity for the promotion of his tag ringbang. Though some observers

333

were not convinced that the "Electric Avenue" ringbang remix made musical reference to soca, Grant was not disturbed. His Ice Records Web site, with its portal link to what it calls "Ringbang University", espoused the tenets of ringbang as drawing from calypso, soca, reggae, dancehall, jungle and hip hop, among other genres. The process of the remix's gaining popularity and the inscription of the label "ringbang" on it raises compelling questions concerning intent, authorship and commercial exertion. What this internationalization of ringbang ultimately reveals is the paradox, uncertainty and complexity inherent in popular culture. But Caribbean culture and music have from time to time reaped success through the input of players extrinsic to the day-to-day practice of the culture – this was nothing new.

While Grant pioneered and transformed the way Caribbean music was played and listened to throughout the 1990s from his Ice Records/Blue Wave Studio empire, other players in the industry have led the way since the late 1990s. This has to do partly with a series of legal battles that preoccupied Ice Records.[20] Machel Montano represents a new, young generation of entertainers and businesspeople who were also embarking on redefining the boundaries of soca fusion. His 1998 song "Torro Torro", although categorized as rapso (rapping calypso), does not sit comfortably or squarely within that vein. For one thing, traditional rapso is founded on a conscious edge and is very much concerned with lyrical message. It might be useful to compare Machel's vocal performance with, say, the rapso duo Kindred, also of Trinidad, whose song "Ha Da Dey" (1999) privileges the "spoken" word. Rapso is certainly characterized by the speaking-cum-singing vocals riding a calypso beat. But although Montano's song begins with near-spoken vocals, it soon loses its reference to rapso when the music takes over, and the vocals ferment into a crescendo of post-rapso aggression. In the music video for "Torro Torro", which also features the Jamaican dancehall artist Shaggy, the atmosphere of total chaos which the vocals and music suggest is kept up by the wild abandon of Caribbean players dressed as matadors. Calypso experts and soca purists have made many disparaging statements about the song. Some commentators have questioned the legitimacy of this song's being entered into a calypso/soca category, since, as one longstanding calypsonian, Chalkdust, has said, the song has no real chorus and the few words which comprise the chorus do not rhyme: "Charge! torro torro / Charge! torro torro".

Though there might be doubts about my placement of "Torro Torro" outside the traditional parameters of rapso, fewer people would disagree with a similar categorization of Montano's music in 1999 and beyond. On the 1999 album *Any Minute Now,* which anticipates the turn of the millennium, Montano teams up with another widely popular Jamaican DJ, the controversial rude boy Beenie Man. On the track "Outa Space", Montano again extends the boundaries of calypso-oriented music. In terms of musical and vocal aggression, this song takes off from where "Torro Torro" flew highest. "Outa Space" is constructed around explosive upfront music samples and tones. Orchestral hits and similar powerful sound samples dominate the mix. In soca during the late 1980s and early 1990s, these tones were used sparingly and at strategic points of songs, for example, on Tambu's 1990 "No No We Eh Going Home". In post-soca music at the beginning of the twenty-first century, these orchestral clusters (punctuations) are played throughout. In "Outa Space", busy drum tracks, Montano's intense warnings to "point your finger in the sky!" and Beenie Man's characteristic infectious chanting all signal the apotheosis of post-soca performance. This song is a fitting representation of how far the early experiments in the 1980s had evolved. All in all, it is a highly commercial, cleverly constructed and extremely likeable production. Montano's audacious Web site, http://www.xtatik.com, showcased all the accoutrements of soca's leading act. The Web video with Beenie Man and Machel cast the two performers as "Men in Black", in search of two female aliens. The video made reference to the Hollywood blockbuster starring Will Smith and Tommy Lee Jones in order to give the video wider mass appeal. Videos of this kind set the standard for other soca music video productions in the early twenty-first century.

Machel Montano's appearance on the "Dancehall Magnificent Seven" music video, which also featured Buju Banton, Beenie Man and Mr Vegas, among others, represented the eclectic nature of soca fusion at the end of the twentieth century. It was therefore not surprising that, throughout the region, soca and post-soca acts began to sing on top of a single rhythm, in the same way that dancehall artists have been doing for years. As the music developed, the distance between it and dancehall grew increasingly closer.

Where his earlier single "Come Dig It" (1996) appeared with a major label, by 2001 Montano had also secured a limited deal with Atlantic Records. This deal subsequently met with problems. Machel was clearly not satisfied with the direction which the record label wanted him to take. He was not happy with the fact that he was working with a lot of producers who seemed bent on doing things other than soca. Ironically, some commentators had also been accusing Machel of not doing soca throughout the mid-1990s. But Machel's stance in the Atlantic deal reflected the tensions that are at work in regional music as well as in the wider music industry. In 2003, after the Xtatik breakup, he reconstituted the band, which appeared as Xtatik 5.0. In 2004, they performed as the Xtatik Road Marching Band, gesturing to the pop culture flick *Drumline*. In spite of some mixed fortunes since 2000, Machel hardly relented in his quest to innovate. His "Mad Man", "Kock Back and Roll" and "Crazyness" revealed the sensibility of an avant-garde soca act in the big league – and on the verge of even more audacious experiments. No other Caribbean artist could compare in terms of innovation and energy.

There were other artists of this type in other territories as well. Tallpree, from Grenada, burst onto the scene in the late 1990s with his "Old Woman Me Taking Home" and soon established his unique style, derived from his dancehall background, with playful lyrics and driving bouyon rhythms. Jaunty, from St Lucia, and Fireman Hooper and Poorsah, from St Vincent, reflected the sensibility of soca fusion while maintaining an identifiable national quality in terms of vocalization. In St Kitts and Nevis, the long-standing King Ellie Matt, on his 2002 release, demonstrated his awareness of new trends on songs such as "See Me Ya" and "Carry On". These drum-driven songs also made no attempt to mask their employment of synthesized brass. "See Me Ya" makes use of a drum styling which fuses soca and hip-hop patterns, while its tonal, pulsating kick drum was closer to house and hip hop than to soca proper. "Carry On", like most other songs on the album, does not attempt to disguise the synthesized character of the brass tones used.

By 2002, the retro craze in sound synthesis had also taken over Caribbean music, and the analogue sound generated by synthesizers was trendy. Slingshot, from Guyana, produced the 2003 album *Jump for Carnival*. Like Ellie Matt's work, it revealed an awareness that the tempo of Caribbean soca was unhindered. It also gave full vent to raw-sounding synthesized horns.

It is significant that many of these artists could be accessed relatively freely via the Internet. Xtatik's official Web site, along with those of other artists like Rupee and Kevin Lyttle (who both signed to Atlantic in late 2003), revealed their stated intention to cross the boundaries of soca as defined before the 1990s. These Web sites were therefore fairly interactive, and by 2000 they revealed the kind of carefully constructed Internet architecture that defined the more commercially advanced arena of dancehall. The presence of sites devoted to national musics intimates that dedicated spaces – places – are being inscribed in cyberspace. Sites such as Lucian Carnival (http://www.luciancarnival.com/) are as much about information and marketing as about harnessing the cultural and musical expression of the nation. St Vincent and the Grenadines Broadcasting Corporation's Web site (http://www.svgbc.com/index2.htm) projects nationalist themes reflected through pages devoted to sports, news, entertainment and music. Its impressive offering of calypso, ragga, soca and other hybrid styles in streaming audio defines this site as a major promoter of Vincy music.

But as many nationalist sites as there are, there are many more which traverse national boundaries and connect through shared musical expression. The energy and innovation of Poorsah and Fireman Hooper are captured at CarnivalPower.com (http://www.carnivalpower.com), but that site also projects artists from other islands. Whereas Caribbean television proved incapable of projecting images of the region, smaller organizations and entities employ the Internet to keep the people in touch with the pulse of cultural expression throughout the region. The impressive showing of CarnivalPower.com means that audiences can experience aspects of regional carnivals through photos, sound and video clips.

The Internet's facility for video clips of artists emblematizes the marriage of even newer forces in the dissemination of Caribbean music. In a symbolic and symbiotic interface, Caribbean music had yet again seen the forging of new technological links, links which reflect the attempts to position Caribbean culture at the cutting edge of global developments. Such links and their manifested contents anticipate the birth of even newer styles.

Music Video to Web Streaming
Cultural Ventriloquism @ the Leading Edge

The Industry and Caribbean Music

Significant developments in technological modes of recording and dissemination at the beginning of the twentieth century inevitably gave rise to revolutionary transformations in the production of music. By the beginning of the twentieth century, there were several major phonograph companies: the Electric and Musical Industries (EMI, founded in 1897 as the Gramophone Company), Columbia Gramophone Company (1889), Victor Talking Machine Company (1901), and Decca (1914). They were all actively engaged in recording and distributing indigenous musics, including those of the Caribbean. These early recording interests saw Caribbean music as part of Latin American music, and so they approached and marketed the region's materials as such.

No later than 1914, Victor sent technicians to Trinidad to record Caribbean folk songs. These exploits were mostly undertaken with the assistance of a limited number of Caribbean interests, people such as the composer, musician and bandleader Lionel Belasco.[1] Belasco was contracted to locate and record songs for major interests: he was responsible for recording more than three hundred songs from the region for Decca, Columbia and other companies. By the 1930s, companies were offering contracts to indigenous singers, mostly calypsonians, for less than US$10 for a song.

The long-standing interest in Caribbean and other regional musics by the recording industry underscores the importance of this music. It also underscores the value of this music as a cultural commodity. It is important to call attention to these early encounters in order to emphasize the tradition of interface and exploitation. When this process is recognized, then a better understanding of contemporary relationships between Caribbean musicians and major players in the industry can be achieved.

Since the 1970s, there have been numerous instances where Caribbean music and musicians were celebrated as breaking through into the international market, and many artists have been rightly lauded for their ground-breaking achievements in Caribbean music.[2] Quite similar moods of euphoria also engulfed performers and their fans in the region during the 1930s. There was much expectation and euphoria surrounding the historic journey of Roaring Lion and Atilla the Hun to New York in 1934 to record sixteen songs.[3] Their exploits were significant and created an avenue for greater exposure.

Since that time, calypso has surfaced and receded on the international scene. Although many artists have seemed about to bring it to sustained international attention, this has not materialized. Leading exponents such as the Mighty Sparrow, King Short Shirt, Beckett, King Obstinate, King Ellie Matt, Ajamu, Rebel, Gabby and Pelay have not managed to insure calypso's permanence on the international stage. This might not necessarily be a reflection of their talent. Rather, it might be an indication of the way the music industry is structured. Talent and potential are not automatic passports to international acclaim. The music industry is a complex phenomenon built on a series of lateral and vertical structures and networks. Indeed, it is not even bona fide calypso performers who have the distinction of first catapulting "calypso" onto the international stage: Harry Belafonte holds this distinction with his 1956 album *Calypso*. But the title and categorization of the album have been the subject of much debate, since what Belafonte sings as "calypso" falls short of what defines the art form in the minds of many commentators, artists and academics.[4]

There is a bittersweet relationship between Caribbean artists and major recording interests in the music industry. Many of the disagreements have surrounded questions of contracts, royalties, copyright, production and marketing. One of the more celebrated cases of antagonism over ownership featured Lord Invader versus the Andrews Sisters and Decca for the composition "Rum and Coca Cola".[5] Another pitted the Cuban Joseito Fernandez against Fall River Publishers and Pete Seeger over "Guantanamera".[6] More recent developments in Caribbean music have demonstrated the negative side effects of "going international".

But there are also many benefits reaped by artists who come into relationship with major industry players. The current situation still finds regional artists going in search of that illusive major deal which will bring unlimited rewards. Nonetheless, the process of crossing over is also fraught with unexpected occurrences. In the final analysis, Caribbean music is not practised within an exclusive zone; it is performed in the context of national, regional and international forces. Today these boundaries are being eroded significantly with the expansion of technology and the introduction of new trade and related practices. Caribbean music has therefore come under increasing pressure to maintain its place and significance. Because of the growing power and presence of major players in the global entertainment industry, Caribbean and other regional cultures have had to contest their position within the system of global culture.

Interactivity and Discourse

Modern technological monoliths such as the telephone, radio, television and the Internet have been responsible for revolutionizing the way human beings interact and communicate. These media have pointed the way towards a more closely knit community of participants.[7] It has indeed become possible for a lot more people to be hearers, viewers and participants in a given communicative event, potentially widening the discursive global space into which local creators can now take their products if they so choose to.

But this proliferation of high-tech facilities also both marks and masks an homogenization of the discursive process. This is the problematic of technological innovation, and it is also the challenge of economic and cultural development. Media such as radio and television have been responsible for opening up the world of communication and entertainment and have functioned to empower those people who have been able to gain access to them. There are, however, those many more people who, unable to gain access to communication, have been subordinated and disabled by the disseminative presence and power of technology. For example, satellite television is still predominately a one-way "interactive" phenomenon. In the Caribbean, satellite television looms large. There is still in the twenty-first century a very small percentage of Caribbean programmes being disseminated abroad; the marketing of regional programmes throughout the region and abroad is a very small trade.[8] The region's potential response to "the world" is hampered by the economic, political and cultural realities of accessing this discursive space. Thus, although in theory it is now potentially more possible to reach wider audiences, there are still major challenges associated with capturing and sustaining the notice of large audiences. Because of these challenges, trendy postcolonial notions of "writing back" to the centre are rendered idealistic, inadequate models for analysing Caribbean cultural response in the domain of technological discourse.[9] Foucauldian discourse and free-trade advocates have asked people to resist imagining a world divided between "the dominant and the dominated one".[10] Indeed, the notion of discourse and dialogics on which this and Bakhtinian thought rely cannot in itself be meaningfully applied to the Caribbean reality. In Caribbean reality, discourse or dialogue is not an immediate, open option; it does not therefore truly exist. What we have instead is "dis/course". There is not a continuous open field for interplay; this possibility is fractured, rendered null and void.

Because of the central position of key transnational corporations and subsidiaries within the entire worldwide network of speakers and hearers, the homogenization and control of communications signifies a further entrenchment of old systems. The "new global world order" is one of the names given to current systems of interaction and control. Caribbean culture thus continues to evolve in the shadow of national, regional and significantly powerful international initiatives. And all of these exert pressure on a set of art forms that are themselves in transition.

Caribbean Music: Sound/Film/Theory

Although there is a substantial body of writing on Caribbean music and culture, there has been relatively little critique of Caribbean popular music in its diverse media. Many studies have tended to focus on historical developments, lyrical texts and socio-cultural contexts, some on the actual music. They have largely, however, eschewed a genre like the music video. It is inconceivable that future Caribbean popular music criticism will continue to ignore this medium of cultural representation and dissemination. This is not to suggest that previous studies have all ignored the visual nature of Caribbean popular music and performance; some have dealt with it in detail. But there is still space for an assessment of the "packaged performance" – the recorded sound-and-image text – and a critique of the ideology inherent in the construction of music videos. The embracing of the Internet by the entertainment industry has witnessed the blooming of Internet radio as well as Internet TV and Internet-disseminated music videos. The Internet has evolved into a major medium for the dissemination of regional culture. It is now possible to gain easier immediate access to Caribbean artists through the Internet than through any other facility.

This chapter examines aspects of the music video – not only specific music videos, but also the music video as a medium of expression. In this consideration, it asks the reader to consider music as possessing an ideology. This is a reasonable request, since we can and do talk of a song's theme or philosophy as being inherent in the lyrics of the work. But the total work can also be considered to be encoded with an ideological statement, one which an artist (and his or her various producers) can create and which an audience can discern.

The music video is a relatively new dimension of the international music industry. As early as the 1940s, there were "soundies", which featured artists in short musical clips on jukebox-type machines called Panorams.[11] In the 1950s, short filmed performances called Telescriptions, which featured artists such as Nat King Cole, were inserted as clips between television programmes.[12] By the 1960s, artists began to create filmic works (such as The Beatles' *A Hard Day's Night*) that captured aspects of their performance. In the 1970s, short musical films made their way to television with greater frequency. By the mid- to late 1980s, video clips were an integral part of the promotional and marketing thrust of major labels. Music television (particularly MTV) was largely responsible for this advancement. Earlier in the development of music videos, there was a tendency to have the music video follow the release of a sound recording, but eventually the music video became a medium for encouraging radio DJs to give airplay to soon-to-be-released sound recordings or to give exposure to soon-to-be-signed artists.[13] Major record companies have devised strategic methods of fashioning their artists and projecting them directly onto music television.[14]

The advancement of Caribbean popular music onto the world stage has paralleled the rise in the prominence of the music video. This is not to infer any direct causal relationship, but rather to point to the fact that Caribbean culture has indirectly come under influence of international developments. In its quest to survive and to thrive abroad, Caribbean music has had to acknowledge the presence of the global music industry and the power of leading-edge technology – to indulge in the music industry's experimentation with sound, music, images, the moving picture camera and video. It is within this domain of the technological interactivity of sound and pictures, audio and video, the real and the virtual, that a significant portion of global discourse has taken place since the 1980s.

Since the development of film, and beginning with silent-film makers, there has been some scepticism about the value of sound, which has always played a secondary role to the visual component (music videos would later reverse this process). Film criticism has tended to treat sound films as being constituted by two simultaneous parallel phenomena, image and sound. Rick Altman proposes a provoking theory about the relationship between sound and image.[15] For him, these two phenomena are engaged in an ongoing play in which each complements the other and also masks its own actions. For example, Altman refers to the practice of moving the camera in search of the sound source (for example, to an actor's lips), which can turn an off-screen dialogue into an on-screen conversation between characters. This practice identifies the source of the sound, thus fulfilling an audience's curiosity; but for Altman, the focusing of a camera on moving lips merely conceals the "true" origin of the sound, which is actually a technological sound source somewhere beyond the film's illusion of moving lips. Altman refers to this play as "sound hermeneutics", whereby every audio signal/speech is constantly asking "Where did that sound come from?" and, subsequently, the zooming-in by the camera on an image signals a response: *"Here!"*

Altman wants to suggest that technology is really behind the process of filmmaking and construction. For example, when, in a music video, we hear ambient rich and "present" strains of music and the camera focuses on a pocket radio, either we believe the rich sound comes from the pocket radio or we come to realize that these strains really belong to another source that is at the disposal of sound engineers and film producers: "We are so disconcerted by a sourceless sound that we would rather attribute the sound to a dummy or a shadow than face the mystery of its sourcelessness or the scandal of its production by a non-vocal (technological or 'ventral') apparatus."[16]

In film the soundtrack can therefore act as ventriloquist, creating the illusion that its image is speaking and further creating the belief that the entire production has a life of its own. Altman places emphasis on sound (and technology) as the hidden or masked factor which manipulates its own relationship with the image. In this chapter I want to build on that suggestion: to further suggest that in popular music video discourse (insofar as the technology is concealed, to varying degrees), there is an even more hideous concealment of the ideology which lurks behind the technology. The upfront carrier of the ideology (the singer/actor) is therefore displaced at the disseminative stage of viewing and consumption. Given the central role of production managers, choreographers and directors in music video productions, these personnel can act as ventriloquists of sorts, manipulating the performer and the performance and controlling the interaction of image and sound in preparation for audiences.

Given the immense impact that some Caribbean artists and their music videos have made on the world stage, the fashioning of these videos should come under scrutiny. This scrutiny is even more desirable because the music videos of these major "international" artists reveal recurring motifs, many of which are not generous to the region. Are the artists solely responsible for the images they project in their videos? Do their record companies support and encourage the projection of stereotypical motifs? Does the signing to a major label render the Caribbean artist at greater risk of being manipulated and influenced by these larger players? Are some Caribbean artists – and, by extension, Caribbean society – at risk of being reconstructed by the music industry? Is it possible that in addition to their players' having a life of their own off-camera, the characters within a number of Caribbean music videos are like dummies, manipulated through technological ventriloquism? We will examine these and other associated issues.

Cultural Ventriloquism

In addressing these issues, this chapter will focus moreso on dancehall because of the number of its artists who have signed to major record companies. Less attention is therefore given to other genres as recognition that other musical genres of the anglophone Caribbean have not had the international profile of dancehall. The international profile of dancehall rose sharply from the early 1990s, and this chapter therefore makes reference to many videos from that period.

Caribbean music videos in general are notable for the emphasis they place on capturing aspects of Caribbean reality. Another notable feature is the emphasis they place on the process whereby the camera goes in search of the body, in particular the female body. Although Suzanne Moore suggests that it is increasingly "more difficult to show naked women in advertisements", Caribbean dancehall and soca videos challenge this claim.[17] These genres are not alone, of course, in this emphasis. Music videos in other genres, such as hip hop, rhythm and blues, and pop have also been heavily criticized for their sexual content, and the high content of violence and materialism has also come under scrutiny. But the wishful thinking that seems to control many music videos has particularly strong presence in the videos of dancehall artists who are or have been affiliated with major labels or with large independent companies. It is important to note that these entities in the music industry operate with a clear set of guidelines, intentions and objectives: they are most concerned with profits, and all other concerns are subordinated to this project.[18]

It might be argued that some dancehall videos are inclined to project "slackness" because the lyrics themselves have tended to foreground sexual and violent themes. This is an important observation, one that is also gestured to by Kala Grant.[19] It would seem to have some bearing on the discussion, especially since the genre of music video developed with sound as the central controlling component and images as the embellishment.

But by the late 1980s, when dancehall music came to the fore, the lyrical text was no longer always in control of the image text in the music-video domain. The independence of lyrics and image can be illustrated with reference to two songs by dancehall acts, songs which are quite similar lyrically but which reflect different treatments in their video representation: Chaka Demus and Pliers' "Murder She Wrote" and Bounty Killer and Beres Hammond's "Living Dangerously". Lyrically, both songs are message based, to do with the speaker's warning against the repercussions of dangerous love or sex practices. Both songs as lyrical texts could stand as preventatives for a wayward Caribbean generation of youths faced with such problems as substance abuse, illicit sex and materialism. The major distinction between these songs occurs in their filmic representations. The subject matter of "Living Dangerously" does allow for some focus on the interplay of female and male bodies since its lyrics highlight the promiscuous activities of individuals, but the music video does not become preoccupied with the woman as object to be gazed upon. Within the relational interplay of sound and video, then, the image does not assert greater power of control within the overall discursive space of the production. The video begins with an identifiable filmic narrative comprising a man, a woman and child – presumably a family. This filmic narrative tends to reinforce the lyrical consciousness of the song. There is a complementary function that the images serve in this video; hence sound/lyric and video seem to produce a cohesive narrative. There is relative synchronicity of word and image.

Conversely, "Murder She Wrote", whose message is no less potent, does not reveal a similar balance between its lyrical track and the video sequences which accompany it. Whereas "Living Dangerously" introduced the dancehall scenario in the middle of the production, its function was not to elicit sexual gratification by foregrounding the body. In contrast, "Murder She Wrote" as video text is a collage of clippings of the female anatomy, especially the buttocks. It is a video sequence that features an incessant dance party – a party at which the point of interest is the rubbing of bodies, male and female.

So here are two songs performed by artists of the same standing in the international world. Lyrically, the songs are quite similar in terms of their message. Both do lend themselves to productions that could exploit and objectivize the female subject, yet one pays greater attention to a wider range of images than the other in the filmic medium. "Living Dangerously" is not as formulaic as "Murder She Wrote". The motivation for choice of images is therefore not tied to a composition's lyrics: there are other controlling factors. The relationship between the lyrical track and its filmic accompaniment is an arbitrary one. These are grounds for asserting the liberation of the camera.

But the repeated shot of the female anatomy in some Caribbean music videos not only demonstrates an absence of creative imagination, it also reveals an obsessive discursive practice whose fixation with the female's body masks a latent ideology at the base of the overall production process. This ideological politics is located to some degree in Laura Mulvey's feminist categorization of unequal power relations between men and women.[20] It is clear, though, that the motivation is even deeper and spreads wider than that: it has very much to do with geopolitical and cultural politics. In the age of ideological deployment through visual and virtual means, controlling agents within the entertainment industry have fought to uphold stereotypical ways of representing regional cultures.

Frantz Fanon's perception concerning the controlling politics of hegemonic powers summarizes the outlook of many major entertainment companies: "Colonialism is not satisfied merely with holding a people in its grips and emptying the native's brain of all form and content. By a kind of perverted logic, it turns to the past of the oppressed people, and distorts, disfigures and destroys it."[21] This is a blunt assessment. It is even more stark since when imported into a post-twentieth-century text in an era of political correctness. But Fanon's statement remains relevant to the way some major corporations relate to smaller entities in present-day society. Edward Said's 1978 *Orientalism* also discusses the ways in which the Orient has been "orientalized", how Western subjects know and control their "other".[22] Caribbean culture is no different in terms of how it is constructed in the West, and large transnational corporations have continued the process of constructing and "Caribbeanizing" the region.

One of the most telling and persistent stereotypes in dancehall videos has been that of the highly excitable black Caribbean person. By confining Caribbean culture to stereotypes, the industry is also confining the society to a safe, non-complex system of meaning within the wider global space. This point is emphasized by the portrayals of Caribbean society in contemporary big-budget films such as *Predator 2, Godzilla, Air Force One, Scary Movie 2* and *Pirates of the Caribbean*. This is not an outlandish claim; as Lawrence Grossberg suggests, music videos indeed represent a set of cultural practices.[23]

Caribbean music videos are defined by their stark realism, but even notions of realism are often debated across disciplines.[24] And Philip Brophy reminds his reader that the video clip is not built on the same narrative components of traditional feature films; that is, it does not center plot, character and actions in the same way.[25] There could be no end to a debate on film, video and realism. Film *is* an illusion. The very use of technology to capture and present video and sound casts doubts on the reality of the material being re-presented. The use of reality and realism can be usefully defined when put in opposition to surrealism. This chapter thus identifies videos as "realist" or "surrealist" based on the dominant motifs and techniques presented in them: "realist" videos are those which have a more solid narrative structure and which are less concerned with post-production distortion of film and sound. For our purposes, then, these key contested terms have less to do with metaphysics and philosophy than with the technological process, with production and post-production.

Caribbean music videos of the 1990s featuring artists signed to major labels tend to be very realist. These videos appear to be less concerned with production and post-production wizardry and hence much more transparent than other genres of music videos. They tend to hold up a mirror to the world of viewers who, in the 1990s, beheld Caribbean culture in rotation on mainstream entertainment channels for the first time ever. Many of these videos present stereotypical images of Caribbean society. Because these videos tend to be realist, they cloak the presence of the technology and hence conceal the ideology behind the construction of the videos. In another music genre like alternative rock, whose reality is also fixed by the industry, audiences are not duped about this reality; the strong presence of technology in alternative videos reminds them that the video is a re-creation. Looking first at a number of alternative and pop-rock music videos, paying especial attention to the construction process, we can therefore identify the codes through which audiences become aware of technology's self-referencing, a practice that produces a displacement between the actual world and the terrain of alternative-music videos. So, because technology in the alternative-music video tends to stand out, audiences know that they are watching not "real" people but representations of them.

Alternative/Alter-native

Like dancehall in the Caribbean, alternative rock is considered in the United States to be the music of rebellion. It also claims substantial popularity among youths in the heart of many US cities. Whereas dancehall emerged in the international domain as a new music of the "Third World", mainstream rock has been the nurtured product of an expanding music industry, led by the hegemony of "First World" major labels. By the mid-1990s, dancehall was gaining the attention of larger audiences. Around this time as well, alternative rock was being embraced within the music industry's mainstream. Groups such as Nirvana had brought alternative music even closer to the heart of the industry.

Thomas Levin has suggested that analyses of sound in film should privilege the technical object itself.[26] James Lastra takes issue with this mode of analysis as a procedure for understanding sound and image.[27] In countering Levin's method, Lastra sides with Raymond Williams, who has tended to foreground the importance of art as practice rather than as object.[28] Like Williams, Lastra argues for technology not as an object, but as "a set of cultural and scribal practices".[29] I consider both sides of the debate to be important: no serious discussion of sound should suggest that technology inherently constructs sound and images or, by extension, that it is the sole instrument in the creation of film and sound. Meaning *is* suggested and evoked based on the perception (by audiences and producers) of what a sound or image should or does represent. Conversely, it cannot be argued that "social and cultural practices" themselves determine the nature of the reception of sound and the image. There would seem to be some overlap of these two opposing approaches in the analysis of sound, image, audience, technologies and the process of reception.

It is difficult to attribute a fossilized set of given responses to a specific set of technological practices. Or, as Altman says, every event, once it offers itself to be heard or seen, "loses its autonomy, surrendering the power and meaning . . . to the various contexts" in which it might be experienced.[30] Altman is correct insofar as there are bound to be different responses to cultural productions once they are disseminated in different contexts. This, however, does not render futile the attempt to scrutinize the nature, source and creation of cultural productions.

The technological practices that manipulate the music video, for example, are not devoid of ideological processes. Music videos do not therefore possess autonomy in that sense. Furthermore, such genres as the music video do not, when disseminated, totally surrender power and meaning to the contexts in which they are experienced; rather, there are varying degrees of this surrendering. Music videos do not always conform to the process that Altman espouses above in relation to film. In some cases, as Jody Berland notes, music videos tend to dominate and arrest viewers, audiences are not always active in the viewing process.[31] The music video, once disseminated, might be marked by *some* "surrendering of power" in various contexts, but unless audiences are alert and willing to grasp this power, there is no real transfer of power.

Whereas many studies and debates have focused on active and passive viewers, fewer, arguably, have closely examined the crucial role that technology plays in shaping popular genres and affecting some audiences. In Caribbean music videos of the 1990s and beyond, technology played a central role in helping to shape responses. Increasingly, technology has stood between the art (that is, the art form, its creation, its creators) and audiences who experience it. The degree of technology's visibility has held implications for the detection of hidden politics in the construction of some music videos.

As an art form which actively engages in the process of transmitting culture through sound bites and film edits, the music video threatens not merely to re-present culture but to become the creator of that culture which it reproduces. It is poised to achieve greater feats in the near future: it stands ready to supplant that which it imitates. This process has quickened with new advances in the realm of virtual technology. Video games and simulations foreshadow the blurring of reality and its other. Unless viewers are reminded of this process (that is, that the music video *re-produces* culture), they are in danger of giving in to the ideology and power of the production, which begins to control the viewer. And one way in which this audience might be reminded that something [ideology] stands between themselves and what they see and hear on the screen is through their discovery of the presence of the technology.

In the music videos of many major Caribbean artists, the presence of technology is not made readily discernable through the production. Music video practices (at the level of production) in alternative rock, on the other hand, allow for an easier discernment of the technology. The Caribbean music videos under examination here are formulaic. They convey predominantly negative images of the region. Further, their production tends to cloak the technology, in disguise offering the videos as "true-true"[32] images of Caribbean culture.

An examination and analysis of selected alternative-music videos can provide support for the comparison being drawn between that genre and selected Caribbean genres. At face value, many alternative-music videos seem to reflect a state of chaos – at least this is the impression that they make on casual observation. It is the prevalence of non-logical, non-sequential filmic narrative, cataclysmic images, inaudible vocals and "noisy" guitars which give rise to this impression.

The (sense of) chaos which many of these music videos exhibit serves to foreground the fact of the videos' self-conscious construction. That is, these videos are able to call attention to the genre as re-creating technologically altered versions of the "true-true" world. Or, put yet another way, the foregrounding of excessive chaos in this category of music video captures the audience's attention initially but subsequently deflects the point of interest away from what is being represented on-screen, refocusing it on the artistry of the technological act. This technological act consists of a number of processes and tendencies that are integral to modern methods of editing, creating special effects and performing self-indulgent practices. Many alternative-music videos do not hide the fact of their constructedness: they declare the presence of technologies in creating them. Think, for example, of the Smashing Pumpkins' "Bullet with Butterfly Wings", the Presidents of the United States of America's "Lump", the Red Hot Chilli Peppers' "My Friends", Green Day's "Brain Stew/Jaded" or Bush's "Glycerine". Audiences are thus at least made aware that a form of technology mediates the discursive space between themselves and the music video. It must be added, nonetheless, that in this experience audiences are not led to seize power within the discursive process. Power is only seized when there is an understanding of the further hidden logic and method which informs the construction, dissemination and reception of music videos.

Although a number of these videos create the impression of non-logical construction through their use of distorted images and sound, there is in actuality a great deal of underlying logic and method to the construction of these videos. It is at the first stage of experiencing – of seeing and hearing – these videos that the impression of non-logic is created. Since audiences do not tend to engage the music video beyond this stage, this is the impression that remains. Although they are invited to gaze at the technology which is "in effect", theirs is only a blind gaze; they do not begin to engage the *workings* of the technology. An examination of the working of this technology (at the second, deeper stage) would reveal the existence of some logic and method. The fact of the presence of logic and of shrewd methodical manipulation in these music videos underscores the pivotal (and clandestine) role that the technology plays in informing the ideology which underlies the construction of some music videos.

Let us look at an example. Lyrically, Deep Blue Something's "Breakfast at Tiffany's" is about the desperate attempt by an individual to find one common ground on which estranged love might reunite. The music video does not by any means represent the most extreme case of chaotic sound and video, but it is representative to some degree. The video's treatment is non-realist, its tone and texture deliberately contorted. The absence of surface realism here is attributable to the hodgepodge editing which seems to have taken place at the production and post-production stages. But this effect, this absence of realism, also comes about because of a number of absurdities: a man on horseback riding through what is obviously a "pedestrians only" walkway in a downtown setting, another man walking out of what appears a posh hotel into a business area of a bustling city, wearing his bathrobe and carrying the morning paper.

One questions the meaning of this video, with its quickly shifting images and its series of absurd occurrences. In the first ten to fifteen seconds, the audience is at sea, dumbfounded, because the early segment of the video flickers between apparently unrelated scenes. The first ten seconds represent a systematic process of disguises. There are five two-second snapshots or blocks of distinctive occurrences:

Shot one (2 seconds): Two men in the distance walk a busy street. They are carrying something heavy (perhaps). In the foreground, two objects – yellow cabs – pass from screen left to screen right and conceal what we began to observe of the two men. We wonder, what did the passing vehicles conceal? Did we see what we thought we did? Are we seeing correctly? Are we seeing at all?

Shot two (2 seconds): There is now a single man, in the mid-distance. He exits a hotel. He wears what seems to be a bathroom robe. He carries what is perhaps the morning paper. He walks towards the camera into (again) a busy street. Again, cars and people pass in the foreground, though these do not totally conceal the man. What! Is this individual mad? Does he also wear bedroom slippers?

Shot three (2 seconds): Coming on-screen from behind the pillar of an edifice is a man on horseback. He rides with familiarity and nonchalance. But this appears to be a pedestrian's haven. What! A horse amidst this downtown city of people and modern vehicles?

Shot four (1.5 seconds): Closer up, a man crosses a busy city street. He wears a black windbreaker. He looks at his watch. What for? Why this urgency? The prior characters would seem to have none of this regard for time. What is the connection? Where is the logic behind all this?

Shot five (2 seconds): Up close again, a man, taking his head out from a book which he is reading, begins to sing: "You say that we've got nothing in common. . . ." The camera again shifts to one or other of the previous scenes. But we still cannot make reasonable sense of this non-logical presentation of distinct events, along with the absurdities that are attendant upon each snapshot.

Now within normal (viewing) time (which represents a first-time experiencing of these ten- to fifteen-seconds of shots) all this is experienced as chaotic. We are not allowed enough of our own real time in this segment of the video to formulate meaning. So we can only gaze at the technology. But the technology then suspends our ability to construct meaning. And so we cannot seize the power of the discourse – we are not able to, not allowed to do so, because of the experiential instability of the sound and image.

Through a deeper engagement with technological processes, it becomes evident that there are calculated strategies in operation within this and similar videos – there is some degree of methodological construction here. The most obvious method in "Breakfast at Tiffany's" is the act of concealment through the dramatic editing (in this instance) of five distinctive events. Each occupies a two-second clip. There are some wide-angle shots which ensure that we do not make out what is really being centred. Obstacles which occupy the foreground obscure central objects in the distance. There is some degree of rotation of these scenes, but they do not begin to amount to a coherent narrative video sequence until the middle of the production, when the semblance of a meaning emerges from the apparent chaos of the music video. As a result of the deliberate obscuring of its own logic, one begins to interrogate the technology which manipulates the music video at the various levels of experience. In a sense, it is as though the technology which recreates these feats is engaged in an ongoing practice of discursive camouflage.

It is important to further examine the systematic method by which the industry's technology calls attention to itself in many alternative-music videos, clearly stating to its viewers that the world of aberration of predominantly white performers and audiences is not their "true-true" world; it is only their technology. There are a number of recurring technological motifs (codes or signs) in alternative-music videos. These codes are evident across a wide range of alternative-music videos but are not always readily discerned or examined for an understanding of their hidden strategies. To locate the recurrence of these repeating codes is to gain greater understanding of the strategic employment of the technology. Four processes (methods or practices) act as signs: the faulty camera, experiential absurdities, digitized sound and video interface, and camera, screen and set aberrations.

"Faulty camera" describes three technological acts. First, it refers to the apparent presence (and use) of a malfunctioning, amateur or home video camera in the actual music video. This strategy is used, for example, in Joan Osborne's "One of Us", Deep Blue Something's "Breakfast at Tiffany's" and Bush's "Glycerine". In "Glycerine", the camera flickers, falters on occasion, so that, for example, within a number of sequences a human figure who sits on a bed is distorted. This is a result of the camera's non-fixity: it does not focus long enough or properly on the human figure. This camera is soon replaced, but the faulty shot returns. The second technological act is the startling precision of the camera – recurring amazing close-up shots of usually unnoticeable objects. For example, in Bush's "Glycerine" the camera suddenly focuses up close on a tiny butterfly. In Collective Soul's "The World I Know", city people mingle with heavy traffic on the way to work, and the camera unexpectedly centres a shoot of grass growing from a crack in the traffic's turf. Smashing Pumpkins' "Bullet with Butterfly Wings" presents an unexpected change of weather from drought to a close-up edit of a little pool of water. The third component of the faulty-camera process is the strategic locating of the camera by the video's subjects. In Oasis's "Wonderwall", Liam Gallagher sits in a chair and throws a self-conscious gaze, finding the camera and peering into it. This is a method used in other genres of music video, but alternative-rock productions make stark use of it. In "The World I Know", the vocalist peers down through the dark interstices of a sewer cover on the street in search of the camera. This deliberate practice of fixing on the technology, like the others referred to above, reflects a self-conscious method, calling attention to the act of creation. Because of this self-conscious referencing, audiences tend to perceive many alternative-music videos as obvious re-creations. To many viewers, these videos are obviously not the "true-true" reality.

Experiential absurdities are numerous in the alternative-music video genre. This refers to a variety of directorial techniques that can make audiences question the plausibility of film or sound events on the screen. The audience carries out this questioning because of the absurd presence of sound or video or both in an experientially discursive frame. For example, in the video for "Lump", the director, Roman Coppola, positions the band members of the band in a swamp with growing marsh plants and knee-deep water in which they play their electric instruments. They are also given microphones, along with a full complement of sound-reinforcement bins and speakers. The sight of musicians in a marsh is itself cause for wonder, but even more problematic is their playing in the domain of impossibility and peril. We know that the instruments the musicians play in this video are not acoustic instruments and so rely on an electrical power source. The presence of water thus highlights the incredulity of this occurrence. The music video's sound is untarnished, and the viewer must reconcile this anomaly. That is, given the technical problems associated with producing "clean" sound in such a water-logged environment, we must interrogate the production's representation of a pristine soundtrack, working in tandem with the video track, this sound which the filmic track professes to produce. It becomes clear that the video track and the soundtrack are in some relationship of conflict: the synchronization of film and sound must be interrogated in this discursive arrangement. Because of the disharmony and tension they share, they call greater attention to larger issues. Because we know that the occurrences presented to us are not experientially plausible, we search for the source of their construction. This leads us to the technology: we discover that it is technology that manipulates the overall setup of the music video. It is technology that calls attention to its own presence. The audience beholds the directorial control of this performance/production.

Attention is drawn to technology similarly in other music videos. In Oasis's "Wonderwall", directed by Nigel Dick, band members play with straight faces on carpenter saws. But the soundtrack does not bear out this visual representation. Audiences must fall back on their suspicion that technology is at work. Like "Lump", Smashing Pumpkins' "Bullet with Butterfly Wings" features the trio performing in a Holocaust-type workspace, a ditch, soon to be a mass grave. There is a full complement of sound-reinforcement gear. Because the audience knows this is not a credible environment for the production of the work's soundtrack, they suspect the hidden presence of technological directives. Alice in Chains' "Grind" presents a similar, anachronistic representation, only this time the music is produced from the arena of ancient coliseums, long before electrified sound was possible.

While this kind of video and sound absurdity forces audiences to gaze upon the technology and serves to create distance between the actors (their world in the videos) and the audience (and their world), there are other music video practices which invite the gaze, but as a result of video and sound collaboration or unity. The most obvious evidence of the technological collusion of sound and video takes place during the guitar solos of a number of alternative-music videos. In the Red Hot Chilli Peppers' "My Friends", the guitar solo seems to take the song into a frantic overdrive. Explosive snare drums and an hypnotic bass are interfaced with heightened visual effects. There is a much faster flicker of visual images. Sound and video seem to be synchronized, each reflecting the other, in the same way that the modern method of linking sound instruments through musical instrument digital interface (MIDI) produces a system wherein separate instruments operate in tandem, by way of a single controller. This process also occurs, but is less pronounced, in Joan Osborne's "One of Us", Green Day's "Brain Stew/Jaded" and Oasis's "Wonderwall". The recurrence of this synchronized process highlights the collaborative involvement of image and sound devices that construct the music video. The audience recognizes this collusion of media. It is technology at work.

Screen and set aberrations are often created by encoding unconventional colours as part of the world in which the music video is situated. For example, in "Brain Stew/Jaded", a hazy green colour is encoded onto the video. In "My Friends", the dominant colour is a dull grey-gold. In "Bullet with Butterfly Wings", the colour is an ashy grey-blue. And in "Wonderwall", black and white give way to the distinctive colouration of selected objects in bright fluorescent tones. In this video, a guitar is at times a very deep blue, as is a band member's hat. Guitars are also coated black, then yellow. The encoding and frequency of these surrealistic colour tones points to a degree of technological gratification. These music videos are thereby inscribed as re-creations of a culture, not as "true-true" presentations of that culture.

The Dance Hall as Caribbean Space

Technology does not bring attention to itself in many of the music videos of Caribbean artists under study here, as it tends to do in the alternative-music genre. The Caribbean music video assumes the anonymity and absence of technology in order to foreground the fallacy of full presence, or "true-true" reality about the world which it creates as the Caribbean. In the absence of a technological focus in Caribbean music videos, the gaze fixes on other constituents of the music-video text. In technology's absence, audiences are asked to believe that the constructions within many Caribbean music videos are not re-creations but "true-true" experience. And, ultimately, what some key music videos make available to unsuspecting audiences worldwide is an X-rated and predominantly unfavourable presentation of Caribbean culture.

An assessment of a wide range of "international" music videos in several genres of music in the mid- to late-1990s reveals their difference from each other. At the production level, music videos in the popular reggae-style of dancehall were not given as much technological attention as those in other genres, such as alternative rock or rhythm and blues. In many instances, reggae videos did not appear to be as professionally done. They also tended to be much more realist than others in the rebel-music categories of rap and alternative rock. An important question must be, why is this so?

It is obvious that alternative music has a much bigger and more established market, hence it attracts bigger production. Video networks such as the Caribbean Satellite Network (CSN) and, later, the Caribbean *Rhythm Express* programme required reasonable broadcast quality for videos to be aired, but the budgets of many of those shown in the mid-1990s and early 2000s came in at well under US$3,000. Caribbean music styles were regarded as fringe expressions, and, as they evolved in the 1990s, the music industry treated them as such. Artists and record companies in turn responded to this perception. It was therefore not prudent to overspend on production and promotion, since market share was limited. As a result, a set of formulaic practices developed around music videos. The shaping of Caribbean music videos rested on the economics of production marketing. But, in another sense, the fashioning of these music videos revealed the semiotics of production marketing.

Dancehall music video's most telling weakness has been not an absence of economic capital input but the absence of a creative focus. Creative input has been replaced by formulaic process. Sexually suggestive video frames have ruled. Alternative-music video privileges technological creativity (and gratification). It is on the technology that audiences are made to fix, and audiences are, as a result, more readily aware of technology's presence and of its mediating role. Alternative-music audiences are therefore able to account for alternative-music video's aberrations as attributable to the technology. The dancehall music video, in contrast, tends to privilege other aspects of the work. Because of the absence of this technology and other creative devices in dancehall – marked by the relative sparseness of post-production techniques – audiences must find fulfilment through other means. But the stark realism of dancehall music videos is, paradoxically, also responsible for the masking of technology's true presence and its hidden agenda.

In examining aspects of selected music videos of dancehall artists signed to major labels, we will focus on the ways in which these videos misrepresent Caribbean culture in the global domain and on the tendency of foregrounding the setting of the actual dance hall and an X-rated culture (through the play of bodies, with the female as "eye-full" presence). To examine how this is done at the first level of observation as well as beneath the surface, reveals the process which is, in effect, in spite of the perceived absence of technology is to confront the ideology which hides further behind the camouflaged technology. Ultimately, it is clearer to observe how the music-video format further situates the Caribbean as subordinate and its artists as puppets. The relationship that the region shares with the international music industry is one wherein the region's artists and culture continue to be manipulated by global economic and cultural imperatives: the process of cultural ventriloquism.

Many of the videos of reggae's superstars of the 1990s are set in the ghetto or 'hood and in the dance hall. In fact, if it is possible to suggest that the recurring setting for the alternative-music video is a transfixed surrealistic world created through colour coding and filmic aberrations, then the recurring setting for dancehall videos is a dilapidated space, one which often houses bouts of "slackness" for the duration of the production. Much in the same way that modernist fiction in the early twentieth century marked a break with the realist tendencies of more traditional literature, the rock video created a set of non-realist practices which it celebrated during its monopoly of MTV. But music-video productions of major dancehall acts remained strategically locked in the realist mode. This is not necessarily a point of concern. The concern rather is with the nature of this realism, which has persistently stuck to limited ways of representing Caribbean culture.

Bounty Killer's "Benz and Bimma", for example, begins with little build up or subtleties, such as one notices in other genres. In "Benz and Bimma", there is little or no self-conscious play with the technology. Very little is hidden from the audience, who are thrown immediately into the middle of a claustrophobic bar with men and women huddled together.

Whereas an alternative-music video such as Deep Blue Something's "Breakfast at Tiffany's" typically builds up an introduction to the video's central performance space (in this case, on an expansive lawn), "Benz and Bimma" begins in a tightly woven space, returns there throughout the video and ends there. Shabba Ranks's "Shine Eye Gal" is given a similar setting, as is his "Ting-a-Ling", Chaka Demus and Pliers' "Murder She Wrote", Terra Fabulous's "Gansta Anthem" and Patra's "Think". A careful further analysis of the semiotics of this positioning of Caribbean artists reveals a type of filmic pleasure attendant upon the act. To an audience displaced from the "true-true" realities of Caribbean society, these videos present an apparently transparent and one-track vision of the islands and their culture.

X-Rated Culture

In these videos, intrigue and interest are not created through the filmic process in itself. Instead, they seem to be sought after at another level: that of basic response to sensuous or sexual overtones. Hence, in these videos, the audience's attention fixes on the monotonous play of bodies which the camera locates. In the alternative-music domain, there is a similar manipulation of the camera, which on occasion goes in search of an image. But in that music genre, one's attention is focused on the technological source itself as a result of its locating unconventional, inconsequential images (a blade of grass, for example), contrasts which are often out of line with the main focus of the video. In the dancehall genre, the camera rarely lets up as it goes in search of images. The audience's attention does not, as in the alternative-music video, refocus onto the camera or technology itself, because the act of focusing on the female body is not presented as being out of line with anything else that takes place. As a result, this focus represents the norm, the ongoing site of central gratification for many dancehall music videos. Audiences therefore celebrate the pleasure of the body rather than the wizardry of the technology. These two genres are, therefore, both noted for their attempts at finding gratification. Alternative music does this by exploitation of technology; dancehall exploits stereotypes of black and Caribbean cultures.

It is not the male's body that the videos exploit. Only the female body undergoes repeated scrutiny. Many of these videos might be considered as celebrating the freedom of Caribbean women. They could also be said to challenge conservative perceptions of the body and sexuality. Music videos of this period therefore redefined the parameters of Caribbean cultural expression. But the deliberate emphasis on women is also a marketing tool: sex sells in the domain of entertainment and commercial culture. It is also arguable that this open display represents a challenge by women to the claims of authority made by male DJs who rule the industry. In this regard, they drive the interest in contemporary Caribbean dance music. They feature heavily in major music videos. Their names are not widely known, if at all, but their sensuality steals the interest of viewers in many videos, including Shabba Ranks's "Mr Lover Man", Buju Banton's "Make My Day", Patra's "Think" and Lieutenant Stitchie's "Prescription".

In "Make My Day", there are two basic positionings of the female body within the camera's fore- and post-play with its audience. These bodies are either back-left and right of the tall and erect male symbol when he is foregrounded or (mostly) positioned upfront and centre screen. It would be no exaggeration to suggest that this particular video is built around the camera's own play with the female body, which it attempts to pin down with gratifying frequency. This series of interconnected suggestive frames constitutes one layer of the video narrative, presented as in grain with the song's own lyrical focus. That is, the song is about the speaker's "bigging up" the female and her potential to satisfy, so the visual narration privileges the full presence of the female. If one were reading the song backwards, as it were – from video to lyrical text – a more appropriate title for this song might well be "Girls You Make My Day": the camera's attempt to locate one subject who embodies the soundtrack's insistence on *girl* falters, but it produces an extended sequence of suggestive frames featuring *girls* in swimwear and cycling shorts.

The illusive nature of the body image can be read as representing the alluring possibility of sexual fulfilment. This expectation is often deferred. The interplay of soundtrack and video track is central to this process of defining the relationship between contending agencies – between men and women and between viewers and actors. Shabba Ranks's "Mr Lover Man" begins with a sultry sample of a female voice repeating the song's refrain, "Mr Lover Man . . . ." The camera goes in search of this sound source, which is voiced off-screen, and attempts to locate it by focusing on a number of women in swimwear, who are brought on- and off-screen. It is the audience, therefore, who interacts with a trailer load of women's bodies, even before the main act begins to chant the song. This foreplay of video and sound clips dramatizes the tense relationship between sound and video in the genre. It also plays out aspects of the relationship between the genders. For some viewers, this initial tease sets the tone for the rest of the music video, which features the sexual exploits of the hardcore male lover, Shabba Ranks.

Patra's "Pull Up to My Bumper" apotheosizes the body – the woman's body. Patra is seductive in presentation. Her flesh is laid bare. It is repeatedly located as centre shot. Indeed, her corporal presence is assumed from beginning to the ending of the music video, and there are few other filmic feats of note. In a recurring scene, Patra performs as if on stage with a single microphone still on its stand. The camera locates her in a wider frontal shot in which the microphone's stand divides her lengthwise down the centre. She caresses the length of the upright device and fondles the head of the actual microphone, which stands hard, upright on the stand. This is a stark symbolic representation. It is made even more suggestive on account of the absence of other filmic or technological diversions. When this scene changes, Patra is located on a sofa with her perpetual lover. They engage in love-play. The next scene focuses on women gyrating their bodies. Next, men kiss their "bumpers". This is the gist of the filmic concentration. The technology presents itself as an innocent bystander to this activity, which it attributes to the dancehall diva herself – to Patra – and to her insignificant others; together they are the embodiment of Caribbean culture.

If these descriptions seem to suggest that little creative thought goes into the production of many music videos of Caribbean dancehall artists of international fame, then this is exactly so. It is evident that different genres of music have their own conventions of production in the music video domain. It is these tropes and conventions which help to identify them in the marketplace. Since the entertainment industry is built upon well-defined categories and clearly marked genres of expression, the various entities within the industry are careful to conform to the conventions inscribed by the major players. But having said this, it is also true that the industry is driven by some degree of creative interpretation and innovation. Caribbean hardcore genres such as dancehall and soca are not sufficiently built on presenting and representing the diversity of Caribbean cultural expression; creative innovation is not their hallmark. They have repeatedly fallen back upon stock realist modes of displaying Caribbean cultural expression, asking the world to take it as it is. In alternative-music video, one is aware (and made to be aware) of the technology which is mediating the discourse – this discourse of which the video is a product. This awareness has a way of situating the actual music video as an artistic representation: the audience is asked to be conscious that this is a music video, a re-creation of "real" life and not life itself. This is done by self-conscious manipulation of the media's technologies. Thus, the alternative-music video tends to reveal the heavy impact of filmic editing, of special effects and other absurdities. Dancehall videos, in contrast, do not call attention to this process, so two deceptive perceptions are formulated. First, these videos tend to convey the sense that what is being presented (on-screen) has not been mediated by technology. Since many viewers formulate their impressions of cultures through popular media, these videos are powerful simulations. Second, this kind of presentation has the effect of concealing the ideology which hides behind the technology that produces the music video and hence controls the discourse – an ideology that is largely the product of the large record companies that have played an important role in shaping the content of music videos.33

The visual component of many of these music videos does not enhance the image of the Caribbean in the global arena. It is possible that the application of the image to this Caribbean export is potentially more damaging to the region's cultural identity than cultural critics are willing to concede. The further dissemination of these texts within the international domain perpetuates a long-standing myth about the physical potency of blacks. Some critical observers, such as Robert Walser, consider the excessive focus on the body to be a marketing tool of the industry.34 This is certainly so. But it becomes much clearer, on deeper analysis, that the objectives of major global interests are potentially more insidious than some people imagine.

At the end of the 1990s, there was little change to this formula for presenting the music video and representing Caribbean place and space. Super Cat's "Girlstown", for instance, which aired quite frequently on BET, upheld the standard for the dancehall video text at the turn of the new century. Super Cat's popularity had remained relatively constant throughout the 1990s. In the late 1990s, he went to Sony/Columbia Records. His "Girlstown" music video, as with all his videos, features Super Cat as the extra cool "don dada". He performs in a semi-posh nightclub, engulfed by "world-o-girls" who surround and caress him while he sings, almost oblivious to their presence. This is the video's main preoccupation. But, unlike other videos, this one tries to weave a subplot. In this subplot, a young fellow pursues an illusive, enticing woman. This gives the video much-needed purpose and direction, since otherwise, it is hardly more than a warmed-over re-enactment of 1990s ritual. But the subplot is merely that – secondary to the video's central concern with its star. The video is about sexual prowess and posturing.

Throughout the video, Super Cat is positioned at the centre of the catwalk. The women clamour to the left and right to be positioned next to him. Although they are repeatedly filmed as swarming him, the production clearly maintains the sharp distinction between him and all others. This distance is marked by the positioning of the supporting cast, who are down from and below him, off the catwalk where he poses and postures. He is object of their desire. The women reach for him. The camera's play with the women's bodies is not as excessive, however, as in other, earlier dancehall music videos. The camera zooms in and out while fixing on a woman's body, but these shots are not sustained long enough to satisfy the gaze. In a significant reversal of the 1990s formula, "Girlstown" treats the dancehall don as its object of greatest desire. Given Super Cat's chic demeanour and sophisticated persona, it is understandable that his marketing strategy has sought to supplant the male gaze with that of the female.

Mr Vegas's music video "Heads High" is less creative than Super Cat's "Girlstown". There is little filmic narrative intrigue. Instead, the viewer must make deeper sense of the play of bodies and their subordination to the director's control. Whereas Super Cat is the epitome of poise, Mr Vegas merely gestures to importance in the video. The video production is constructed around the dance-party motif. Mr Vegas's function in the production does not appear to have been sufficiently carved out and defined. Though dance moves are choreographed, the central performer appears somewhat out of place, thrown into the production by the director without full briefing about the video's overall dynamics. The director's placing of him in and out of the video's sequenced routines reinforces the disconnection of the performer from the tools of the trade, such tools as the music industry requires for active participation in the global entertainment culture. Mr Vegas's exaggerated antics are a memorable feature of this very popular music video. Arguably, this is what the video wanted to achieve; music videos are often constructed with the premise that some memorable signature within them can ensure lingering impact. In that respect, therefore, "Heads High" succeeds. Audiences would remember the camera's close-up shots of Vegas. They would certainly recall, in the same frame that captures his face, carefully placed gyrating hips and waistlines. All this is captured as the music video progresses to its climax, when Mr Vegas beats his chest in uninhibited glee. Nonetheless, although this was the dominant tendency in music videos of some artists signed to big labels, there were many more acts whose videos did not conform to this stereotype. I Jah Bones's "One Love in a Jah House", Yami Bolo's "Too Much Blood Stain" and Capleton's "Never Get Down" are some of the videos which wrestled with the formula.

From the mid-1990s, Caribbean television carried the popular music video programme *Rhythm Express*. Hosted by the affable Philomena Roberts, it showcased recent music videos by leading artists in calypso, soca, reggae, dancehall and other styles. Indeed, the roster of successive shows reveals the many artists whose music videos explored other, creative visual and aural narratives. These were not all dancehall acts; they included I Jah Bones, Beres Hammond, 4de People and Morgan Heritage. Some artists who resisted stereotypical conventions and overtly sexist motifs are known to have some power over their videos. For example, Eddy Grant has made the point that he has always sought to have some control over his music videos.[35] But, admittedly, not too many artists now aspiring to international stardom can sway the intentions of their new labels and promotion managers. Since it is felt that genre formulas in video are already set, production companies and directors working in consort with record companies are convinced that their task is to work within these parameters. Unfortunately, this process has contributed to the recycling of straight-up, realist productions. Since the productions are apparently transparent re-creations of Caribbean place, culture and space, they uphold a limited set of ways of seeing the region.

The music video is not merely a tool of entertainment. More than this, it is a medium of possibility. For some people it is the central medium by which they gain access to other cultures. Since this process is vested with so much potential, it is important to begin to understand how it is also loaded with cultural politics. The creation of music videos is also by extension the creation of ideological statement. Accompanying the projection of sound and images there is always an underlying ideology, more overtly expressed in some videos than in others. This is one reality of global popular-culture production and dissemination, and Caribbean artists are a part of this wider global politics of cultural manipulation. Like other aspiring artists around the world, some Caribbean artists appear to be at the mercy of the entertainment industry and its controllers who pull the strings while masking their own industry-driven imperatives and ideologies.

Clear and Present Virtual Realities

If music television represented the frontier of entertainment broadcasting in the 1980s, then the late 1990s and the beginning of the twenty-first century found new expression through other means and media. Movies such as *Run Lola Run* celebrated late 1990s post-MTV film and video aesthetics. The film was a music-driven, technologically self-conscious work, reflective of new trends in entertainment production. In this phase, music television, as conceived in the 1980s, underwent radical transformation. The Internet surfaced as a viable medium for facilitating mass participation within and consumption of popular culture. Video on demand, interactive programming, additional music television channels and closer interlocking of the music and film industries refashioned the old ways of thinking about music and video. Industry dynamics and consolidation also brought new practices and realities to light. Mergers such as that between America Online (AOL) and Time Warner in 2000 signalled that the industry was poised to maximize the returns from interfacing the film and news industry with computer technology. DVD audio format was developed to take advantage of the proliferation of DVD players and multichannel surround sound. Technology companies moved to position themselves at the centre of the entertainment industry. Sony's purchase of Capitol and its ownership of Sony Pictures (including Columbia Pictures) reflected the intention of companies. In 2003, Apple was in talks to purchase the world's largest record company, Universal Music. The antitrust saga in the United States surrounding the computer giant Microsoft anticipated the new wars that would be fought in and for cyberspace. Media platforms jostled for supremacy of the streaming audio and video formats.³⁶ Microsoft's Windows Media, RealNetworks' RealPlayer and Apple's QuickTime shared honours in hosting Caribbean videos on the Web. The Internet, wireless technologies, MP3, and mobile and other hybrid gadgetry sounded the effective decline of more conventional ways of expressing, experiencing and exploring popular phenomena.

By the end of the twentieth century, some of the formulaic patterns established in dancehall music videos throughout the 1990s still remained. By 2003, major record labels still showed interest in dancehall acts. In October 2002, Atlantic Records signed a worldwide deal with leading dancehall/reggae label VP Records. The deal meant that Atlantic assumed responsibility for the international marketing of leading dancehall acts. Some of those bundled to Atlantic were Sean Paul, Lady Saw, Tanto Metro and Devonte, Beres Hammond, Capleton and T.O.K. The music video for Sean Paul's 2002 smash hit "Gimme the Light" received quite heavy rotation on MTV and BET but does not challenge the formula of 1990s dancehall music videos in terms of visual emphasis on women's bodies. The music video for Wayne Wonder's "No Letting Go" also hugs the stereotype. On show at Atlantic Records Web site (http://www.atlantic records.com), under the category called "world music/reggae", the video aptly enacts the song's love theme through a captivating interplay of the sexes and on the lovely beaches of what must be the Caribbean.

Although the overall formula of the dancehall music video has remained intact, there have been changes – the genre has not remained static in all respects. Some recent productions reveal the extent to which the music video in the post-2000 era has evolved. The Sean Paul's "Gimme the Light" appears much more streamlined than videos of the previous decade. Sean Paul's image is also responsible for the overall effect and style of the production. Like Super Cat before him, he is a smooth-looking, cool, dapper DJ. Unlike many other videos of the 1990s, this video does not convey the rough, gritty feel of the Caribbean's "dungle" (a term coined by Kamau Brathwaite in the poem "Wings of a Dove", meaning "dark suburban jungle"). It is well shot and edited, and its set is not the standard run-down yard but a soundstage or small video set, the setting used by many hip-hop artists from Missy Elliot to Busta Rhymes. The production sets the action on a suspended catwalk where Sean Paul shares the stage with a motley crew of brightly dressed, skimpily clad women, who perform choreographed routines to the camera. The video does not ultimately come across as a trashy commercial product; its apparently large production budget attempts to salvage it from that category of videos. Of significance, though, is the realization that in productions like this, the boundaries are being breached. Like Shabba Ranks and Patra before him, Sean Paul's elevation to just left of mainstream anticipated his excursion into other musical genres. These post-dancehall productions were a reminder that Caribbean culture was ever changing as it came into contact with other phenomena. In the same way that soca's boundaries were challenged throughout the 1990s, dancehall had also gone through changes. Acts such as Shabba Ranks, Patra, Beenie Man and Bounty Killer had taken the genre to new heights, especially through their collaborations with artists in hip hop and other hardcore genres outside of dancehall proper. Dancehall was now post-, as was hip hop.

Market research in the United States shows that many more people feel the computer is the medium of the present and future and suggests that young people who view products on the Internet are more inclined to purchase them than are those people who see them on conventional media.[37] Record companies took notice of this research and invested time effort and money in promoting their wares on the Internet. In August 2003, VP Records splashed across their home page a sign that read "LOOK OUT FOR ELEPHANT MAN'S NEW VIDEO: PON de RIVER PON de BANK". Though predictable in its interpretation of the dancehall reality, the video, like many others at the time, captured the energy of dancehall and of the black experience and gained favourable rotation on BET. On another site, the video stream of Beenie Man's "Feel It Boy", featuring Janet Jackson, accentuates a number of stereotypes. Because of the thinning of the stream and freezing of video, stock features are even more foregrounded: scantily clad natives, leisure activity on the beach, coconut trees, fruit-eating locals and blank-faced Rastafari. Shaggy's Web video "Hey Sexy Lady" cast images of the solo act in the company of women who adore him. In this respect it was similar to Super Cat's "Girlstown". Even more than Super Cat, Shaggy represented good looks and charm; he seemed to carry little ideological baggage. But his sense of humour and wit helped to define his image within post-dancehall culture. The 2002 Web video to his flamenco/orchestral/hip hop/reggae song "Hey Sexy Lady" accentuated his crossover ambitions. The production quality of the video distanced it from some other videos of the mid-1990s. Despite the shortcomings of streaming video, the production held together through a set of recurring colour and character motifs. Its introductory frames promised to weave an engaging narrative. The camera pans across a sleepy looking rural town. It zooms in on the doors of a saloon. Two female hosts open the door to greet viewers. The singer utters the word "sexy" and the rest of the video is devoted to the singers and their support cast of women dancers.

Lady Saw's video (also broadcast on the Net) "I Don't Need to Know", from the 1997 VP Records album *Passion*, proved it was indeed possible to break the stereotypes in some respects. The video features the artist alone; the only "props" are her dazzling outfits and shifting backdrops. Ce'Cile's MPEG-format video "Hot Gal", featuring Lady Saw and Mad Anju, was hailed at Rudegal.com as a "quality video shot in Jamaica",[38] but its download at that site did not do justice to the promotion. Surfers on such sites were forced to compensate for the limitations of technology. Because of the broadcast quality it was difficulty to grasp the full definition of the video's glam-clad women. But since the music video revolved around established visual motifs, navigators were able to fill in the missing parts.

Beenie Man's first major signing, his 2000 *Art and Life* on Virgin Records, featuring collaborations with Steve Perry, Wyclef Jean and Redman, revealed a wide range of influences from rock, hip hop, rhythm and blues, and Latin music, reflecting the creative marketing direction of the industry. The album was therefore difficult to locate in terms of its appeal and ideology. This work, though not the first of its kind, became increasingly popular and began to open up a new space in terms of artistic, aesthetic and commercial expression. The VP/Atlantic deal was a recognition that dancehall had gone through significant reconfiguration: it was now decidedly post-dancehall. Sean Paul therefore collaborated freely with Jay-Z and Busta Rhymes on the tracks "What They Gonna Do" and "Make It Clap" respectively. The extent of collaboration, fusion and cultural overdubbing was marked by the confusion displayed by people within the industry who were marketing performers such as Shaggy, Elephant Man and even Kevin Lyttle as rap, hip hop, and rhythm and blues acts.

In the same way that dancehall was now post-, hip hop, through its renewed interface with dancehall and other genres, was also being transformed. The post–hip-hop era was also being fashioned through a set of experiments and through commercial and technological developments. Sean Paul's second video release, "Get Busy", from his album *Dutty Rock,* was marred while being filmed in Canada when a youth was killed near the set. Though not directly related, the incident was a reminder of the close relationship between dancehall and hip hop and seemed to portend that hip hop's ongoing saga of lyrical play and gunplay was not too distant from happenings within segments of dancehall culture. The subsequent showing of Sean Paul's video on the Internet upheld stark stock images of hip-hop/dancehall video and signalled the future blurring of genres: Cadillac's SUV Escalade, big designer coats, a well-packed venue, bling bling (jewellery), tightly clad women, close-up body shots.

It is clear that the music video phenomenon has changed worldwide. When music television was created two decades ago, television and then cable television were the dominant media through which viewers could access the latest videos. By the end of the twentieth century, there were signs that the computer would challenge the pride of place of the dedicated television set. The advent, demise and rebirth of free music-swapping sites such as Napster foreshadowed the challenge that the music industry would face in the immediate future. In June 2001, it was announced that Napster had signed a deal with three of the world's major record companies, allowing Napster clients access to more than half of the mainstream music of those companies for a fee. But other legal and illegal sites surfaced, and the industry continued to fight. What became evident to those involved in the industry was that the new technology of the Internet stood poised to reconfigure models of the relationship between creators, producers and audiences, models that have been instituted by major players in the music industry.

For many artists, therefore, the Internet and cyberculture have become a space wherein greater creative and commercial freedom can be exhibited. Caribbean cyberculture has tapped into this new mainstream, where other global artists and practitioners are also at work and play. The traditional music video is therefore not only experienced on the dedicated television set, but is now also streamed over the Internet. Since many computer users do not have the capacity to quickly download large multimedia files, they turn to audio and video streaming, the process whereby data is transferred from a source to the user's plug-in or computer on a continuous stream. Because there are many sites that offer the possibility of sharing sound and video clips with anybody who cares to listen or view them, Caribbean and other artists have begun to explore streaming music video. Major record labels also provide this facility for some of the artists on their rosters, although some artists feel that major labels are not as good as smaller hosts at maintaining dedicated Web pages. Because of the challenges of policing the Internet, it has become relatively easy to access sound and video clips of artists from the Caribbean, leading and not. Given the quirky nature of non-commercial everyday video streaming, some industry people and artists do not accord high status to it. Broadband offers the potential for better quality and easier access, but broadband cable, DSL and satellite technology are not yet widely distributed. Nonetheless, in spite of these limitations, many Caribbean youths and other cyberculture participants now experience the music videos of Caribbean artists through the computer, over the Internet.

Sites such as RealVibes.net and MTV.com provide access to leading artists. But sites have also sprung up to promote events, fêtes and bashments. They often feature video clips of artists' live performance but seem to thrive on showing clips featuring the audience. Web streaming has therefore grown in popularity partly because it supports a number of underground shows. The ordinary patron has become an active participant in video clips. Since video clips are in many cases low-tech streams, they conceal the full identity of people in the crowd. Their gritty feel is in keeping with the raw, uncensored cut of many Caribbean festive parties. The best streaming videos are often transmitted as blotchy, jerky and badly produced clips when the data being transmitted does not transfer fast enough. Regardless, Web sites such as RudeGal.com and the Bahamian Society (http://www.angelfire.com/wi3/bahama/v203/music .html) promote older and cutting-edge videos by artists such as Sizzla, Degree, Ce'Cile and Spragga Benz as downloads and streams. There are still many niggling technical problems associated with Internet music video, but, in spite of this imperfection, cyberculture embraces the limitations, making do with what technology has to offer. Videos on the computer are consumed with full knowledge that the challenges posed to their new medium of consumption will be surmounted in the near future. In the interim, many artists, companies and consumers use streaming video as a support for the other, better-established facilities by which the stars of popular culture are accessed. Record companies and leading-edge artists throughout the Caribbean have steadily vested interest in sound and video clips since they know that this creates buzz among fans and the buying public.

Cybertheory and cybercriticism have only just begun to understand the ideological politics of cultural fashioning on the Internet. Whereas individual artists might delight in the supposed democratic set-up of the Internet, it is vital to remember that even in cyberspace, ideological and cultural confrontation and negotiation are taking place. Unless individual artists have some measure of control over their Web site and its material, they face the danger of standing outside of their own construction. There is potentially much more control over a dedicated site put up with the sanction and directive of the individual artist. But there are sites that promote a bundled set of artists and genres, as does the commercial yet informative Artists Only! Records site, http://www.artistsonly.com. Artists Only! Records is careful in its treatment and presentation of artists affiliated with the label, but some other sites of this kind are much more prone to error, especially if their objective is out-and-out commercial. Sites that host a range of signed artists have the propensity to construct layers of encumbered information through which users must navigate before they can access an artist of choice. These layers also have the tendency to conceal aspects of an artist's individuality since the Web site is constructed on the premise of shared cultural, artistic, philosophical or ideological values. On the Atlantic Records Web site, for example (as accessed on 19 March 2003), the dancehall fan must circumnavigate the front page, which announces the return of Hootie and the Blowfish, then go to the section called "Genres" and scroll to the bottom of the rung for the category "World/Reggae"; they can thereafter locate a limited number of elite acts, including Sean Paul and Wayne Wonder, then read about their status and popularity and have access to audio and video clips. This virtual positioning often mirrors what takes place in the real world. At the 2004 Grammy Awards, Lady Saw was placed so far away from the action that she could not make it to the stage to celebrate her collaboration with the Southern California punk/ska band No Doubt. She could only exclaim from a distance, "I'm here!" Her name was also not listed on the official Grammy Web site as a contributor.

Whereas the conventional music video has managed to mask the presence of technology as a vital constituent in the construction of some Caribbean videos in the 1990s, the advent of video webcasting does not achieve this as successfully. Because of the embryonic state of this medium, Internet technology's faulty virtual reproduction of the music video foregrounds the active presence of the technology. Does this therefore mean that audiences who encounter Caribbean culture on the Internet via Web streaming are better placed to recognize the role of technology and production politics or ideology in music videos? Given the current dependence on technology for getting the music video right and for transmitting it in real time, audiences are bound to view the video stream more critically. They are bound to be troubled when their attempts to consume seamless Caribbean music video turns up jerky tracks of data and they are forced to behold the process that attempts to transmit representational tracks of Caribbean experience. Whereas the more trendy youthful audiences and cyberfiends have negotiated this technological handicap, many other viewers or hearers come face to face with the imperfections of Web filmic/video simulation. This experience has in some cases brought about interrogation of the computer, entertainment and multimedia, and the entertainment industry has therefore come under greater scrutiny – there are now many more debates about the music industry, its intentions and capabilities.

Though Web streaming has failed to totally capture the music-video market, it has sought ways of collaborating with more traditional media. Music and video on the Internet are not an end in themselves. The Internet provides hyperlinks to other sites and sources that audiences can access, some of them also found in the real world of commerce. For example, although most major Caribbean acts provide access to their wares online, they also give clear directions for reaching them at "hard" addresses and locations in the Caribbean and abroad. The ongoing reliance on more traditional methods of practising culture emphasizes the relative distance between past, present and future cutting-edge technologies. Even given the apparent limitations of Web technology in the early twenty-first century, video streaming can be said to gesture towards a process of simulation rather than of representation, drawing the viewer more readily into confronting the technological process and its accompanying politics, which lurk somewhere in the machine, trying to fit it and to get it right, so that some day there would be a near-seamless play between the real and the virtual worlds.

The "Big Technology" Question

"What is this gadget?"
– Brian Gooding, a young musician

Who We Is, Where Technologies Are

Music technology has made such an impact on Caribbean music and culture that it has proven a burdensome task for musicians to keep up with the latest gadgets and instruments. In the music industry there are basically two types of music-instrument users: One gets to know them by their reactions on seeing state-of-the-art music instruments and gadgets. There are those who pretend to be abreast of *all* new developments and who pose their questions about the technology in silence. Then there are the others who openly express their surprise when confronted by leading edge wizardry, who voice their awe and excitement loudly: "What is this big technology!"

The last two decades of the twentieth century and the early years of the twenty-first have witnessed intriguing developments in musical instruments themselves and in their application. Caribbean music owes great debt to the radical advances in state-of-the art musical-instrument technology. Since the region and its criticism have not yet meaningfully surveyed and interrogated this technology to keep up with developments, I will both pose and respond to the big technology question here.

This book claims to explore issues that are in some respect on the cutting edge, but I have not attempted to misguide readers into thinking that all cutting-edge phenomena are related to high-tech culture. I have also been suggesting, especially through aspects of calypso history and development, that there are many linkages between past and present phenomena. In spite of the fact that many observers think of Caribbean music as moving linearly – forever away from its past – this is not always the case. This is a flawed perception of how music and music genres exist and develop. New technologies are still very much dependent on pre-existing ways of doing things. Even as Caribbean music goes forwards, it is also always in many ways referencing the past. This referencing is noticeable through lyrics, performance and sound. Because Caribbean societies generally tend to segment what is "popular" from what is "traditional" or "folk", music culture practices have also tended to uphold this division. But the traditional and the popular are not necessarily opposites or even at odds with each other. Indeed, the Caribbean music industry would benefit greatly from the connection of its popular music arm to the "traditional", even folk, roots. In another ten years, when society looks back on itself, it will possibly feel a little embarrassed at how our current musical styles, once at the cutting edge, have become passé. Just as the traditional and the popular are relative – and related in time – so definitions of what constitutes the cutting edge are relative. It is perhaps more accurate to talk of the "former cutting edge" and the "present cutting edge".

Caribbean societies have in the past evolved with a clearly defined sense of binary opposites. That is, within the English-speaking Caribbean (and the wider region as well), there is a tendency to clearly conceptualize issues as "either/or". This dual mode of operating has filtered into every sphere; it has even affected the way the society has viewed its cultural material. I have already alluded, for example, to the division between the secular and the religious within music culture. This type of separation does have some basis in Caribbean history, in the divisive forces that fought for the power to define the region for themselves, but it is not the only way of seeing things.

Interestingly, as the region moved into the twenty-first century, external forces still continued to affect the Caribbean's way of seeing. In the late twentieth century, Western philosophy and key institutions propagated the pleasures of plurality, hybridity and "in-betweenness" as desirable traits. These tenets were also locked up in "new world order" initiatives. They continue to be enshrined in various ways in World Trade Organization, the United Nations and other global institutions. But in the first decade of the twenty-first century, Caribbean society has had to make sense of its own existence. It is faced with the challenge of remaining distinctive in its expression of selfhood, but at the same time it cannot ignore the growing impact of external phenomena. It is clear that there can be no turning back, no wholesale return to old ways of being and knowing. There has to be a partial acceptance, at least, of new ways of self-fashioning.

Caribbean culture at the turn of the twenty-first century has already gone through two decades in which its cultural practitioners came under immense pressure to handle First World technology. Since the early 1980s, its musicians have had to learn the music industry's gadgetry. Then they have had to learn to manipulate this technology to suit their own distinctive cultural needs. Arguably, there is no other grouping that has had to constantly and consistently negotiate cutting-edge technology more than the musicians who operated in the analogue-to-digital-to-virtual-analogue revolution from the early 1980s to today. However, this aspect of Caribbean culture has hardly been documented or consistently assessed over the years. The way in which Caribbean culture will or can respond to promised future advances in technology can perhaps best be thought about through an assessment of how its practitioners handled leading-edge music technology in the recent past.

During the past twenty-five years, there has been a great effort by musicians to empower their standing in the entertainment industry by enlisting state-of-the-art technology. But cultural and artistic empowerment does not necessarily exude from the state-of-the-art. Ultimately, "state-of-the-art" derives meaning from the cultural arena which manipulates the technology for its own local purposes. The act of tweaking represents an awareness that technology can be re-engineered and reconfigured. *Tweaking* is an important term in itself. As used in contemporary technical environments, it refers to minute fine-tuning, but it also carries the meaning of technological undermining.[1] One major failing of Caribbean music continues to be the failure to systematically and creatively tweak the technology to harness national and regional sound identities.

Technology and tradition can indeed interface. The perpetuation of tradition is often marked by a culture's reconnection with the past through new technologies. Technology can harness power and bring about change. It also has the potential to propel local and regional culture into the international limelight in ways never before possible. Caribbean artists have therefore invested heavily in technology in hope of success. But another reality is that in spite of the employment of cutting-edge

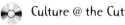

technology, many regional artists will remain unheard: they are part of a larger scramble for power.

Although Caribbean society has become more aware of this last dynamic in recent times, the depth and intensity of this struggle has not always come home to artists. In the late twentieth century, the struggle for control of international markets was akin to trying to get a word in edgewise during a supposed conversation with similarly motivated but more powerful person: passive auditors do not stand a chance in this environment. Caribbean practitioners have therefore to refine and define their "voices" in order to secure power. The region cannot seek to tear its music from ideological roots in this politically charged global set-up; it cannot afford to separate the music from its source of power. Caribbean society also cannot afford to play popular music without grounding it in some philosophy or agenda – there is a source of inspiration that surrounds a national act. It is from this source that creativity and meaning derive. Indeed, it is very difficult to think of committed artists who do not draw from their own realities and experiences. It is these realities which give them the inspiration and power to create. Crowded House, out of New Zealand, for example, explores and exploits Maori myth and Aboriginal hollow, earthy, wooden textures in their compositions, as in the song "Weather with You". Artists who give in to the environment that they inhabit are like inventors, taking the raw material of the society and harnessing its potential. It is instructive how, for example, Jamaican reggae burst out of the nation to become a visible world-music category. The current popularity of many reggae, dancehall and post-dancehall acts cannot be attributed, however, solely to these individuals. Theirs is a legacy that reaches back to mento, Rastafarianism and a history of struggle and cultural assertion.

The Caribbean's success in the international music industry also relies on the development of a shared understanding of what constitutes Caribbean cultural expression. This process has then to be taken further, in a conscious project of harnessing cultural motifs and sounds, and disseminating them not only as music but also as culture and as ideology. Since the region has been so ad hoc with its culture over the years, and since in recent times islands have assumed a superficial mask of revelry, little notice is given to the hidden resources that can fuel a regional culture music engine. These hidden resources include phenomena that define our difference from others (for example, our language and speech).

Those who frown on the notion of connecting with past musical and cultural experience should perhaps be reminded of the retro fever that infected the international music industry in the 1990s. In the United Kingdom, retro has always seemed to be the way forward. Groups such as The Cure and Oasis come to mind here. Rhythm and blues and soul acts such as Whitney Houston, Mariah Carey and Michael Bolton depended on remakes for their success. Sampling was an industry buzzword, especially in hip hop, where artists such as Will Smith, LL Cool J and Puff Daddy (Sean Combs) all rapped over samples of 1970s funk and older hits.

Perhaps Caribbean popular music has not worked steadfastly to exploit the region's soundscape because popular music has had to preoccupy itself with other things. One such preoccupation has been leading-edge music technology. Contemporary music technology has captivated its users, and many Caribbean users have stood in awe of its magnificence as spectators and as passive consumers. They have beheld the power of technology. The 1980s, 1990s and beyond can said to be marked by the struggle of people in the music industry, particularly musicians, to come to terms with the sheer might of musical technology. With them, Caribbean users have spent long periods of time trying to negotiate developments by purchasing state-of-the-art after state-of-the-art technology, and perhaps have not spent enough time analysing, interrogating and dominating this technology, bending it to serve their own purposes. Caribbean cultures are therefore guilty of not tweaking with clear intentions and with ideological motives.

The past twenty or so years have thus been about the application of cutting-edge technology within the regional music project. Indeed, this period represents the most contested moment for control of the region's cultural products, including music. This chapter is founded on the premise that a better understanding of future conflicts over identity, ownership, authenticity and self-fashioning can be grasped through analysis of the ways in which the region's music-instrument users have reacted to the music industry's power gadgets, and how these state-of-the-art gadgets have affected and are affecting the region's music and culture. So, because technology has so mesmerized the region over time, it is a fitting exercise to exorcize our subordination and to look again at some of the technological moments that shaped Caribbean music culture in recent times. One objective will be to point to the specific devices and practices that propelled Caribbean music to greater international attention. With our current knowledge, we can more objectively assess the relationship that the culture shared and now shares with the very technology that shaped the Caribbean soundscape and held Caribbean society in awe over the past twenty or more years.

In this descriptive survey, I do not set out to glorify the technology itself. If I want to achieve anything, it is to introduce readers to some of these instruments and to their role in shaping Caribbean popular music. Although this chapter can therefore stand on its own, it is perhaps more rewarding when read in the context of the book as a whole. This chapter provides fuller description and explanation of some of the gadgetry mentioned in earlier chapters.

Some Technological Moments: Amplification, Amplifiers, Speakers, Power

Electronic musical instruments and audio amplifiers had their beginnings in the early 1900s with radio sets. In the international world of live music performance, sound amplification came into wide usage around the early 1930s. One of the earliest electric instruments to gain acceptance worldwide was the steel string guitar. In the early 1930s, players began to experiment with these, manipulating their volume and tone controls. In the Caribbean, mass utilization of sound amplification came about only in the late 1960s and in the 1970s. Before this, many individual guitar players prided themselves as owners of guitar amplifiers by Fender, Gibson and Marshall. The popularization of reggae, calypso, zouk and other genres hinged on the dissemination of sound and song by live bands, and the concept of the sound system integral to the development of reggae depended on sound amplification, through the use of power amplifiers, self-contained power speakers or both. Many live bands during the 1970s made use of these self-contained power speakers. For the most part, these were powered guitar speakers; that is, they were designed to be used in projecting the sound of the guitar. But the tendency among musicians was to use the guitar amp's two or more inputs to plug in additional instruments as well, so that it was common to see and hear a clustering of many instruments being sounded through a single powered amplifier. Since the wattage of these amplifiers was relatively tame – no more than 150 watts (the output of a conventional boom box) – it meant that system overload was a common headache for many bands. In any case, a speaker designed to carry, say, the six-stringed guitar did not handle well the heavy-weighted booms of the 1970s Gallan bass guitar.

The popularity of dedicated power amplifiers was well established in the Caribbean in the 1980s. Manufacturers such as Peavey, Yamaha, Crown and JBL found their power amps being used by many acts (a dedicated power amp is an amplifier which does not have built-in speakers but whose prime function is to generate power). In the 1980s, musicians and sound DJs also demanded increased wattage to project their heavier, fuller mixes, which were made possible by the advent of multi-track recording. Most amplifiers needed two channels of power supply in order to power two sides of a stereophonic speaker stack. If two sets of electronic speakers were set up in a venue, each side of the amplifier could drive a separate set of speakers. Amplifiers were often required to deliver at least 200 watts per channel in the mid-1980s. By the late 1980s, this had become the lower end of the power amp scale. Peavey therefore popularized a range of amplifiers, in its CS series including the CS400 and the CS1200, which were capable of delivering 210 to 630 watts per channel at four ohms (if their electrical resistance is set at a lower resistance of two ohms, they are capable of delivering twice the power capable at four ohms).

By the end of the century, though, this power wattage represented a modest output level; amplifiers by Crown, JBL and Chevin Research boasted over 3,000 watts per channel. For example, the Chevin A6000 delivered over 3,000 watts of power per channel. Whereas these were some of the brands preferred by sound and band music professionals, music DJs who were into live dance functions preferred the "underground" marketing and sound capabilities nurtured by amp makers such as Gemini Sound Products, Audio Pro and QSC Audio. Most modern amplifiers give soundmen the option of operating in what is called "bridge mode", the sum harnessing of power assigned to separate channels. An amp designed to deliver 630 watts per channel can be bridged to deliver over 1,750 watts of total power. DJs have maximized the use of this function, as have sound engineers at big live shows such as Reggae Sunsplash and national calypso finals such as St Lucia's at the Marshand Grounds, demanding over 50,000 watts of power. Caribbean sound systems have played a vital role in promoting and disseminating Caribbean music. The sound system is credited with having driven reggae, soca and other dance-oriented music. Although sound trucks have been marked by their banners and speaker stacks, the real core of the sound system is the power generator and power amplifier. Beginning in the 1980s, sound systems grew in popularity. Sound companies also ventured into this domain on occasion, as they already had the hardware. Companies such as Trinidad's Rent-A-Amp came into being in the mid-1980s; Rent-A-Amp grew from a small business which rented power amps into a large company which has provided power and other facilities for Charlie's Roots, St Lucia's Jazz Festival, Carifesta in St Kitts and Dominica's World Creole Music Festival.[2]

Industry users in the Caribbean also showed some interest in powered mixing boards, mixing consoles with built-in power amplification. The Peavey XR series in particular has been used quite widely. These powered mixers restrict the need for dedicated amplifiers in some cases, such as in small performance contexts where only 1,000 watts of power were required. Most of these powered boards are not expected to carry power loads for larger shows, with crowds of over two hundred, for example. Yamaha's post-2000 EMX series, for example, provides powered mixers for solo artists, but also for bands and ensembles.

Since the power capacity of amplifiers increased significantly in Caribbean music usage in the last two decades of the twentieth century, it was also necessary that speaker enclosures, which disseminated the sound, be capable of handling the power load produced by these state-of-the art power amplifiers. In the 1980s, therefore, musicians began to demand and make use of specialist and special-purpose speaker systems. Guitar players demanded and used speaker enclosures designed specifically for the guitar; those made by Rane, Fender and Peavey have been popular. Bass guitarists also required a fuller, heavier sound on stage at their backs. Serious cutting-edge performers did away with knee-high, fifteen-inch, single-speaker enclosures, and by the mid-1990s would only be seen playing next to a human-sized double-stacked enclosure which housed multiple speakers ranging from twelve to eighteen inches. Marshall has popularized this look among international bands; in the Caribbean, stage set-ups copied this look. Synthesizer speakers were also in popular usage, especially when the 1980s and 1990s were dominated by the synthesizer workstation.

In addition to the separate demands of independent musical instrument-alists on stage, sound engineers also had demands in live contexts. Their output demands were also the demands of audiences, who began to experience Caribbean music in the live context more often in the late twentieth century. The live concert was central to promotion. Reggae Sumfest and the various carnivals around the region attracted audiences from around the world, and Caribbean promoters had to produce a sound quality on par with live shows in the United States and Europe. This had to be done by stepping up sound quality, making use of sound-enhancement gadgets such as the sonic maximizers from BBE Sound and Alesis.

But sound management also had to be attended to at the level of stage management. In the 1980s, therefore, it became standard practice to provide separate monitoring for individual musicians on stage. Musicians' needs were looked after by a stage-based engineer who sat somewhere slightly hidden from the audience but visible to the performers. The individual input-to-sound (what each performer produces), was also patched through a wired "snake" into the main mixing console, controlled by the main sound engineer, who was some distance away from the performers, somewhere elevated within the crowd of listeners. The main engineer, or house engineer, was therefore responsible for controlling what audiences heard. Whereas during the 1960s and much of the 1970s independent musicians controlled the fluctuation of the band's output levels, in the 1980s and thereafter tight reins were put on output sound level and texture by the newly vested authority of the soundman.

Like the sound-system street DJs who signalled the power of their systems by amassing huge speaker stacks, many Caribbean bands also valorized the presence of monstrously heavy speaker-reinforcement bins by the likes of Peavey (particularly the HDH series and the UDH), Yamaha, SoundTech and Elite Systems. But the end of the twentieth century witnessed the move away from heavy stacks towards the efficiency and enhanced output ratio of bins by Electro-Voice, JBL and EAW. Some of these speaker bins came with built-in power and stressed such features as the ability to throw sound far and to disperse it at wider angles from the pointed direction of the speaker cabinet. This evolution marked a victory of sound quality over the appearance of power.

Guitars

The electric guitar became a standard component of most popular combos in the Caribbean in the 1970s. The guitar has always been an important instrument within Caribbean music, of course. Acoustic guitars in particular were widely used before the 1970s, especially to provide accompaniment for "folk" performances. Many roving singers throughout the region in the twentieth century depended on this instrument.

The guitar has proven to be a functional instrument for a number of reasons. First, it is portable. Second, it has never been a very expensive instrument. This is not to say that guitars were widely purchased throughout the islands. Some indigenous woodworkers have used their talents to construct acoustic guitars. Others, not so skilled but eager practitioners, have also constructed guitars, tuning the strings to the required pitch.

Although the popularity of the guitar has ebbed and flowed over the decades, it has remained an important fixture in ensemble set-ups. The guitar's functional capacity has assured its popularity in Caribbean music. It is capable of providing rhythmic, harmonic and melodic accompaniment. Because of this, its potential for performance embellishment is significant, and roving singers have been able to employ it for a number of purposes. It has been used to provide an accompanying rhythm, largely by the free hand's strumming over the guitar's circular sound port. It is also capable of melodic properties, since it is possible to pick the melody of a song on the four higher strings. Fewer guitar users have been able to master the playing of complex harmonies. Whereas solo acoustic acts have tended to excel in this vein, more contemporary music use has not made good use of this method. Many bands have therefore used the guitar in a more fluid role.

By the 1970s, when sound amplification came into wider popular usage, the guitar's function as a solo instrument gave way to its greater use as part of the combo set-up, sharing the stage with many other instruments. The guitar now shared the same sound space as the presynth, bass and vocals, since all these were filtered through the same speaker. In the 1970s as well, the six-string guitar shared a new relationship with the four-string bass guitar. The popularizing of the four-string bass guitar meant that the six-string guitar was restricted to a specific function; it was rhythm-oriented and also played melody or lead segments, while the lower registers of sounds were now assigned to the bass guitar. With amplification as well, many bands influenced by pop, rock and roll, and country music added a second six-string guitar, whose function was primarily to play lead parts, to mirror the song's melodic line and to play solo parts.

The major producers of guitars have sold their wares throughout the Caribbean. Companies such as Fender, Yamaha and Gallan have had their guitars appear in Caribbean music over the years. Popularly known artists such as Bob Marley, Eddy Grant and Joan Armatrading have come to be synonymous with the steel-string guitar. Reggae performances have instituted the guitar as a central instrument. The rhythm guitar has evolved as critical to the delivery of the "skanking" rhythm and style within reggae, which is evoked by the upward strum across the guitar's strings. When reggae became internationalized, it also made greater use of rock and pop aesthetics by employing the guitar. Bob Marley's devotion to his guitar is not only noticeable through its central role within his song texts, but also in his many appearances with this instrument on and off stage.

Calypso has also used this instrument throughout the music's development. With the popularization of amplification, the guitar has not gained radically new applications in calypso, however. If anything, the instrument's status has diminished overall, while it has continued to play a supporting role for other instruments. Throughout the 1970s, it largely served the function of sustaining a song's insistent rhythm. Throughout the 1980s, the guitar rose and then was submerged within the construction of calypso. In the 1980s and thereafter, its place has been challenged by the synthesizer. But the guitar has, nonetheless, remained. Although the six-string has at times been used to deliver brief interludes or rock-influenced solos, its sister instrument the bass guitar has gained greater presence.

The four-string bass guitar became a core constituent in the new style which was coming into calypso in the early to mid-1970s. This style was soca. The bass guitar was elevated to major significance, along with drums, in this music style. (Drum and bass were also central constituents in reggae's evolution at this time.)

Throughout the 1980s, guitar applications were influenced greatly by trends in pop and rock. The rock guitar style was appropriated by Caribbean music. In the 1980s, multiple-distortion devices were widely available to musicians for the first time. Before then, of course, such sound features as tremolo, wah-wah and distortion were built into guitars using additional levers which musicians had to manipulate with their strumming hands. This meant that guitarists had to be quick to both strum and manipulate the extension device with the same hand. Even then, these devices were limited in the kind of effects they offered to musicians. To solve these problems, many instrument companies began in the 1980s to produce guitar sound-altering devices that were independent of the instrument itself. These devices could now be activated by the guitarist's foot. With the tip of the shoe, they could be turned on (for effect) or off (for normal sound). By the mid-1980s, most Caribbean musicians were in possession of such foot-gadgets, which were operated in a chain. The major effects available were distortion, chorus, flange (an echo with variable delay), overdrive and octaves. Some of the more popular guitar effects among Caribbean musicians were by the world's leading maker of compact effects pedals, Boss, by Yamaha and by Fender. By the late 1980s, instead of purchasing several independent footpedal effect gadgets, which were quite costly and untidy on stage, musicians were opting for an all-in-one foot unit that housed a range of effects within a relatively small casing. Korg's AX30G, a guitar hyper-performance processor, was being sold in the region around 1995. This foot-operated device boasted twenty-eight different dynamic effects. It also claimed to have build-in the world's first pressure pedal, with which the player could gain greater expressive control over the sound than with more conventional volume-type controllers. In the 1990s, guitarists in the Caribbean tended to move away to some extent from foot-operated guitar effects. They were intrigued by what the music industry marketed as "rack-mount" processors, gadgets which could be housed within a portable rectangular casing and positioned on stage near the musicians, not on the floor. Rack-mount gadgets were used not only for guitar effects but also as sound enhancers for a range of instruments, from drums to synthesizers to vocals. Boss's late-1990s rack-mount guitar-effects processor, the GX-700, in addition to thirteen powerful, simultaneously accessible effects, also housed a built-in preamplifier (which gives initial amplification to a relatively weak signal and then transmits it to a main amplifier) and tuner. Guitarists have found this useful.

For a period in the 1980s and early 1990s, Caribbean band members began to perform with portable synthesizers (remote keyboards), such as Roland's Axis, strapped around their shoulders like guitars, but this trend died in the early 1990s. During the same period, the question concerning the necessity of a guitar within live band set-ups was also broached.

Because of the popularity of the synthesizer and its endless array of sounds, including the guitar clone, some bands began to subordinate and even do away with the guitar. But it is significant that the guitar made a new re-entry on the back of cutting-edge technology through music interface: the very technology which allowed the synthesizer to clone a range of sounds also empowered the guitar to approximate whatever sound was possible by the synthesizer, from orchestral strings to piano to police sirens. Roland's late-1990s VG-8 in its V-Guitar System, for example, with its sixty-four preset patches, enabled Caribbean users to emulate anything from classic guitar sounds to extraordinary synthesizer-type sounds.

The bass guitar has, within the past fifteen years, moved from being a four-stringed instrument to being, first, a five-stringed, then a six-stringed instrument. The music industry's rationale for this transformation has been musicians' desire for a much more flexible instrument in terms of pitch and harmonics. In the Caribbean, most popular bands were making use of either five- or six-string bass guitars by early in the first decade of the twenty-first century. These guitars were very popular in the reggae and calypso dance contexts. The effect of these instruments on Caribbean music has been to enhance the bass contours of sound. Caribbean music now possesses a deeper bottom end within both recorded and live performances.

Having gone through some transformation, the role of the guitar is currently diverse. It is sometimes indistinguishable from some of the other instruments with which it now operates in the digital domain. As the music technology has changed, so has the function and application of the guitar as it has appeared within Caribbean music. The guitar has survived.

Drums

Drums have also undergone a process of digitization since the 1980s. The acoustic trap set was very much present in most band set-ups by the late 1970s. The traditional drum set comprised the kick drum, the snare, two toms (low and high), the floor tom, high hats and at least one crash cymbal. By the mid-1980s, there was a significant revolution in the production of drum sound, a revolution which also involved what drums looked like.

In the mid-1980s, the acoustic drum set was being challenged by the advent of electronic drums. Certainly, by the late 1980s the majority of bands in the Caribbean had partially or totally replaced their old acoustics. They opted instead for the new, sleek, digital, powerful and more expensive electronic kits by Yamaha, Simmons, Tama and Roland. Suddenly, acoustic trap sets were deemed to be deficient in a number of respects. Yes, acoustic drums could be used in small venues without having to amplify them, since their sound carried naturally in certain acoustic spaces. But once a venue was larger, it was customary – and necessary – to place microphones around the drum set in order to give an amplified band a truer, fuller sound. By the mid-1980s, most Caribbean musicians saw the direct-line connection of electronic drums as providing the answer to the problem of having to find at least three additional microphones and three additional channels on the mixing board to assign to acoustic drums.

Electronic drums indeed made some tasks very easy. Although new electronic drum kits varied in appearance based on the manufacturer, they all functioned according to the same basic principle. The drum pads were made of sturdy, rubbery plastics to simulate the feel of vibrating drum skins. Each drum pad had an output line that was connected to a tone-generating source. The tone-generating source was then fed into a mixing board, where the levels of individual instruments could be controlled. Although it was also possible for the drummer to control certain aspects of the drums' sound, such as their tone, pitch, sound contours and attack, drummers and bands in the Caribbean were especially taken in by the claim to power which many advertising brochures made. Indeed, worldwide, 1980s music was driven by big sounds, and many of the big sounds heard throughout this period were driven by electronic kits. International bands such as the Jets, Genesis, Tears for Fears and REO Speedwagon all used electronic kits. Throughout the Caribbean, the electronic drum craze hinged on the newfound power that these drums harnessed. But musicians and sound engineers were especially fascinated with the routing of control over this once untamed collection of instruments directly to the soundman at the mixing board. Thus, groups as wide-ranging geographically and musically as Blacksand in St Vincent, Burning Flames in Antigua, Reasons in St Lucia, Spice in Barbados, Atlantic in Trinidad, and Byron Lee and the Dragonaires in Jamaica have all come into contact with the power of electronic drums.

The functionality of these kits did not end there. It was possible to connect these drums to other electronic instruments within the band and to have the drums react to or initiate a range of pre-programmed sounds. Since these instruments were connectable to a range of sound sources, drums could now also sound like non-drum instruments. For example, they could be connected to a synthesizer, which itself was set to play piano; on striking the toms, a range of piano sounds would be produced.

Many Caribbean songs of the mid-1980s and the early 1990s reflect the heavy use of electronic drums. It is easy to distinguish the use of electronic drums from acoustic drums in the early days of the electronic kit, since, over 95 per cent of the time, electronic-drum users sought to inscribe their sense of difference from the acoustic set. They usually made their drums sound like high-tech pads. Michael McDonald's 1985 album *No Looking Back* provides a good example of the Simmons electronic sound on such tracks as "Lost in the Parade" and "By Heart". Crazy's 1989 "Nani Wine" also reveals the presence of similarly tuned pads. It was only in the latter days of the electronic drum that producers and musicians seemed to demand much more realistic sound samples from their drum kits. In the early days of electronic drums, popular brands were produced by Simmons; the SDS9 and SDS8 have had many loyal followers throughout the Caribbean. But these early models were highly "electronic" in their sound. By the mid-1990s, there was a tendency to want the highly technologized drum sound only as an option; Caribbean musicians desired, again, the sound, feel and texture of real acoustic skins.

There was therefore a movement back towards acoustic drums by the mid-1990s, though many bands saw the wisdom of retaining their electronic drums as additions to the standard acoustics. Drum sets thus began to appear more full. At the time, many leading popular bands featured acoustic drums and electronic drums on the same stage. Those bands that did not retain electronic drums as part of their central drum kit assigned the playing of electronic pads to a dedicated percussionist.

Although the electronic drum kit significantly affected the creation and sound of Caribbean music, the greatest revolution in drum technology concerned the drum machine and drum programming. The electronic drum kit depended on a tone-generating brain (which was a separate unit from the actual pads) to replicate the sound of drums; it thus seemed inevitable that music technology would discard the outer casing, which was really just an embellishment. In the mid-1980s, therefore, portable devices called drum machines began to appear in greater regularity with major Caribbean acts. These handy drum machines, which could connect through a direct line to the mixing board, contained coin-sized simulation pads which could be struck with the finger to produce drum sounds when amplified through speakers. But their programmability made them even more exciting. Drum machines were used at first along with live drumming, serving like metronomes to keep a band's live performance in strict metrical time and, in some cases, depriving many live sets of freer spontaneous performance. Many popular bands, especially small steel-pan groups, still use the drum machine for this purpose. Some recordings of live performances from the 1980s even reveal, with varying degrees of audibility, the metronome-like ticking of some drum-machine programming. The Linn Drum was used quite frequently in the region as a time-keeping device. Bands began to pre-program the machines and play them back during "live" performances. This made the presence of the live drummer dispensable. Indeed, many regional bands replaced the live drummer with the drum machine. This was especially true of those bands that sought to maximize their profits by achieving a cleaner sound mix through upfront drums while doing away with an additional member – one less person to pay. Some bands which operate in the hotel and nightclub context still perform with the drum machine doing all the drum and percussion parts. Although there are varying degrees to which bands incorporated aspects of pre-programmed drums into their sets, by the end of the 1990s bands again ascribed greater value to live drum performance and attempted a more creative and less ostentatious use of the drum machine.

Whereas in the late 1980s many drummers were dependent on drum machines such as Akai's Linn, Roland's RX5 and Alesis's HR16B, these machines now have their greatest presence and application in the recording studio. Since the drum machine came into use, it has indeed replaced the actual trap set in the recording studio. Musicians and producers have found that much time can be saved in the studio by using programmed drums. This also minimizes the number of errors that might otherwise accompany live drumming in studio recordings. After all, as long as a drum sequence is programmed beforehand, all that is required in the studio is the touch of a button to trigger an entire drum accompaniment for a song. These drum sequences are also connected to synthesizers and their sequences; hence, one full pre-packaged song arrangement can be played with the start of the drum machine. Dancehall and soca have evolved through this process.

By the 1990s, synthesizer technology also threatened to spell the death of the dedicated drum machine. A range of synthesizers, such as Korg's M1, began to offer built-in drum sounds as part of their package. More and more musicians and producers worked in the self-contained domain of the synthesizer. At the end of the 1990s, this was the preferred practice among many music arrangers and producers in the Caribbean. Since Caribbean musicians and producers have operated on limited production budgets, an imperative for many musicians has been to record a product that is of good quality while making wise use of costly studio time.

MIDI and SCSI

Musical instrument digital interface, or MIDI, has become a standard term for musicians and the music industry since 1982. MIDI was conceived a necessary progression in the music industry's attempts to create instruments which could "speak" to one another. Through the acceptance of a universal interface standard for all musical instruments, MIDI was born and came into use around 1982. The keyboard company Sequential Circuits produced a keyboard called the Prophet 600, which carried sockets in its rear panel that allowed it to be hooked up to another keyboard and to be played together with it. When two synthesizers were connected through MIDI, the playing of one synthesizer could be enhanced by the other. The texture of the synthesizer's sound could be embellished since it was sucking or borrowing from the sounds mapped out on the other connected synthesizer. Soon MIDI allowed for sharing of data and for the playing of programmed sequences between keyboards, drum machines and all other digital electronic musical instruments.

The development of MIDI affected Caribbean music practices significantly. Because musicians and producers have always been conscious of studio time and the money factor, MIDI meant that musicians who wanted to go into the studio could pre-program their songs and store them as electronic data, releasing them in the studio onto master tape with the press of a button. Since all the instrument parts were storable on MIDI-capable instruments, musicians could go into the studio armed with few music gadgets and download their sound data and songs with relative ease and without fear of having to redo "live" mistakes, as had often been the case.

The industry also began to standardize an interface between musical instruments and the computer. Small computer system interface (SCSI) became a popular buzzword among many Caribbean musicians who were into recording, editing and sound production. SCSI paved the way for advances in computer music, anticipating post-2000 full composition on the computer. It was now possible for musicians to connect instruments directly to the computer and to bypass intermediary gadgets. Since by the mid-1990s many synthesizers had built-in disk drives, their storage method was compatible with the computer. MIDI, SCSI and instrument-to-instrument interface spawned the development of soca, dancehall and other digitized music styles.

The Studio: From Reel-to-Reel to Computer Music

Within the recent history of Caribbean music, the recording studio has had major responsibility in shaping the soundscape of the region. It is the recorded sound text that has circulated within the region and abroad to establish the label "Caribbean music". It is ironic that this is so, and yet the region has not fully comprehended how its cultural hub is propelled, how its recording engine functions at the core. One would expect creative industries to concern themselves with and be attuned to the various components that drive the industries.

The role of the recording studio is still obscure in academic discourse on Caribbean song. In order to construct a more sound knowledge, it is imperative to walk the dark corridors of the recording studio and to come face to face with the state-of-the-art gadgets, hardware and software which fill the sound room and which give pleasure and anguish to producers, engineers, musicians and audiences at home and worldwide. The engine of music, sound and image construction has undergone many changes over the years. The future will witness an even sharper growth in the number of non-professional, home-based studios than was experienced during the 1990s.

The centrepiece of the early recording studio in the Caribbean was the tape machine. Reel-to-reel tape machines by the likes of Philips and Sony have been used in many studios. Earlier recording practice in the Caribbean found musicians and singers huddled together in radio stations' soundproof facilities singing and performing over a single microphone centrally placed to capture the various instruments. These recordings were filtered onto quarter-inch tape as two tracks. The tapes therefore became the record master, which was then carried or sent to one of the few pressing houses in the region, where it was transferred onto LP or 45 rpm format. Many of these vintage recordings have remained on old recording formats or hidden away among stacks of unexplored material. Up to the 1970s, this recording practice still remained as standard for some groups recording in the region.

By the late 1970s and certainly by the early 1980s, greater attention was devoted to the process of transferring live sound onto a fixed master format. Whereas older techniques treated the performance as a composite act, new techniques influenced by the advancement in technology shattered the old concept of squeezing all instruments into a single recording moment.

The presence of the recording mixing console changed things greatly. The notion of a dedicated studio mixing board was not widely accepted and appreciated in the Caribbean until the 1980s. Internationally these were widely used in the 1970s. Many studio boards provided enhanced sound-control features, which gave engineers more facilities to alter sound contours by manipulating frequency knobs assigned to individual channels. Popular makes in studio mixing boards in recent times have been by TASCAM, Soundcraft and Mackie. Over the years, studio mixing boards became bigger in terms of track facilities. Many studios in the 1980s stepped up from using four-track boards to eight-track and sixteen-track mixers. By the early 1990s, many decent-quality studios boasted sixteen-track status, and at the end of the 1990s, they laid claim to being twenty-four-track-ready. They also offered ready connectivity (through patch bays and auxiliary returns) for sound-effects processors such as delay and reverb gadgets as well as sub-output channels, which meant that sounds produced during recording could be filtered back to earphones worn by performers and also returned to the engineer through studio monitors. Many pre-1990s mixing consoles measured sound input and output by VU needle levers, which were not always assigned to all the channels. Indeed, in some cases a VU reading was possible only for the total output level. Most professional mixing consoles at the end of the 1990s assigned a separate reading for each channel, such as the Alesis X2. The popularity of LED lights (coded flashing light signals) has also grown over the years.[3]

Modern mixing consoles in the studio are at the core of sound creation and sound shaping. To capture the original sound, it is passed from instrument to microphone to the mixing console. It is the engineer who then subjects that sound to a process of filtering, recording and storage for future retrieval and enhancement. Since modern recording techniques allow a number of instruments to be filtered through separate channels – sometimes more than thirty-two – recording engineers have worked in pairs in order to better manage the busy mix. By the late 1990s, some studios boasted of having fully digital recording facility, including a fully digital mixing console. The digital mixing console allowed a single engineer to pre-program the individual channel settings for every part of the song during its recording (and during post-recording production).

But sound-recording techniques and practices in the Caribbean cannot be understood only in relation to the mixing console. The mixing console has, after all, been connected to a number of critical instruments. Chief among these, for many Caribbean recording engineers, has been the actual recording machine. By the early 1990s, analogue tape recorders were being rapidly replaced by recorders that claimed to operate in the digital domain. Some studios maintained both analogue and digital capability, such as Bronese Recording Studio in St Maarten.

In less professional studios, there was considerable interest in what the music industry marketed as complete compact recording studios. These were relatively inexpensive portable recording machines that used cassette tapes to store the recorded tracks. Around 1995, curiously enough, TASCAM was still trying desperately to market this product in the region, in the form of the eight-track 488MKII Portastudio. But around this time, reel-to-reel machines and less expensive cassette-based four- and eight-track analogue tape recorders were being resold relatively cheaply by enthusiasts who wanted to be a part of the digital craze which was sweeping the Caribbean.

A number of digital tape-based recorders by TASCAM caught the fancy of engineers. These recorders, such as the DA-88, were using Hi-8 (8mm) videotape for storing the tracks. For a time this was considered the most up-to-date tape-transport technology, and it prided itself on providing up to 108 minutes of recording time, as compared to 40 minutes on the VHS format. Other models, by Alesis, used wide-band Super VHS half-inch tape to store eight tracks of recorded data. Many of these recorders provided facility for erasing an individual track without affecting any of the others. They also offered punch-in and punch-out options, which meant that a mistake made anywhere on a track during recording did not necessitate re-recording the entire part from start to finish; the recorder could be stopped at the point where the mistake was made, and the performer had the chance to splice in a corrected chord or note.

The editing facilities were endless on these new digital recorders. Although TASCAM won the admiration of higher-priced studios, many other aspiring studio owners opted for the much more economical ADAT eight-track digital recorder by Alesis, the same company which had made the drum machine available to a wide cross-section of musicians a decade earlier. Recording machines like the ADAT provided traditional quarter-inch input and output jacks for connecting to instruments or to the mixing board. But they also offered digital I/O (input-output) connecting ports, which meant that these recorders could operate totally in the digital domain. They could be connected directly to digital mixing consoles or to a computer for such functions as file management. Because sound was being stored digitally, it was possible to locate and scrutinize and alter any part of the song, however minute. These recorders were also sometimes used to store the final two-track mix-down of a song, although most serious studio engineers preferred to mix down their songs to two tracks on DAT (digital audio tape) recorders such as TASCAM's DA-30 MK II. Machines such as this boasted a shuttle wheel for fast program search and an inner data wheel for marking specific points in the tracks. These DAT tapes were then treated as the master, which could then be taken for duplication.

In the late 1990s, industry musicians and engineers drifted towards hard-disk recording. Tape was done away with altogether; instead, the recording went straight from source (say, a guitar) onto the hard drive of a new wave of track recorders. Hard-disk recording caught on among musicians because multi-track recording on hard disk claimed to deliver a higher-quality recording. It also promised powerful editing functions, compactness and simple operation. The biggest difference between conventional recording and recording on a tapeless system was that to locate a particular spot on a conventional system, one had to wade through the tape. Hard-disk recorders such as the DR 4d, by industry leader Akai, recorded sound data on random access hard disks, so it was possible to jump to any location at any time. Storage was also possible on computer disks. Some of the hard-disk recorders which were found in the Caribbean were manufactured by Roland and Ensoniq, but hard-disk recording had been a preoccupation of Akai for a long time. Akai's hard-disk recorders have never been widely accessible to Caribbean music users, however, because Akai's products have tended to attract the higher-priced end of the music market. Its DPS twenty-four-track workstation hovered in the range of US$4,000. In contrast, at the end of the 1990s, near similar hard-disk recorders by other manufactures were available for less than US$2,500.

Most serious recording studios today make use of the computer for sound-recording projects. Leading-edge technology offers software that turns the desktop computer into a powerful multi-functional, multi-tasking instrument. These workstations can input, output, record, edit, score and produce a finished master on CD. The secret component of these machines is the software that allows them to carry out a range of functions all in one package. Among the more popular software is Steinberg's Cubase, whose SX series boasted of being the best virtual sequencer of 2002. Cakewalk's Sonar was another software package used. This type of software gave musicians a near-unlimited number of tracks, although, ultimately, many engineers must continue to invest in new software and hardware upgrades regularly. But computer music is a growing phenomenon; many small and home-based studios find it less expensive to do recordings now. Similarly, many artists and bands have established their own in-house studios. Thus, while the music industry has expanded to affect a wider range of regional cultures, there has been a corresponding compression of the creation and recording process. The potential of digital transfer and file sharing means that artists can create in the privacy of their own space and transfer music files to collaborators for feedback or for further processing.

With the advent of the CD as a new format for song storage and distribution, musicians have had to rethink the production process. Where, before, recorded master tapes could be sent to pressing houses in Jamaica and Barbados, the absence of a CD-pressing plant in the Caribbean meant that recorded masters had to be sent outside of the region, to Canada and Miami, for mass CD duplication. While some studios used CD recorders (such as Pioneer's PDR-O4) to give their clients limited copies of songs on one-off CDs – for example, for radio distribution – bulk CD reproduction distanced artists from their music products in the last critical stages of sound-to-disk impression. The technology has therefore allowed musicians to achieve near-perfect sound quality, but it has also brought about a transformed relationship between musicians, engineers and the music product. Many Caribbean musicians have been forced to abdicate the power of control in the latter stages of sound transfer to the manipulation of a detached technological process. Not all artists have the capacity to take their master tapes overseas personally.

There are no recording studios today in the Caribbean which have not relied heavily on the use of signal, or effects, processors. These are devices that enhance or alter the sound of an instrument or vocals. Since most studio recording boards have built-in parametric equalizers (knobs which alter high, mid and low frequencies), then this form of signal processing – or altering, rather – can be said to have been around for a long time in Caribbean recording studios. But more recent recording trends have made the introduction of graphic (horizontal rows of faders) equalizers standard. Graphic equalizers provide engineers with up to thirty-one bands of sound frequencies that can be adjusted. In the studio, equalizers began to be used on selected instruments, but by the end of the twentieth century, with tuning built-in on many electronic instruments, equalization became a necessary sound enhancement, usually at the later stages of production. It became customary to employ a couple of equalizers at final mix-down stage. Digital programmable equalizers have also come into vogue, especially when a musician has stored and wants to recall a number of sound-filter settings for an instrument in an instant, at the press of a button.

Next to equalization, compression and limiting were two of the most sought-after functions in Caribbean studios in the late 1990s. Compressors are basically responsible for controlling the amplitude of sounds, reducing the dynamic range. Limiting is an extreme form of compression. Limiters are often used to keeps the total output of instruments from getting too loud, regardless the volume of the input signal. In response to the perception that international radio privileges a tight, punchy mix, recording engineers, musicians and producers sought the help of limiters and compressors. For many producers, like the innovative Dennis Bovell, who wanted to create in-your-face mixes for international distribution, the compressor-limiter (sometimes sold as a single unit) allowed them to drive hot signals to the track recorder without producing distortion. Dancehall music, with its excessively weighty bass ends, has depended quite heavily on the shrewd use of compressor-limiters; so has calypso, whose dance derivative has increasingly made greater use of deeper basses and a more dynamic sound range. A comparison of most 1970s recordings with any from the 1990s will reveal a higher recording output level (in terms of volume and presence) on the more recent recordings. Since the birth of the CD, this punchy upfrontness has come to epitomize digital sound production.

Sound enhancers and sonic maximizers have also come into popular use. Usually at the mix-down stage, sound enhancers have been employed by Caribbean engineers to breathe more life into the entire mix. Products by BBE, Lexicon, DBX and many other manufacturers have filled the rack space of recording engineers. Reverbs, delays, flanges and choruses, such as Alesis's Quadraverb and Ensoniq's DP Pro twenty-four-bit effects processor, are also vital signal processors (sound enhancers) in the construction of Caribbean popular music. Audiences are not always aware of the presence of these instruments in recordings, but these tools are partly responsible for the impact of reggae vocals and chanting. Dancehall chanters in particular owe much to these effects. A dry-voiced, chanting Buju Banton would not achieve the potent impact of Buju Banton's vocals manipulated in the stereophonic spectrum. An overall coating of reverb carries his vocals to the expanded depths of the mix, and two unequally panned delays (left and right) wrap his voice comfortably around the musical constituents that cohabit the mix. We therefore hear his voice upfront in the mix. In soca music, recording technicians have used more than one effect at once for vocals. Songs such as Kevin Lyttle's hugely popular 2002 "Turn Me On" reflect the presence of multi-effects processing.

The future of Caribbean music sound-mixing looks towards the unlimited use and abuse of these sound-processing devices. So complex is the range of uses to which these are put that engineers are divided on the proper application and function of these effects gadgets. Because Caribbean engineers have learned the trade largely by trial and error, there are divergent mixing practices and little respect for conformity. Aspiring young engineers have been noted for their daring experiments.

Some mature listeners have accused music creators at the leading edge of moving more and more towards cacophony. But, on the other hand, many youths continued to show their approval of the new mixing standards and procedures by supporting post-soca and post-dancehall tendencies.

Synthesizers

In the Caribbean since the 1980s, no single piece of music technology has had more impact on music than the synthesizer.[4] The 1980s was really the decade of musical synthesizers. Before then, there were electronic keyboards in use, such as the Moog Minimoog, which had a production run from 1970 to around 1982. Throughout the 1970s, the Fender Rhodes Stage 73 piano was many a musician's instrument of desire. It produced icicle-coated piano tones, but it was a burden to transport. Whereas the instruments of greatest use in the 1970s were guitars and acoustic drums, the decades of the 1980s and 1990s and early 2000s certainly belonged to the synthesizer. This was not a situation peculiar to the Caribbean – the synthesizer revolution had an impact worldwide. But in the Caribbean it became increasingly trendy and commonplace for musicians to own, play and display their synthesizers with a passion. Many of the early instruments by the synthesizer giants Oberheim and Sequential Circuits tended to be expensive: the Oberheim Matrix-12 sold for around US$6,400, Sequential's Prophet T-8 for around US$6,000. But musicians could opt for other, less imposing instruments, such as the extremely popular Roland SH-101, which could be had for around US$500.

In the very early 1980s, the real value of the synthesizer – apart from its trendy image – was the array of sounds that it provided. It was used to add layers of sound. In some instances, it was used as a melody-accompanying instrument; that is, musicians would mirror parts of the song's melody as sung by the lead singer. It also became a lead instrument; that is, it played the bridges and interlude segments of songs. This was a role tailor-made for the monophonic capacity of most synthesizers in the very early 1980s – most synthesizers at the time were capable of producing only one (mono) tone or voice or sound at a time. This made the synthesizer an ideal instrument for interplaying with live brass in the calypso genre.

The synthesizer was also used to emulate the steel pan. Significantly, most digital synthesizers from the mid- to late-1980s and onwards offered build-in steel-pan samples; Korg's Poly 800 caught the attention of some users in the mid-1980s because of this feature. Since the 1980s, there has, in fact, been much debate surrounding ownership and patent rights of the steel pan. But there has hardly been any substantial debate regarding the processes by which music-industry technology has reconfigured the steel pan, both as instrument and as sound referent. The synthesizer had already through its popularity begun the process of internationalizing steel pan (as a voice) while also granting power of control and reconfiguration of this sound to all potential users.

The synthesizer was also used outside of calypso, in reggae and other pop-oriented musical styles. The degree of delight and gratification which many musicians felt for synthesizer technology can be heard in many compositions recorded in the early 1980s. Some good examples might be heard on recordings by calypso, reggae and gospel acts. Beckett's "Stranger Man" (1985), for example, creates an audacious interplay between the vocalist and a highly technologized "percus" tone (fusion of steel pan and piano), a tone which delightfully takes over the song during its interlude segments. Ivory's "Print Out" (1984) is also a classic example of the foregrounding of the synthesizer. This well-constructed song celebrates and laments the inevitability of computerized technology. In the composition, other instruments are slaved to the programmed computerized bass line. The flanged guitar, even the rock lead and drums, must give way to the programmed bass. The instruments and sounds used in "Print Out" can be counted on one hand. There is a certain bareness and dryness to the mix. This was deliberately done to call attention to the highly technologized bass loop and to buttress the song's theme of high-tech exertion.

By late 1984, the poly-synth, or multi-voiced synth, such as Kork's Mono/Poly, though allowing only four voices to be heard simultaneously, gave musicians even greater flexibility in creating textured layers within their compositions. Kork's Mono/Poly Synth was not the first instrument to offer polyphony. But certainly the start of the 1980s marked the twilight years of the monophonic synthesizer, although many monophonic synthesizers remained in use. Whereas the monophonic synthesizer was limited in its delivery to only one voice at a time, the polyphonic synthesizer allowed musicians to form chords by holding more than one note at a time. This phenomenon was not a totally new concept to Caribbean musicians – full polyphony had always been achievable on the piano, the organ and string instruments. But the availability of this feature on the portable electronic synthesizer provided the option of not only playing lead melodic lines, but also creating textured soundscapes. Casio's CZ101 in particular made an impression because it was inexpensive and offered multi-timbral features.

Musicians were being offered the tools to stretch the boundaries of technology and to re-engineer the sound of Caribbean music, but this new facility caused a number of contentious debates in the region. Some music creators and users got into trouble attempting to negotiate the role of the instrument and to apply its sounds to Caribbean musical traditions. For example, early attempts to produce "live brass" served up a series of thin-sounding factory-built sounds. These were used liberally in the calypso domain as well as in reggae; many of these unconvincing synthesized brass tones were coming out of St Lucia, Barbados, Trinidad, Antigua, Grenada, Montserrat and Jamaica.

But there were some moments of magic. The Grenadian composer, arranger and music-technology buff Desmond "Kalabash" Campbell challenged the parameters of music-technology application in the region. He harnessed, among other instruments, Yamaha's TX 816 – a rackfull of about eight DX7s, each capable of responding with sixteen voices. This 1984 instrument was one of the earliest multi-timbral instruments. Relatively few musicians in the Caribbean and elsewhere at the time could figure out why it was needed, but they stood in expectant wonder. Campbell's 1987 *Calypso Variations* made blatant use of this machinery in the calypso idiom. Its synthesized brass gave much more "stab" or expression than most others heard around this time. Campbell made much use of brass solos and brass clusters on the album, as heard, for example, on the song "We Jumping". On *Calypso Variations*, Campbell also used the Commodore Sx-60 computer. Computers were very much a rarity at the time. This album epitomizes the immense impact of the synthesizer and early computer technology on calypso and crossover music in the 1980s – computer music in the late 1990s built on the relatively limited capabilities of the 1980s. This album was an eye opener for many when they first heard it; for Campbell himself it represented an attempt to master the technology that was coming into vogue. Back in the mid-1980s, Campbell talked on radio about the nostalgic desire to reconnect with his homeland in the song "Me Island" from the same album. Here was an early acknowledgement that it was indeed possible to make the technology bear the burden of cultural expression; it was possible to make the technology do what the user intended. Campbell therefore bared his soul to the Caribbean. He expressed his desire through the technology: he admitted that it was possible to openly yearn for Grenada through the driving loops of computerized, synchronized analogue-sounding drums, bass and ambient strings. This was how the technology allowed him to think and to create.

Impressive sound synthesis could be found on dedicated samplers such as Akai's S900 and S1000. Such machines, in addition to storing factory sounds, allowed music users to record and play back their own sounds, either as a one-off event or as a sound loop. Musicians could plug a microphone into their synthesizers and record, say, breaking waves on the beach, then replay a few seconds of this sound by pressing the keys on the synthesizer. Akai's samplers have tended to be expensive, and so Caribbean musicians have aspired to them. Caribbean musicians have also been very keen on selected samplers from the company E-MU Systems (now merged with Ensoniq). E-MU's Emulator series has not been as visible in the Caribbean as has been the 1986 darling called Emax. This instrument reproduced a familiar array of jungle-type sounds heard in the music of many bands in the mid- to late-1980s. Second Avenue's "Here Comes the Rain Again", for example, began with this sample. A few of these instruments were still being offered up for sale on the Caribbean second-hand market in the mid-1990s. Some retailers were still asking ridiculously high prices (beyond US$650), vaguely reflective of what the Emax was worth in its glory days, around 1987; but music retailers, like the musicians they service, have frequently seemed to be caught up in a trance. Another outstanding instrument, visible because of its awesome power, size and hype, was the Stevie Wonder–inspired Kurzweil 250. In the 1980s, this instrument boasted one of the highest sampling rates. This meant that it could record sound events longer and more clearly than most other samplers. Because of its extensive sound library, updated by the manufacturers, it boasted built-in upgradeability. Fewer than twenty of these could have been owned by regional musicians. They retailed for approximately US$16,675 during their production run from 1984 to 1989. The K250 was visible wherever it appeared, for example, with the soca band Spice.

Digital sampling came home to many more Caribbean musicians through the then (1982) new company Ensoniq. Their Mirage, "the poor man's sampler" (so called by musicians), could be had for under US$2,250, and its thirty thousand-plus units sold worldwide included a fair representation in Caribbean stage set-ups, both secular and gospel. This sampler produced one of the most credible built-in brass sections. Samplers provided many possibilities. Musicians could actually record a few seconds of a live steel band and loop together the beginning and ending of the sample so that it became a continuous sound when a key on the synthesizer was pressed. That said, many music users felt satisfied to simply make use of the built-in sounds.

The three big synthesizers of the 1980s, 1990s and early 2000s in the Caribbean must be Yamaha's Dx7, Roland's D50 and Kork's M1. Worldwide, the DX7 sold over 160,000 units, the D50 over 200,000, and the M1 over 250,000. These three instruments have shaped the music of the Caribbean in no small way: their influence is unmatched by any other electronic musical instrument in recent Caribbean history. The DX7's FM synthesis and its trademark Rhodes-cloned FullTines sound were heard in many gospel recordings, from the Grace Thrillers to Promise. There are few serious groups that have not owned or used the trademark Chiffy sounds of the D50 and its Digital Native Dance. In consuming and disseminating these tones, musicians were sharing in the joys of creating on an instrument similarly revered by Prince, Sting and Genesis. The M1's chunky piano, as heard on London Beat's "I've Been Thinking about You", was played everywhere in the Caribbean in live sets and on recordings from calypso to gospel to Caribbean-alternative, when the M1 ruled between 1989 and 1996.

When the M1 came on the market in the region, it was said to possess the first serious collection of well-mapped-out drum kits and sounds across the length of the keyboard; this threatened to put to death the dedicated drum machine. The move towards do-it-all-here synthesizers, called "workstations", meant that many musicians retreated to the solitude and vacuum of their creative spaces. It is no secret that some musicians became ultra-private. At the same time, there were many built-in sounds being echoed throughout this period from island to island. In spite of the fact that the D50 was the first big synth with built-in editing features (as with the DX7 four years before it), at least 95 per cent of all regional users were satisfied to make use of the factory-preset sounds. It is, indeed, possible to trace the regional industry through these few instruments and the trademark sounds that they produced.

In addition to standing in awe of these synthesizers, musicians threw out their acoustic instruments, whose sounds could be emulated on the synthesizer. Synthesizers began to be used as self-contained systems. With their programmability and multi-functional facilities, synthesizers redefined music performance and music-recording procedure.

In the 1980s, because musicians, engineers and producers stood in awe of the technology embodied in these musical wares, they became less flexible in shaping the raw material of these machines. So, although there was some experimental work with refashioning factory programs, there was really little conscious tweaking of the technology to make it carry the strains of the Caribbean tonal cultural milieu – that is, there was no conscious strategy or policy by the national or regional industry or among musicians to enlist the technology to empower the Caribbean soundscape. This could have been done by using local, iconic sounds, such as the mumming or tuk band, for example. Synthesizers from as early as Korg's Poly 800 (1984) had built-in steel-pan tones. But throughout the 1980s, many steel-pan samples on records tended to stay close to the tones built-in at the factory.

The status of the synthesizer shows few signs of waning. In the late 1990s, Caribbean musicians followed the rest of the music world in returning to the analogue sound. This retro wave affected dancehall and soca in particular. Artists such as Bounty Killer, Elephant Man, Machel Montano and Maddzart made significant use of virtual analogue sound effects in their recordings. The workstation synthesizer was also referred to as a "production station", pointing to its potential to accommodate the total production of songs, from start to finish, on a single instrument. Kurzweil projected this term to music users in the region on their K2500, as did Yamaha in their popular Motif series.

Technology with a Passion

Although some Caribbean musicians have edited and reused built-in tones to create culturally relevant sounds, there does not seem to be an overriding systematic ideology to link these experiments. This is not to say that music producers do not possess ideologies – indeed, all creators work from some ideological perspective. However, there has hardly been a systematic engagement with the potentialities of sound (sound creation, shaping and dissemination) as a culture-constructing agent.

Because the Caribbean has been slow in this regard, it has lost some opportunities. The internationalization of the steel pan was not done, therefore, by Trinidad and Tobago alone. It was driven by other players, who studied its sound and reconstituted it (and Trinidadian culture) in the digital domain. Similarly, too, reggae has had a significant degree of sound (and culture) reconstruction in the international domain by extra-national acts such as Eric Clapton, the Eagles, the Police, Men at Work and Ace of Base. This is not a challenge peculiar to the region; many small territories have had to consciously lay claim to their creative rights. Since intellectual property represents a new site of struggle, Caribbean societies are faced with the task of asserting their claims and upholding their national and regional status. Music, and in particular sound creation, is an area that has gone unnoticed by technocrats and practitioners in the attempt to demarcate the limits of sovereignty and cultural identity.

From as early as 1985, regional musicians were in possession of the know how which allowed them to tap into Caribbean soundspace and to employ music technology with a lot more attitude and ideology on tow. There was plenty of technology and relatively little ideology in that period of development. In the mid-1980s, big sound was very much in vogue worldwide. Indigenous percussion bands of the Caribbean have been producing big sounds for a long time. These bands are big on tonal contrasts and rhythmic interest. The international market might have been intrigued by these ensembles; they would have listened with greater trepidation in the technological domain on hearing these cultural symbols. Songs such as Steve Winwood's "Highlife" and Tears for Fears' "Shout" are reminders to the region of what was possible in earlier decades. Not that "Shout" has Caribbean rhythmic components, but as a recorded track it carries an attitude that makes one think critically of the possibilities for extant Caribbean percussion bands – it has a certain underlying rhythmic aggression, though technologized. Unfortunately, interpretations of Caribbean percussion bands in the recorded format in the 1980s were comparatively tame. Producers had to be sufficiently committed to make the call on the final mix. Since there were relatively few ideologically or technologically charged producers in terms of sound-construction, it was up to the artists and to engineers to make the call on the state of the final mix-down. Not enough producers consistently took the chance.

Then in St Vincent and the Grenadines in 1986, the aspiring young sound engineer Cleve Scott entered into the fray. By 1988, he was doubling as a recording engineer. A brief overview and examination of some of his work can suggest the kinds of changes that sound recording and management have undergone and can locate some of the "big technology" in actual sounds.

Scott has now engineered for many bands, including Touch, Resurrection, X-Adus, Blacksand (later Blaksand), National Youth Band, New Life Ambassadors and Signal. He has also recorded for Touch, Blaksand, Signal, Kevin Lyttle, Islandvibes (of Trinidad) and many others. Since 1994 he has done between thirty and forty songs a year. He has worked with the Vincentian sound companies Dynamic Guys and BDS. He has also done sound for Vincy Carnival since 1991. In the 1980s, Scott's studio gear included the TASCAM sixteen-track with one-inch tapes, reel-to-reel tapes, the Soundcraft 500B console, the Yamaha DX7 synthesizer, the Yamaha RX7 rhythm processor, the E-MU Emax sampler and the E-MU SP1200 drum machine. This gear would have been instrumental in producing Scott's first ever recording, "Back Off", along with head engineer Jerome Franciqué, in 1988. It was recorded at Windy Ridge Studio, Careenage, Trinidad, and became St Vincent and the Grenadines' 1988 Road March. "Back Off" was later used to advertise Eku Bavaria beer on Caribbean radio and TV. Scott's first solo project was "Friends of Freedom", by Allan "Pappy" Oliver in 1988, recorded in BDS Studio, Dorsetshire Hill, St Vincent. He also made use of this technology for the 1989 Road March "Jam Dem", by Touch featuring Ifill Shortte, produced at Blue Wave Studios, Bayley's Plantation, St Phillip, Barbados. Most of his productions of this 1980s period, like that of other contemporaries, reflect a certain reverence for the technology being used. His musical and recording experiments at the time were not as radical as in the later period. This can be reflected in drum machine application. In many recordings of this time there was near regimented application of quantization (metrical exactness) within drum tracks. These tracks were programmed to keep strict metrical timing. Many of the drum and percussion tracks of the time were produced out of the rhythm box. Although it was the arranger who programmed the drums and other instruments, the engineer inscribed the recorded texture and output level. The drum textures of this period call attention to their electronic makeup.

Mechanized electronic drum and percussion tones abound. The synthesized brass samples of the time were credible, if not "true", since they did not have the rip or the punch and simulation capacity of the later period.

By the mid-1990s, Scott was using an Alesis ADAT tape machine, the TASCAM DA88 tape machine, DAT tapes, the Yamaha RY70 drum machine, the Ensoniq EPS 16 synthesizer-sampler, Korg M1 synthesizer, the Yamaha SPX 90 effects processor, the Otari MTR90 tape recorder and the State Logic (SSL) G series mixing console, which was used at Blue Wave on various projects. Scott currently uses Steinberg's Cubase recording software, the Soundcraft Digital 328 console, the MPC software tutorial, the Korg Triton synthesizer, the Korg Trinity synthesizer, the Yamaha SPX 990 effects processor and the AKG Acoustics BL414 microphone.

This gear and its application can be heard on songs like "To Take Away", by Godfrey Dublin of Touch, a song co-produced in Ruff Lab Studio, Beachmont, Kingstown, St Vincent, in 2000; it became the Road March. Also from that studio in 2001, Scott co-produced "Hairy Bank", by Cornelius "Poorsah" Williams, the 2001 Road March. This equipment can also be heard on the hugely popular "Turn Me On", by Kevin Lyttle in 2001, as well as on 2001's "Poor People Song", by MaddZart of Blaksand, and on the 2002 Road March by Poorsah, "Chucking".

Scott's own struggle with the technology is reflected in the way he has kept abreast of the latest in sound innovation, collaborated with other producers, and interacted with artists of different genres and from different islands of the region. A major challenge he has faced has been maintaining a distinctive sound for various individuals. For example, the Kevin Lyttle song "Turn Me On" reveals acute attention to signal and effects processing on the vocal tracks. The vocal tracks are not "pure" sounding, since their waveform seems to have been altered. This innovation on Scott's part certainly caught the ear of other producers, who attempted a series of experiments to approximate this method. Carl Jacobs and Roger George's 2004 song "Sugar Island" reflected further experimentation with vocal tracks.

By the end of the twentieth century, the sound quality produced by Caribbean producers had moved closer to what the international industry was projecting as an adequate standard. Whereas music of the late 1980s was reverent to emerging digital technology, twenty-first-century

Caribbean engineers and producers such as Scott were more confident and daring. They knew that they had easier access to the latest software packages and that they could download the samples also being used by people entrenched at the centre of the Western music industry. Recordings of this period therefore reflect the kinds of virtual analogue tones also being used in hip hop and pop. Kevin Lyttle's "Turn Me On" was therefore not expected to be subjected to radical reworking of music tracks when Lyttle was signed to Atlantic. Songs of this era were generally tight and punchy in terms of overall weight at the final mix-down stage. The increasing reliance on real and virtual synthesizers within soca placed hardcore soca in the same category as dancehall and in league with the post-dancehall sound. As reflected in Scott's productions of this period, bass tones were even more pronounced and drum patters were closer to leading-edge reggae and hip hop. Drum and instrument sound samples moved away from strictly distinctive Caribbean sound iconographies. This was not a case of engineers selling out. But here was recognition by engineers that a set of sound textures and practices were being offered up by way of computer hardware and software and that the future of sound construction demanded a fearless use and appropriation of emerging technology. Although many of recordings have begun to participate in the global domain of sound generation, it was impossible for Caribbean engineers and producers to leave Caribbean aesthetics behind. Indeed, most producers did not seek to do so. Many productions therefore reflected some retention of distinctive Caribbean vocal intonation.

Eddy Grant's innovations, referred to in previous chapters, also represent moments of possibility. Grant managed triumphs over machinery which kept some regional users in submission throughout the 1980s. But he was not alone in this struggle. There were many other producers and studios around the region: Kenny Phillips in Trinidad, Boo Hinkson in St Lucia, Dynamic Sounds in Jamaica, Darron Grant in Barbados and, of course, Cleve Scott in St Vincent and the Grenadines.

The innovations that all of these producers and studios have attempted do not, however, signify the end of the creative process for Caribbean musicians. Musicians, engineers and producers are still confronted by technical issues; they still have to come face to face with technology's power. A firm posture and stance will have to be taken. Caribbean musicians must engage with the technology and thereby sound their response to global and local issues through these very innovations. In St Lucia, Boo Hinkson has demonstrated how creative composing, programming and production can undermine the structures which the music industry has artificially constructed and imposed. The aggression of the Guyanese Eddy Grant and his studio-inspired music represents a cry of both victory and rage: victory in having to some degree conquered leading-edge technology, rage at the ideologically charged institutions which continue to subordinate regional entities and their culture. It is imperative that more music creators take control. The major creators of cutting-edge technology market their wares to those who will then use them to maintain the current relationship of leaders and followers in the music industry. It is no coincidence that the industry has kept its system of power relations intact. For this reason, Caribbean musicians should share a common goal.

In the ideologically charged domain of technological construction, a new site of contestation is being formulated. Technology does not come to the region innocently. It has always come with an attendant bias and ideology in its very functionalities. Caribbean users must become aware of this. This point can be illustrated with an aspect of early drum-programming technology called "quantization". This feature offered the exciting possibility of regulating the metrical pattern of all instruments and sounds within a musical set-up. But the popularity of quantization discouraged free-hand programming and experiments with polyrhythms. Ignorance that conceptual and ideological principles are built into some leading-edge technology, such as quantization, could seriously affect the region's ability to compete effectively and seriously in the new global arrangement. In this new global arena, users of technology must find ways of tweaking it by reconfiguring the set of relations that govern the process of production, consumption and redeployment.

Because the Caribbean was so hopelessly slaved, connected to a limited pool of core instruments, it has not gone on to explore other tonal, textural and compositional possibilities. The overreliance on a small pool of musical synthesizers has not been a good thing for the region. There has always been a more powerful range of instruments out there, but market trends have tended to lead Caribbean music creators to believe that only a specific core of instruments can do the job effectively. Roland's JD800, for example, could have supplemented the M1 in big sound and textures, yet the JD800 hardly appeared on the big Caribbean stage.

Relatively few musicians opted for synthesizers from Kawai, whose K1 was still being produced when the D50 was discontinued after only two years, around 1989. The K1 could be had at about half the price of the D50, while boasting multi-timbralism. The region also underutilized one of the most impressive of them all, the Kurzweil K2000, phenomenally popular outside of the Caribbean. It is significant that this instrument is regarded by many industry connoisseurs as one of the very rare modern classics of its time. Yet it was hardly used in the Caribbean when it was in active production because of the perception created in the Caribbean that manufacturers like Kurzweil were radical, unstable, and hence their instruments, though highly priced and immensely powerful, were not good investments. But Caribbean musicians failed to realize that the entire industry was volatile. So regional users of technology fell into the trap of marketers who wanted to maintain the profile and sound base established by Yamaha, Korg and Roland. There is a clearly mapped-out strategy that has pinned music users down to specifically branded manufactured music wares. For these reasons, therefore, the market for synth and other music equipment in the Caribbean seems to offer a narrow collection of gadgets for those who shop in the region.

By the late 1990s, many bands also clamoured to collect one of Roland's sixty-four-voice polyphony XP-80s, which were primarily used for their punchy dance-type sounds. By 2002 there were signs of popularity for the Yamaha Motif line. But there were other neglected alternatives, such as the seventy-six or eighty-eight-note Kurzweil K2500, with VAST technology on tow, and also the K2600 and K2661. Many more musical acts now employ Kurzweil wares, as does the leading production company CRS Music studio. Indeed, it must be said that from the late 1990s, there appeared to be a tendency on the part of musicians across the region to go in search of their own equipment, either while on tour or by individual importation. The Guyanese band Jahrusalem is such an independent outfit. Throughout the 1990s and into the present, Jahrusalem has not been afraid to experiment. Central to the band's distinctive sound has been the investments they have made in a mixed collection of leading-edge hardware and software. Jahrusalem has made use of synthesizers by Alesis(QS8), Korg (N364 and Triton) and Kurzweil(PC88). They have also employed Kurzweil for MIDI control. These instruments feature on the 2001 two-disc release, clips of every song which were posted online at http://www.geocities.com/jahrusalem/music.html.

At the turn of the new millennium, physical modelling synths seemed the instruments of the future. According to one definition, physical modelling is "a method of synthesis in which a mathematical model of the instrument being synthesized is used to create the sound. It is the best way of approximating a real instrument".[5] But keyboards like the Yamaha Z1 and retro virtual analogues like Clavia's Nord Lead 2, Roland's JP8000, Yamaha's AN1X and Kurzweil's VA1, though extremely expressive machines, were still the possessions of a relatively small number of musicians who were creating new sounds throughout the region.

A much more liberating revolution has already started to take root, through computer music and innovations such as "virtual instruments". But greater access to musical instruments and creative tools carries the burden of wresting control of the technology. This is a point that resonates even more widely given the fact that the computer appears to be the instrument of choice for more professional and amateur musicians than any other piece of equipment. Given its popularity, it is likely that Caribbean musicians will continue to labour diligently to construct new sound metaphors, genres and subgenres. All this represents the continuation of the process of creating new and renewed cultural forms. The future of the region might very well not only reveal the extent to which Caribbean society has projected its culture by way of technology, but, paradoxically, it might also come to reflect the ways in which technology has created and recreated facets of this very culture.

Quick Mix-Down

In Caribbean history, particularly our very recent history, we have gone in search of musical styles which would help to define us. In the 1980s, digital processing and programmability allowed technologized variations on calypso, reggae and other genres. Throughout the 1990s, the music was in a state of greater flux as a result of the fusion of "traditional" categories (reggae, calypso) with many other styles. It is therefore still difficult to say conclusively what many of the new styles are called or what they will evolve into. I have ventured to say that many of the styles being produced today have certainly outstripped the labels that were ascribed to them a decade ago. The impact of new techniques of music creation, coupled with the blurring of boundaries between extant music genres, signals the passing of music styles such as soca and dancehall/ragga. In the first decade of the twenty-first century, Caribbean music is without doubt in a post-soca, post-dancehall phase. New evolving attitudes to and styles of playing, recording, producing and disseminating the music are important signs of a culture in transition.

It is evident that Caribbean society is being greatly affected by global politics and the culture that both supports and exudes from globalization. The new global site of virtual contestation is in the arena of culture. Caribbean societies are no less implicated in the culture wars than they are in other kinds of struggles that take place with respect to trade, offshore finance-sector arrangements, whaling and money laundering. In the new global dispensation, Caribbean societies have had to negotiate a path of development in the context of tightened legislation relating to trade practices. Banana regimes of the Caribbean have, for example, had to face challenges to their preferential access to markets in Europe. Challenges from larger Latin American and North American interests have revealed the role that trade, finance, economics, politics and (necessarily) culture play in the repositioning of nations. Since 2000, Caribbean governments have found themselves under pressure to navigate the course towards progress. In addition to local challenges relating to race, ethnicity, attitudes and age, they increasingly have to deal with the Organization for Economic Cooperation and Development, the World Trade Organization and other international organizations. While they struggle to satisfy major powers and major treaties, their cultural integrity is under threat. Indeed, since 2000, Caribbean culture has undergone significant transformation. Social and cultural planners have hardly critically examined the causes and effects of this transformation on the region in a timely manner.

It is within the domain inhabited by the music, movie, fashion and Internet industries that the new contest for power will be fought most vigorously. The achievement of global pre-eminence is now to be had through the control of these media. Like graffiti taggers who once fought for space in the inner cities and subway systems, high-tech global industries now hustle to control cyberspace and related terrains. The music industry and its affiliates worldwide have for some time been shaping human attitudes to local and global culture through the production, marketing and dissemination of music. The major record companies and their associates have had a range of effects, but one significant impact has been to streamline and dominate global cultural production. The major companies have laid down the criteria by which other entities who wish to compete head to head must play. Although there is room for some autonomy – offered by the potentially liberating world of the Internet – Caribbean artists and societies as a whole seem increasingly to be at the mercy of transnational interests.

As Caribbean culture evolves, academic criticism is also faced with the challenge of upgrading itself and of finding the language with which to critique the new developments. What will the Caribbean produce for itself and the world in the coming years of a new dispensation? This is a world of real and virtual instruments, a world of real and virtual culture. It is not easy to say what will transpire. But it is clear that innovation will abound. It is clear that some of the debates addressed in this book will preoccupy Caribbean society for a long time. The hope must be, however, that whatever is produced is created with tradition in mind, with critical insight that interrogates the technologies used and with a definite attitude that reflects a meaningful ideology.

Notes

Track 1: Reading Culture as Multi-tracked

1. Gordon Rohlehr, *Calypso and Society in Pre-independence Trinidad* (Tunapuna, Trinidad: H.E.M. Printers, 1990).
2. Carolyn Cooper, *Noises in the Blood: Orality, Gender and the "Vulgar" Body of Jamaican Popular Culture* (Warwick: Macmillan, 1993).
3. Peter Manuel, et al., *Caribbean Currents* (Philadelphia: Temple University Press, 1995); Peter Van Koningsbruggen, *Trinidad Carnival: A Quest for National Identity* (London: Macmillan,1997); John Cowley, *Carnival, Canboulay and Calypso: Traditions in the Making* (Cambridge: Cambridge University Press, 1996).
4. John Perry Barlow, "A Declaration of the Independence of Cyberspace", *Electronic Frontier Foundation* (1996), http://www.eff.org/~barlow/ Declaration-Final.html.
5. See such cyberculture texts as Pierre Babin and Angela Zukowski, *The Gospel in Cyberspace: Nurturing Faith in the Internet Age* (Chicago: Loyola, 2002); Adam Joinson, *Understanding the Psychology of Internet Behaviour: Virtual Worlds, Real Lives* (Basingstoke, UK: Palgrave Macmillan, 2002); Stephen Lax, ed., *Access Denied in the Information Age* (Basingstoke, UK: Palgrave, 2001); Andrew Murphie and John Potts, *Culture and Technology* (New York: Palgrave Macmillan, 2003); Allucquere Roseanne Stone, *The War of Desire and Technology at the End of the Mechanical Age* (Boston: MIT Press, 1995); and Mark Poster, *What's the Matter with the Internet?* (Minneapolis: University of Minnesota Press, 2001).
6. "Multitrack Recording", *Wikipedia,* http://en2.wikipedia.org/wiki/ multitrack_recording.
7. For an example of a state-of-the-art sound-mixing console in late 2003, see the MH3 from Soundcraft, at http://www.soundcraft.com/product _sheet.asp?product_id=6.

8. For a diagrammatic explanation, see Jeffrey Hass, *Mixing Console Input Channels* (Bloomington: Indiana University School of Music, Center for Electronic and Computer Music, 2001), http://www.indiana.edu/~emusic/mixer.html.

9. For an explanation of the process with particular equipment, see Aviom, "Connecting Audio from a Mixing Board to the A-16 Transmitter" (2003), http://www.aviominc.com/setup_overview02.html.

10. For some elaboration on multi-timbrality, see Curwen Best, "Reading Graffiti in the Caribbean Context", *Journal of Popular Culture* 36 (2003): 828–52.

11. Paul Wiffen, "Multitimbrality: A Brief History", *Sound on Sound* (June 1994), http://www.soundonsound.com/sos/1994_articles/jun94/multitimbrality.html.

12. For example, compare a monophonic instrument, such as the Sequential Pro-One (http://www.synthmuseum.com/sequ/seqproone01.html), with a multi-timbral synthesizer, such as Kurzweil's K2600 (http://www.kurzweilmusicsystems.com/html/k2600.html).

13. For an example of equipment that can perform these functions, see the Alesis ADAT HD24 (http://www.alesis.com/products/hd24/index.html).

Track 2: Sounding Calypso's Muted Tracks, Past and Present: Barbados + St Lucia

1. Kendel Hippolyte, "Calypso through the Years", *Lucian Kaiso,* no. 1 (1990): 7–9, 16.

2. In addition to live entertainment packages, there were specific radio programmes both in Barbados and Trinidad which carried the title *Bajan Invasion.* See also "Fetes and Parties: Bajan Invasion – Pier 1, Jan 31", *Carnival on 'de Net 1997,* http://www.visittnt.com/Carnival1997/.

3. See one such comparison by the respected Guyanese literary critic Al Creighton, "The Satanic Rehearsals", in *The Pressures of the Text: Orality, Texts and the Telling of Tales,* ed. Stewart Brown, 37–46 (Birmingham, UK: University of Birmingham, Centre of West African Studies, 1995).

4. See James Reese Europe, *Readings in Black American Music* (New York: n.p., 1983); Jocelyn Guilbault, "The Politics of Labelling Popular Musics in the English Caribbean", *Revista Transcultural de Música/Transcultural Music Review* 3 (1997), http://www.sibetrans.com/trans/trans3/indice3.htm.

5. Keith Q. Warner lists many of these origins of the word *calypso* in *The Trinidad Calypso: A Study of the Calypso as Oral Literature* (Washington, DC: Three Continents Press, 1982).

6. This is according to Errol Hill, a leading writer on carnival and calypso, in *The Trinidad Carnival: Mandate for a National Theatre* (London: New Beacon, 1997), 61.

7. Raymond Quevedo, *Atilla's Kaiso: A Short History of the Trinidad Calypso* (St Augustine, Trinidad: Extra-Mural Department, University of the West Indies, 1983), 4.

8. Roaring Lion [Rafael de Leon], *Calypso from France to Trinidad* (Port of Spain: General Printers, 1986).

9. See Gordon Rohlehr, *Calypso and Society in Pre-independence Trinidad* (Port of Spain: Gordon Rohlehr, 1990).

10. On the griot tradition, see Ruth Finnegan, *Oral Literature in Africa* (London: Clarendon, 1970).

11. Richard Allsopp, *Dictionary of Caribbean English Usage* (1996; Kingston, Jamaica: University of the West Indies Press, 2003), 131.

12. Rohlehr, *Calypso and Society*, 1.

13. Quevedo, *Atilla's Kaiso*, 2.

14. Roger Abrahams and John F. Szwed, eds. *After Africa: Extracts from British Travel Accounts and Journals of the Seventeenth, Eighteenth, and Nineteenth Centuries concerning the Slaves, Their Manners, and Customs in the British West Indies* (New Haven: Yale University Press, 1983); Mervyn Alleyne, *Roots of Jamaican Culture* (London: Pluto, 1988) and *Contemporary Afro-American* (Ann Arbor: Karoma, 1980); E. K. Brathwaite, "Jazz and the West Indian Novel", *Bim* 44–46 (1967–68): 275–84, 39–51, 115–26; Melville Herskovitz, *The Myth of the Negro Past* (Boston: Beacon, 1958); Orlando Patterson, *The Sociology of Slavery: An Analysis of the Origins, Development and Structure of Negro Slave Society in Jamaica* (London: MacGibbon and Kee, 1967).

15. Trevor Marshall, *Notes on the History and Evolution of Calypso in Barbados* (Cave Hill, Barbados: University of the West Indies, 1986). See also Trevor Marshall, Peggy McGeary and Grace Thompson, *Folk Songs of Barbados* (Kingston, Jamaica: Ian Randle, 1996).

16. Richard Ligon, *A True and Exact History of the Island of Barbados* (London, 1657). Other sources also commented on Barbadian customs, for example, J. W. Orderson, *Creoleana; or, Social and Domestic Scenes and Incidents in Barbados in Days of Yore* (London, 1842), and John Oldmixon, *The British Empire in America: Containing the History of the*

Discovery, Settlement, Progress and Present State of All the British Colonies, on the Continent and Islands of America, vol. 2, *Being an Account of the Country, Soil, Climate, Product and Trade of Barbados, St Lucia, St Vincents* . . . (London, 1708).

17. William Dickson, *Letters on Slavery* . . . *to Which Are Added, Addresses to the Whites, and to the Free Negroes of Barbadoes; and Accounts of Some Negroes Eminent for Their Virtues and Abilities* (London: J. Phillips, 1789), 74–94.

18. Ibid., 93–94.

19. George Pinckard, *Notes on the West Indies: Written during the Expedition under the Command of the Late General Sir R. Abercrombie* (London, 1806), 1: 127.

20. Jerome Handler and Charlotte Frisbie, "Aspects of Slave Life in Barbados: Music and Its Cultural Context", *Caribbean Studies* 11, no. 4 (1972), 5–46, is a very good source for information on aspects of slave culture.

21. See Pinckard, *Notes on the West Indies*, 1: 264–65.

22. Dickson, *Letters*, 74.

23. Bryan Edwards, *The History, Civil and Commercial, of the British Colonies in the West Indies* (Dublin: Luke White, 1793), 2: 79–82.

24. Pinckard, *Notes on the West Indies*, 1: 127.

25. Quevedo, *Atilla's Kaiso*, 18.

26. Ibid., 19.

27. Reference to Shilling's statements are derived from an interview aired on CBC Radio, November 1994.

28. Charmer, Voice of Barbados Radio, *c*.1994.

29. Some of the material used in discussing St Lucian music is derived from radio programmes and discussions on St Lucian radio over the years, as well as on Helen Television. The yearly carnival magazine *Lucian Kaiso* has also been a valuable source, as have Jacques Compton, ed., *Carnival Expose: Memories of St Lucia Carnival, 1950s to 1990s* (Castries, St Lucia: Expose Publishing, 1998), and various articles in the *St Lucia Voice*. Useful Internet sites include *Kaiso Newsletter*, 26 July 2000, http://www.mustrad.org.uk/articles/kaiso37.htm; St Lucia Carnival 2004, http://www.luciancarnival.com; Radio St Lucia Online, mas results, http://www.isisworld.lc/rsl/masresults.htm; Summer Cove Limited, http://www.iere.com; Carnival Power.com, http://carnivalpower.com; TropicalFete.com, http://www.tropicalfete.com; SugarK.com Soca Experience, http://www.sugark.com; and Caribbean-Search.com,

Caribbean Carnival page, http://www.caribbean-search.com/carnival.cfm.

30. Gordon Rohlehr, "We Getting the Kaiso We Deserve: Calypso and the World Music Market", *Drama Review* 42, no. 3 (1988): 82–95.

31. "The Mighty Pelay Speaks Out on the State of Calypso", *St Lucia Star,* 5 July 1999, http://www.stluciastar.com/Wednesday%20STAR%20 Online/wedjul5/news4.htm.

32. Ambassadors' Calypso Tent Web page, http://ambassadorscalypsotent .netfirms.com/.

Track 3: Towards a Caribbean Gospel Aesthetic

1. See, for example, Ted Olsen, "Weblog: Are Gospel Music Grammys Religious Bigotry?" *Christianity Today,* 24 February 2003, http://www .christianitytoday.com/ct/2003/108/13.0.html.

2. Center for Black Music Research, "Gospel Music", http://www.cbmr .org/styles/gospel.htm.

3. Eileen Southern, *The Music of Black Americans: A History,* 2nd ed. (New York: Norton), 446.

4. Jack Nesbitt, "Go Ye into All the World: St Lucia" (2001), http://www .saved.com/t&t/archive/2001/t2001058.htm.

5. See Roger D. Abrahams, *The Man of Words in the West Indies: Performance and the Emergence of Creole Culture* (Baltimore: Johns Hopkins University Press, 1983).

6. Curwen Best, *Barbadian Popular Music and the Politics of Caribbean Culture,* 2nd ed. (Rochester, Vt.: Schenkman, 1999).

7. Emmanuel Joseph, *Twenty Five Years of Joseph Niles* (St Michael, Barbados: Alpha Productions, 1985), 4.

8. See, for example, Fransisco Records, http://www.fran-co.u-net.com/ prod03.htm (26 November 2003).

9. Best, *Barbadian Popular Music.*

10. Although Peter Manuel seems to hint at a close relationship between gospel and other performers, there is no marked reciprocation in this relationship; Peter Manuel, *Caribbean Currents: Caribbean Music from Rumba to Reggae,* with Kenneth Bilby and Michael Largey (Philadelphia: Temple University Press, 1995), 171–72.

11. Curwen Best, *Roots to Popular Culture: Barbadian Aesthetics, Kamau Brathwaite to Hardcore Styles* (London: Macmillan, 2001).

12. "Gospel Music Sales Show Double-Digit Growth", Industry News,

GospelCity.com, 25 August 2002, http://www.gospelcity.com/industry
_news/0208/gospel_sales.php.

13. Gary Kinnaman, *The Beginner's Guide to Praise and Worship* (Ann
    Arbor: Vine Books, 2003). For a perspective on "Word of Faith"
    theology, see D. R. McConnell, *A Different Gospel: Biblical and
    Historical Insights into the Word of Faith Movement* (Peabody, Mass.:
    Hendrickson, 1995).

14. Daniel Miller, "Deconstructing 'Praise and Worship': The Myth of the
    Sacred versus the Secular", *Next-Wave* (2001), http://www.next-wave
    .org/jul01/deconstructing.htm.

15. "The Dynamic Force", *IUMA*, http://artists.iuma.com/IUMA/Bands/
    THE_DYNAMIC_FORCE/index-0.html (28 November 2003).

16. "Junior C", *IUMA*, http://artists.iuma.com/IUMA/Bands/Junior_C/.

17. Main Street Music is a company based in Washington, DC, that markets
    itself as being one of the most reliable sites offering music downloads over
    the Internet.

18. For a representative descriptive overview of Caribbean gospel, see Rosita
    Forde and Adisa Andwele, "The Evolution of Caribbean Gospel",
    Ringbang Magazine 1, no. 2 (1997–98): 13.

Track 4: Discourses on AIDS (+ Sex) in Caribbean Music

1. "The Caribbean Partnership Commitment, 2001" (14 February 2001),
   http://www.caricom.org/archives/partnershipcommitment.htm.

2. UNAIDS, http://www.unaids.org/aidspub/index.asp. See, for example, the
   article "AIDS Education: A Battle against Ignorance" (27 June 2001).

3. Andy Humm and Frances Kunreuther, "The Invisible Epidemic: Teenagers
   and AIDS", in *AIDS: Opposing Viewpoints*, ed. Michael Biskup and
   Karin Swisher, 141–48 (San Diego: Greenhaven, 1992).

4. William Graebner, "The Erotic and Destructive in 1980s Rock Music",
   Soundscapes.info 1 (Winter 1998), http://www.icce.rug.nl/~soundscapes/
   DATABASES/TRA/The_erotic_and_destructive.html.

5. Peter Manuel, *Caribbean Currents: Caribbean Music from Rumba to
   Reggae*, with Kenneth Bilby and Michael Largey (Philadelphia: Temple
   University Press, 1995), 178.

6. John Fiske. *Understanding Popular Culture* (London: Routledge, 1992),
   2.

7. Manuel, *Caribbean Currents*.

8. See Richard Chirimuuta and Rosalind Chirimuuta, *AIDS, Africa and Racism* (London: Free Association, 1987), with updates at http://way .net/dissonance/aidsafrbk.html; Annabel Kanabus and Sarah Allen, "The Origins of AIDS and HIV and the First Cases of AIDS", *Avert.org*, http://www.avert.org/origins.htm.

9. Randy Dotinga, "Study Ties Rap Videos to Violence, Promiscuity", *Detroit Free Press*, 10 March 2003, http://www.freep.com/entertainment/ music/rap10_20030310.htm.

10. Baz Dreisinger, "Dancehall Star's Key to Success", *Miami Herald*, 27 October 2002, http://www.miami.com/mld/miami/entertainment/ 4368579.htm.

11. Corey Moss, "Snoop Dogg, Ja Rule, Beenie Man Busted for Swearing", *VH1.com*, 31 August 2001, http://www.vh1.com/artists/news/1448575/ 08312001/beenie_man.jhtml.

12. This debate between Bartholomew and Rudder is discussed by Kevin Baldeosingh, "Show Me Your Enemies", *Caribbean Commentary*, 5 August 1999, http://www.caribscape.com/baldeosingh/religion/sober/ 1999/enemy.html.

13. David Mangurian "A Musical Role Model", *IDBAmerica*, June 2001, http://www.iadb.org/idbamerica/index.cfm?thisid=885.

14. Maha Sabha, "Carnival and the Death of Culture", *Trinidad Express*, reprinted in *VICS Newsletter* 2, no. 2 (1998), Virtual Institute of Caribbean Studies, http://pw1.netcom.com/~hhenke/news3.htm.

15. Jason Sifflet, "St Lucia, Simply Spiritual . . . Right?", *St Lucia Mirror*, 20 September 2002, http://www.stluciamirroronline.com/2002/sep20/ art2.htm.

16. C. Barillas, "Caribbean Countries Resist Gay Reform" [editorial], *The Data Lounge*, 20 February 1998, http://www.datalounge.com/datalounge/ news/record.html?record=2764&continuebutton=Not +Now; C. Barillas, "Cayman Islands Spurns UK Request to Lo[o]se Gay Law" [editorial], *The Data Lounge*, 2 April 1999, http://www.datalounge.com/datalounge/ news/record.html?record=4105.

17. Tania Branigan, "BBC Withdraws 'Homophobic' Reggae Tracks", *Guardian*, 30 August 2002, http://www.guardian.co.uk/arts/news/story/ 0,11711,783015,00.html.

18. Zadie Neufville, "Jamaica: Taking a Stand against Homophobic Violence", *SHAAN Online* (2001), http://www.ipsnews.net/hivaids/new _2612_3.shtml.

19. Tanya Baker, "Tobago: Culture, Calypso and Sexual Education", *Watchdog* 4, no. 3 (2001), http://www.youthcoalition.org/watchdog/engine.php/v4n3/128/.

20. Gillian Murphy, "LIFEbeat: Building Bridges, Making Music", *Body Positive* 14, no. 4 (2001), http://www.thebody.com/bp/apr01/lifebeat.html.

21. "Rock News: Red Hot + Positive", *Rolling Stone,* 5 September 1996, 23–24.

Track 5: Finding the New Hardcore in Caribbean Music

1. Peter Manuel, *Caribbean Currents: Caribbean Music from Rumba to Reggae,* with Kenneth Bilby and Michael Largey (Philadelphia: Temple University Press, 1995); John Cowley, *Carnival, Canboulay and Calypso: Traditions in the Making* (Cambridge: Cambridge University Press, 1996); Peter van Koningsbruggen, *Trinidad Carnival: A Quest for National Identity* (London: Macmillan, 1997); Michael Erlewine, ed., *All Music Guide: The Best CDs, Albums and Tapes: The Experts' Guide to the Best Releases from Thousands of Artists in All Types of Music,* with Chris Woodstra and Vladimir Bogdanov (San Francisco: Miller Freeman, 1994); Peter Mason, *Bacchanal: The Carnival Culture of Trinidad* (Kingston, Jamaica: Ian Randle, 1998); Louis Regis, *The Political Calypso: True Opposition in Trinidad and Tobago, 1962–1987* (Kingston, Jamaica: University of the West Indies Press, 1999). See also Hollis Liverpool, *Kaiso and Society* (Diego Martin, Trinidad: Juba Publications, 1990); John Patton, "Communication and Cultural Identity through Calypso and Poetic Discourse", *Bulletin of Eastern Caribbean Affairs* 19, no. 3 (1994): 53–68; Stephen Stuempfle, *The Steelband Movement: The Forging of a National Art in Trinidad and Tobago* (Kingston, Jamaica: University of the West Indies Press, 1995). Gene Scaramuzzo provides an overview, "Calypso and Steelband Music of the Caribbean", and other, smaller reviews of Caribbean calypso and soca in Erlewine's *All Music Guide,* but these are highly descriptive, terse and detached.

2. Mike Alleyne, "The Transnationalization of Caribbean Music: Capitalism and Cultural Intertextuality" (PhD dissertation, University of the West Indies, Cave Hill, Barbados, 1996).

3. Dick Hebdige, *Cut 'n' Mix: Culture, Identity and Caribbean Music*

(London: Methuen, 1987); Christian Habekost, *Verbal Riddim: The Politics and Aesthetics of African-Caribbean Dub Poetry* (Amsterdam: Rodopi, 1993); Carolyn Cooper, *Noises in the Blood: Orality, Gender and the "Vulgar" Body of Jamaican Popular Culture* (London: Macmillan, 1993); Kwame Dawes, *Natural Mysticism* (Leeds, UK: Peepal Tree Press, 1999), and *Wheel and Come Again: An Anthology of Reggae Poetry* (Leeds, UK: Peepal Tree Press, 1998); Kevin Chang and Wayne Chen, *Reggae Routes: The Story of Jamaican Music* (Kingston, Jamaica: Ian Randle, 1998); Colin Larkin, ed., *The Guinness Who's Who of Reggae* (Enfield, UK: Guinness, 1994). See also Nathaniel Samuel Murrell, William David Spencer, and Adrian Anthony McFarlane, eds, *Chanting Down Babylon: The Rastafari Reader* (Kingston, Jamaica: Ian Randle, 1998); Geoff Small, *Ruthless: The Global Rise of the Yardies* (London: Warner, 1995); Norman Stolzoff, *Wake the Town and Tell the People: Dancehall Culture in Jamaica* (Durham, NC: Duke University Press, 2000).

4. See also Curwen Best, "Culture-thru-Technology" (paper presented at first UWI Cultural Studies Conference, Mona, Jamaica, 1997); Best, "Reading Graffiti in the Caribbean Context", *Journal of Popular Culture* 36 (2003): 828–52; Best, *Roots to Popular Culture: Barbadian Aesthetics, Kamau Brathwaite to Hardcore Styles* (London: Macmillan, 2001).

5. Ted Greenwald, *The Musician's Home Recording Handbook: Practical Techniques for Recording Great Music at Home* (San Francisco: Miller Freeman, 1992). Important magazines include *EQ, Project Recording and Sound Techniques, dB Magazine* and *Keyboard.*

6. *Trinidad Express,* http://trinidadexpress.com

7. Curwen Best, *Barbadian Popular Music and the Politics of Caribbean Culture,* 2nd ed. (Rochester, Vt.: Schenkman, 1999).

8. Earl Lawrence, "Ras Shorty I: Pioneer of Soca", *Sensay Dominica Soca Page* (n.d.), http://www.angelfire.com/ny/Playmas/shorty.html (1 December 2003).

9. Scott Rollins, "Eddy Grant Talks about Ringbang", *Zeeburg Nieuws* (2000), http://www.zeeburgnieuws.nl/kofi/kofi- ringbang2.html.

10. Jocelyne Guilbault touches partly on the ringbang phenomenon in "The Politics of Labelling Popular Musics in the English Caribbean", *Revista Transcultural de Música/Transcultural Music Review* 3 (1997), http://www.sibetrans.com/trans/trans3/indice3.htm.

11. See J. H. Kwabena Nketia, *The Music of Africa* (London: Gollancz, 1975), especially see chapter 7.

12. Colin Larkin, ed., *The Guinness Who's Who of Reggae*, 104.

13. For more on these tools, see Geoff Martin, "Compressors, Limiters, Expanders and Gates", chapter 2 of *Introduction to Sound Recording* (2002), http://www.tonmeister.ca/main/textbook/electroacoustics/02.html.

14. See Jo-Ann Greene, "Eddy Grant", *All Music Guide*, http://www.allmusic .com/cg/amg.dll (1 December 2003).

15. Jocelyne Guilbault, "Beyond the 'World Music' Label: An Ethnography of Transnational Music Practices", *Grounding Music* (May 1996), http:// www2.rz.hu-berlin.de/fpm/texte/guilbau.htm.

16. See, for example, "Ringbang University" on the Ice Records Web site, http://www.icerecords.com/univ.php.

17. Gillian Calliste, "Does Being New Wave Make It Ragga Soca?" *Sunday Guardian*, 21 February 1999, http://www.nalis.gov.tt/music/music _raggasoca.html.

18. Best, *Barbadian Popular Music*.

19. For a simple explanation of frequency in music, see PSB Speakers International, "The Frequencies – and Sound – of Music", http://www .psbspeakers.com/FrequenciesOfMusic.html (2 December 2003).

20. N'delamiko Lord, "Breaking the Ice", *Executive Time Magazine: Caribbean Edition* (n.d.), http://www.angelfire.com/journal/executivetime/ eddie.htm.

Track 6: Music Video to Web Streaming: Cultural Ventriloquism @ the Leading Edge

1. See Linton Corbie, review of *Goodnight Ladies and Gents* by Lionel Belasco (Peterborough Folk Music Society, 1999), http://www .acousticmusic.com/fame/p01100.htm.

2. See, for example, Tom Weber and Brian Jahn, *Reggae Island: Jamaican Music in the Digital Age* (Kingston, Jamaica: Kingston Publishers, 1992).

3. Ray Funk, obituary for Roaring Lion, *Kaiso Newsletter*, no. 25 (14 July 1999), http://www.mustrad.org.uk/articles/kaiso25.htm.

4. Michael Garnice, "Harry Belafonte and Mento Music", 2003, http:// www.mentomusic.com/HarryBelafonte.htm.

5. Ray Funk, "Andrews Sisters", *Kaiso Newsletter*, no. 33 (14 January 2000), http://www.mustrad.org.uk/articles/kaiso33.htm.

6. John Ross, "Cuban Music's Forgotten Man", *San Francisco Bay Guardian*, 20 October 1999, http://www.sfbg.com/News/34/03/3world.html.

7. Jon Anderson, "New Media and Globalization in the Internet Age", keynote address, Middle East Virtual Community (MEVIC) conference, August 2000, http://www.mevic.org/keynote.html.

8. Lynette Lashley, "Television and the Cultural Environment in Trinidad: A Need for Policy", *Bulletin of Eastern Caribbean Affairs* 20, no. 4 (1995): 7–16. These points are also emphasized in Mbye Cham, ed., *Ex-Iles: Essays in Caribbean Cinema* (Trenton, NJ: Africa World Press, 1992); Rex Nettleford, ed., "Communication Arts", *Caribbean Quarterly* 40, no. 2 (1994), special issue; Keith Q. Warner, *On Location: Cinema and Film in the Anglophone Caribbean* (London: Macmillan, 2000); and the television documentary *And the Dish Ran Away with the Spoon*, dir. Christopher Laird and Anthony Hall (Banyan/BBC, 1992).

9. See Bill Ashcroft, Gareth Griffiths and Helen Tiffin, *The Empire Writes Back: Theory and Practice in Post-Colonial Literatures* (London: Routledge, 1989).

10. Michel Foucault, *The History of Sexuality,* vol. 1, trans. Robert Hurley (Harmondsworth: Penguin, 1978), 100.

11. "Soundies", UCLA Film and Television Archives, http://www.cinema .ucla.edu/collections/Profiles/soundies.html.

12. Jeff Vilencia, Billy Ingram, et al., "TV's First Music Videos", *TVParty!* (n.d.), http://www.tvparty.com/vaultvid.html.

13. Steve Levy, "Ad Nauseam: How MTV Sells Out Rock and Roll", *Rolling Stone,* 8 December 1986.

14. Bill Aicher, "Video Created the Revenue Star: How MTV Works with Major Record Labels to Create Stars", *Music-Critic.com* (n.d.), http://www.music-critic.com/articles/revenuestar.htm. See also Alan Cross, *Alternative Rock* (Burlington, Ont.: Collector's Guide Publishing, 1999).

15. Rick Altman, "Moving Lips: Cinema as Ventriloquism", *Yale French Studies* 60 (1980): 67–79.

16. Ibid., 76–77.

17. Suzanne Moore, "Here's Looking at You, Kid!", *The Female Gaze: Women as Viewers of Popular Culture,* ed. Lorraine Gamman and Margaret Marshment (Seattle: The Real Comet Press, 1988), 47.

18. Christopher Knab, "Inside Record Labels: Organizing Things", *Music Biz Academy.com* (2001), http://www.musicbizacademy.com/knab/ articles/insidelabels.htm.

19. Kala Grant, "The Dynamics of Female Empowerment in Jamaican Dancehall" (paper presented in the Warwick University Centre for Caribbean Studies Seminar Series, Warwick, UK, January 2003).

20. Laura Mulvey, "Visual Pleasure and Narrative Cinema", *Screen* 16, no. 3 (1975): 6–18.

21. Frantz Fanon, *The Wretched of the Earth*, trans. Constance Farrington (New York: Grove, 1963), 170.

22. Edward Said, *Orientalism* (New York: Pantheon, 1978).

23. Lawrence Grossberg, "The Media Economy of Rock Culture: Cinema, Postmodernity, and Authenticity", in *Sound and Vision: The Music Video Reader*, ed. Simon Frith, Andrew Goodwin and Lawrence Grossberg, 185–209 (London: Routledge, 1993).

24. Renee Hobbes introduces some of these debates in "Classroom Strategies for Exploring Realism and Authenticity in Media Messages", *Reading Online* 4, no. 9 (2001), http://www.readingonline.org/newliteracies/hobbs/.

25. Philip Brophy, "Non Narrative Film Lecture: Video Clip Textuality: *Flashdance*" (1985–87), http://media-arts.rmit.edu.au/Phil_Brophy/MMAlec/Flashdance.html.

26. Thomas Levin, "The Acoustic Dimension: Notes on Film Sound", *Screen* 25, no. 3 (May–June 1984): 55–68.

27. James Lastra, "Reading, Writing and Representing Sound", in *Sound Theory/Sound Practice*, ed. Rick Altman, 65–86 (New York: Routledge, 1992).

28. Raymond Williams, *Problems in Materialism and Culture: Selected Essays* (London: New Life, 1980).

29. Lastra, "Reading, Writing and Representing Sound", 73.

30. Rick Altman, "Material Heterogeneity of Recorded Sound", in *Sound Theory/Sound Practice*, ed. Rick Altman (New York: Routledge, 1992), 19.

31. Jody Berland, "Music Video and Media Reconstruction", in *Sound and Vision: The Music Video Reader*, ed. Simon Frith, Andrew Goodwin and Lawrence Grossberg, 25–43 (London: Routledge, 1993).

32. "Real; genuine; actual"; Richard Allsopp, *Dictionary of Caribbean English Usage* (1996; Kingston, Jamaica: University of the West Indies Press, 2003), 568.

33. Christopher Knab, "What's a Record Label Deal All About?" *Music Biz Academy.com* (2002), http://www.musicbizacademy.com/knab/articles/recorddeal.htm.

34. Robert Walser, "Forging Masculinity:Heavy Metal Sounds and Images of Gender", in *Sound and Vision: The Music Video Reader*, ed. Simon Frith, Andrew Goodwin and Lawrence Grossberg, 153–81 (London: Routledge, 1993).

35. Eddy Grant, interview with the author, 1996.

36. Stefanie Olsen, "Media Players Play Musical Chairs", *CNET News.com*, 21 June 2002, http://news.com.com/2100-1023- 938423.html.

37. "Web Tops TV for Next Gen", *cvbTV.com*, 1 October 2002, http://www.cvbtv.com/industry/news100102-2.html.

38. Rudegal.com, http://www.rudegal.com/vidmenu.htm (5 December 2003). See also Michael A. Aczon, "The Changing Deal", *Electronic Musician*, 1 July 2000, http://millimeter.com/ar/emusic_changing_deal; Michael Bertin, "Indentured Servitude: The Cold, Hard Truth about Recording Contracts", *Austin Chronicle* 17, no. 41, http://www.austinchronicle.com/issues/vol17/issue41/music.labels.html; Deanna Campbell, Elizabeth Buck and Marlene Cuthbert, *Music at the Margins: Popular Music and Global Cultural Diversity* (Newbury Park, Calif.: Sage, 1991); Chester Francis-Jackson, *The Official Dancehall Dictionary* (Kingston, Jamaica: Kingston Publishers, 1995); David Kleiler, Jr, and Robert Moses, *You Stand There: Making Music Video* (New York: Three Rivers, 1997); Lynne Margolis, "Independents' Day", *Christian Science Monitor*, 11 April 2003, http://www.csmonitor.com/2003/0411/p13s02-almp.html; Peter Shapiro, *The Rough Guide to Hip Hop* (London: Rough Guides, 2001); and the Web sites PartyInc, http://www.partyinc.com/features/vp_deal.htm, and NetHistory, http://nethistory.urldir.com/napster.php.

Track 7: The "Big Technology" Question

Although I have actively participated in the use of some of the instruments and technologies discussed in this chapter, much of this knowledge is supported by hundreds of instrument brochures which I have collected for many years, featuring many of these technologies, particularly those from the following companies: 360 Systems, Akai, Alesis, Ampeg, ARP, Atwater Kent, Bachmann, Baldwin, BBE Sound, Beilfuss, Bit, Boss, Buchla, Burns, Casio, Cheetah, Chevin Research, Chroma, Clavia, Commander, Conrad-Johnson, Control Synthesis, Crown, Crumar, Cubase, Daewoo, Davis, Davoli, dbx, Denon, Digisound, Digital Keyboards, Doepfer, Dream, Dumble, EAW, EDP, EKO Sound, Electro-Harmonix, Electro-Voice, Elgam, Elka, Elvins, EML, EMS, E-MU Systems, Ensoniq, Evolution, Fairlight, Farfisa, Fender, Forat, Freeman, Furman Sound, Furstein, GEM, Gemini Sound Products, Generalmusic, Gibson, Gleeman, Goodwin, Goldstar, Greengate, Gretsch,

Groove Tubes, Hammond, Hartke Systems, Helpinstill, HIWATT
Amplification, Hohner, Hondo, JBL, Jen Electronics, Jennings, Jeremy
Lord (later, Lord), JHS, JVC, Kawai, Keytek, Kinetic Sound, Korg,
Kurzweil Music Systems, Kustom Amplification, Lexicon, Logan
Electronics, Lync, Mackie, Magnatone, Marion Systems, Marshall,
Matchless Amplifiers, McIntosh, Mesa/Boogie, Mellotron, Moog,
Multivox, Music Man, New England Digital, NLG Griff Audio,
Novation, Oberheim, Octave, Octave-Plateau, Orange, Orla, Oxford
Synthesizer Company, Pearl, Peavey, PianoDisk, Pioneer, PPG, Pyramid
Electronics, Quasimidi, Remo, Rhodes, Rickenbacker, RMI, Roland,
Samick Guitar, Selmer, Sequential Circuits, Shure, Siel, Simmons
Electronic Percussion, Soldano Custom Amplification, Solton, Soundcraft,
SoundTech, Steinberg, Studio Electronics, Tama, TASCAM, Technics,
Teisco, Tube Technology, Unique, Viscount, Voco, Vox, Waldorf,
Watkins, Wavestream, Wersi, White, Will Systems, Wurlitzer, Yamaha
and Zildjian.

The Internet was also a vital support source for information, some
of which initially was only widely available in the brochures mentioned
above. Dedicated Web pages also now exist for many of these companies.
Additional vital information on these companies' work, equipment and
gear was collected through informal discussion and interaction with
producers such as Eddy Grant and Cleve Scott, with personnel at NLG
Griff Audio, and with other industry personnel.

The following sources have also been particularly helpful: Glen Ballou,
ed., *Handbook for Sound Engineers* (Indianapolis: Sams, 1991); Don
Davis and Carolyn Davis, *The Sound Reinforcement Handbook*
(Milwaukee: Hal Leonard, 1988); Don Davis and Carolyn Davis, *Sound
System Engineering* (Indianapolis: Sams, 1987); Michael Doyle, *The Art
of the Amplifier* (Milwaukee: Hal Leonard, 1996); Phillip Giddings,
Audio Systems Design and Instalment (Boston: Focal, 1990); Daryl
Gilbert, *Guitars and Basses* (Milwaukee: Hal Leonard, 1998); Wade
McGregor, *Sound Systems* (Milwaukee: Hal Leonard, 1998); Nitebob,
Microphones (Milwaukee: Hal Leonard, 1998); Andrew Schlesinger,
Signal Processors (Milwaukee: Hal Leonard, 1998); David Trubitt,
Concert Sound: Tours, Techniques and Technology (Milwaukee: Hal
Leonard, 1993); David Trubitt, ed. *Making Music with Your Computer.*
Emeryville, Calif.: EM Books, 1993; and Jim Tucker, *Amp Basics*
(Milwaukee: Hal Leonard, 1998).

1. *Webopedia*, c.v. "tweaking", http://www.webopedia.com/TERM/t/tweak.html (12 December 2003); *The New Hacker's Dictionary*, http://www.jargon.8hz.com/jargon_35.html#SEC42.

2. Angela Pidduck, "Rent-a-Amp" (n.d), Angela Pidduck's home page, http://www.sputnick.com/angela/rent_a_amp.htm (15 December 2003).

3. For more on the functions of mixing boards, see Mike Sokol, "Mixing Board Basics: Part I", *TV Technology Magazine*, April 1997, http://www.modernrecording.com/articles/soundav/link25.html.

4. For a general history of the synthesizer, visit Synthmuseum.com, http://www.synthmuseum.com/magazine/archive.html. See also Julian Colbeck, *Keyfax Omnibus Edition: The Real Story behind the Synthesizer Revolution* (Emeryville, Calif.: Mix Books, 1996); Mark Vail, *Vintage Synthesizers* (San Francisco: Miller Freeman, 2000); Paul Théberge, *Any Sound You Can Imagine: Making Music/Consuming Technology* (Hanover, NH: Wesleyan University Press, 1997).

5. Mark White, "Glossary" (n.d.), *Virtual Synth Page*, http://www.markwhite.com/vsp/glossary.html.

Bibliography

Abrahams, Roger. *The Man of Words in the West Indies: Performance and the Emergence of Creole Culture*. Baltimore: Johns Hopkins University Press, 1983.

Abrahams, Roger, and John F. Szwed, eds. *After Africa: Extracts from British Travel Accounts and Journals of the Seventeenth, Eighteenth, and Nineteenth Centuries concerning the Slaves, Their Manners, and Customs in the British West Indies*. New Haven: Yale University Press, 1983.

Aczon, Michael A. "The Changing Deal". *Electronic Musician*. 1 July 2000. http://millimeter.com/ar/emusic_changing_deal.

Aicher, Bill. "Video Created the Revenue Star: How MTV Works with Major Record Labels to Create Stars". *Music-Critic.com*. N.d. http://www.music-critic.com/articles/revenuestar.htm.

Alleyne, Mervyn. *Contemporary Afro-American: An Historical Comparative Study of English Based Afro-American Dialects of the New World*. Ann Arbor: Karoma, 1980.

———. *Roots of Jamaican Culture*. London: Pluto, 1988.

Alleyne, Mike. "The Transnationalization of Caribbean Music: Capitalism and Cultural Intertextuality". PhD dissertation, University of the West Indies, Cave Hill, Barbados, 1996.

Allsopp, Richard. *Dictionary of Caribbean English Usage*. 1996; reprint, Kingston, Jamaica: University of the West Indies Press, 2003.

Altman, Rick. "Material Heterogeneity of Recorded Sound". In *Sound Theory/Sound Practice*, edited by Rick Altman, 15–34. New York: Routledge, 1992.

———. "Moving Lips: Cinema as Ventriloquism". *Yale French Studies* 60 (1980): 67–79.

Anderson, Jon. "New Media and Globalization in the Internet Age". Keynote address, Middle East Virtual Community (MEVIC) conference, August 2000. http://www.mevic.org/keynote.html.

Ashcroft, Bill, Gareth Griffiths and Helen Tiffin. *The Empire Writes Back: Theory and Practice in Post-Colonial Literatures*. London: Routledge, 1989.

Babin, Pierre, and Angela Zukowski. *The Gospel in Cyberspace: Nurturing Faith in the Internet Age*. Chicago: Loyola, 2002.

Ballou, Glen, ed. *Handbook For Sound Engineers*. Indianapolis: Sams, 1991.

Berland, Jody. "Music Video and Media Reconstruction". In *Sound and Vision: The Music Video Reader*, edited by Simon Frith, Andrew Goodwin and Lawrence Grossberg, 25–43. London: Routledge, 1993.

Bertin, Michael. "Indentured Servitude: The Cold, Hard Truth about Recording Contracts". *Austin Chronicle* 17, no. 41. http://www.austinchronicle.com/issues/vol17/issue41/music.labels.html.

Best, Curwen. *Barbadian Popular Music and the Politics of Caribbean Culture*. 2nd ed. Rochester, VT: Schenkman, 1999.

———. "Culture-thru-Technology". Paper presented at inaugural UWI Cultural Studies Conference in honour of Rex Nettleford, Mona, Jamaica, 1997.

———. "Reading Graffiti in the Caribbean Context". *Journal of Popular Culture* 36 (2003): 828–52.

———. *Roots to Popular Culture: Barbadian Aesthetics, Kamau Brathwaite to Hardcore Styles*. London: Macmillan, 2001.

Brathwaite, E. K. "Jazz and the West Indian Novel". *Bim* 44–46 (1967–68): 275–84, 39–51, 115–26.

Brophy, Philip. "Non Narrative Film Lecture: Video Clip Textuality: *Flashdance*". 1985–87. http://mediaarts.rmit.edu.au/Phil_Brophy/MMAlec/Flashdance.html.

Campbell, Deanna, Elizabeth Buck, and Marlene Cuthbert. *Music at the Margins: Popular Music and Global Cultural Diversity*. Newbury Park, Calif.: Sage, 1991.

Cham, Mbye, ed. *Ex-Iles: Essays in Caribbean Cinema*. Trenton, NJ: Africa World Press, 1992.

Chang, Kevin, and Wayne Chen. *Reggae Routes: The Story of Jamaican Music*. Kingston, Jamaica: Ian Randle, 1998.

Charles, Embert. "Judging Calypso". *Lucian Kaiso*, no. 1 (1990): 28–29, 33.

Chirimuuta, Richard, and Rosalind Chirimuuta. *AIDS, Africa and Racism*. London: Free Association, 1987.

Colbeck, Julian. *Keyfax Omnibus Edition: The Real Story behind the Synthesizer Revolution*. Emeryville, Calif.: Mix Books, 1996.

Compton, Jacques, ed. *Carnival Expose: Memories of St Lucia Carnival,*

1950s to 1990s. Castries, St Lucia: Expose Publishing, 1998.

Cooper, Carolyn. *Noises in the Blood: Orality, Gender and the "Vulgar" Body of Jamaican Popular Culture*. London: Macmillan, 1993.

Cowley, John. *Carnival, Canboulay and Calypso: Traditions in the Making*. Cambridge: Cambridge University Press, 1996.

Creighton, Al. "The Satanic Rehearsals". In *The Pressures of the Text: Orality, Texts and the Telling of Tales*, edited by Stewart Brown, 37–46 Birmingham, UK: University of Birmingham, Centre of West African Studies, 1995.

Cross, Alan. *Alternative Rock*. Burlington, Ont.: Collector's Guide Publishing, 1999.

Davis, Don, and Carolyn Davis. *The Sound Reinforcement Handbook*. Milwaukee: Hal Leonard, 1988.

———. *Sound System Engineering*. Indianapolis: Sams, 1987.

Dawes, Kwame. *Natural Mysticism*. Leeds, UK: Peepal Tree Press, 1999.

———. *Wheel and Come Again: An Anthology of Reggae Poetry*. Leeds, UK: Peepal Tree Press, 1998.

Dickson, William. *Letters on Slavery . . . to Which Are Added, Addresses to the Whites, and to the Free Negroes of Barbadoes; and Accounts of Some Negroes Eminent for Their Virtues and Abilities*. London: J. Phillips, 1789.

Doyle, Michael. *The Art of the Amplifier*. Milwaukee: Hal Leonard, 1996.

Dyott, William. *Dyott's Diary, 1781–1845: A Selection from the Journal of William Dyott, Sometime General in the British Army and Aide-de-Camp to His Majesty King George III*. Edited by Reginald Jeffrey. 2 vols. London: Constable, 1907.

Edwards, Brian. *The History, Civil and Commercial, of the British Colonies in the West Indies*. 2 vols. Dublin: Luke White, 1793.

Erlewine, Michael, ed. *All Music Guide: The Best CDs, Albums and Tapes: The Experts' Guide to the Best Releases from Thousands of Artists in All Types of Music*. With Chris Woodstra and Vladimir Bogdanov. San Francisco: Miller Freeman, 1994.

Fanon, Frantz. *The Wretched of the Earth*. Translated by Constance Farrington. New York: Grove, 1963.

Finnegan, Ruth. *Oral Literature in Africa*. London: Clarendon, 1970.

Fiske, John. *Understanding Popular Culture*. London: Unwin Hyman, 1989.

Forde, Rosita, and Adisa Andwele. "The Evolution of Caribbean Gospel". *Ringbang Magazine* 1, no. 2 (1997–98): 13.

Foucault, Michel. *The History of Sexuality: An Introduction*. Vol. 1. Translated by Robert Hurley. Harmondsworth, UK: Penguin, 1978.

Francis-Jackson, Chester. *The Official Dancehall Dictionary*. Kingston, Jamaica: Kingston Publishers, 1995.

Franklyn, Gilbert. *A Reply to R. B. Nicholls*. London, 1790.

Frith, Simon, Andrew Goodwin, and Lawrence Grossberg, eds. *Sound and Vision: The Music Video Reader*. London: Routledge, 1993.

Giddings, Phillip. *Audio Systems Design and Installation*. Boston: Focal, 1990.

Gilbert, Darrell. *Guitars and Basses*. Milwaukee: Hal Leonard, 1998.

Graebner, William. "The Erotic and Destructive in 1980s Rock Music". *Soundscapes.info* 1 (Winter 1998). http://www.icce.rug.nl/~soundscapes/ DATABASES/TRA/The_erotic_and_destructive.html.

Grant, Kala. "The Dynamics of Female Empowerment in Jamaican Dancehall". Paper presented in the Warwick University Centre for Caribbean Studies Seminar Series, Warwick, UK, January 2003.

Greenwald, Ted. *The Musician's Home Recording Handbook: Practical Techniques for Recording Great Music at Home*. San Francisco: Miller Freeman, 1992.

Grossberg, Lawrence. "The Media Economy of Rock Culture: Cinema, Postmodernity, and Authenticity". In *Sound and Vision: The Music Video Reader*, edited by Simon Frith, Andrew Goodwin and Lawrence Grossberg, 185–209. London: Routledge, 1993.

Guilbault, Jocelyne. "Beyond the 'World Music' Label: An Ethnography of Transnational Music Practices". *Grounding Music* (May 1996). http://www2.rz.hu-berlin.de/fpm/texte/guilbau.htm.

———. "The Politics of Labelling Popular Musics in the English Caribbean". *Revista Transcultural de Música/Transcultural Music Review* 3 (1997). http://www.sibetrans.com/trans/trans3/indice3.htm.

Habekost, Christian. *Verbal Riddim: The Politics and Aesthetics of African-Caribbean Dub Poetry*. Amsterdam: Rodopi, 1993.

Handler, Jerome, and Charlotte Frisbie. "Aspects of Slave Life in Barbados' Music and Its Cultural Context". *Caribbean Studies* 11, no. 4 (1972): 5–46.

Hebdige, Dick. *Cut 'n' Mix: Culture, Identity and Caribbean Music*. London: Methuen, 1987.

Hill, Errol. *The Trinidad Carnival: Mandate for a National Theatre*. London: New Beacon, 1997.

Hippolyte, Kendel. "Calypso through the Years". *Lucian Kaiso*, no. 1 (1990): 7–9, 16.

Hobbes, Renee. "Classroom Strategies for Exploring Realism and

Authenticity in Media Messages". *Reading Online* 4, no. 9 (2001). http://www.readingonline.org/newliteracies/hobbs/.

Humm, Andy, and Frances Kunreuther. "The Invisible Epidemic: Teenagers and AIDS". In *AIDS: Opposing Viewpoints,* edited by Michael Biskup and Karin Swisher, 141–48. San Diego: Greenhaven, 1992.

Joinson, Adam. *Understanding the Psychology of Internet Behaviour: Virtual Worlds, Real Lives.* Basingstoke, UK: Palgrave Macmillan, 2002.

Joseph, Emmanuel. *Twenty-Five Years of Joseph Niles.* St Michael, Barbados: Alpha Productions, 1985.

Kanabus, Annabel, and Sarah Allen. "The Origins of AIDS and HIV and the First Cases of AIDS". *Avert.org.* http://www.avert.org/origins.htm.

Kinnaman, Gary. *The Beginner's Guide to Praise and Worship.* Ann Arbor: Vine Books, 2003.

Kleiler, David, Jr, and Robert Moses. *You Stand There: Making Music Video.* New York: Three Rivers, 1997.

Knab, Christopher. "Inside Record Labels: Organizing Things". *Music Biz Academy.com.* 2001. http://www.musicbizacademy.com/knab/articles/insidelabels.htm.

———. "What's a Record Label Deal All About?" *Music Biz Academy.com.* 2002. http://www.musicbizacademy.com/knab/articles/recorddeal.htm.

Kurzweil Musician's Guide. Cerritos, Calif.: Young Chang USA, 1992.

Kurzweil Musician's Guide Supplement. Cerritos, Calif.: Young Chang USA, 1995.

Larkin, Colin, ed. *The Guinness Who's Who of Reggae.* Enfield, UK: Guinness, 1994.

Lashley, Lynette. "Television and the Cultural Environment in Trinidad: A Need for Policy". *Bulletin of Eastern Caribbean Affairs* 20, no. 4 (1995): 7–16.

Lastra, James. "Reading, Writing and Representing Sound". In *Sound Theory/Sound Practice,* edited by Rick Altman, 65–86. New York: Routledge, 1992.

Lax, Stephen, ed. *Access Denied in the Information Age.* Basingstoke, UK: Palgrave, 2001.

Levin, Thomas. "The Acoustic Dimension: Notes on Film Sense". *Screen* 25, no. 3 (1984): 55–68.

Levy, Steve. "Ad Nauseam: How MTV Sells Out Rock and Roll". *Rolling Stone,* 8 December 1986.

Light, Alan. *The Vibe History of Hip Hop.* New York: Three Rivers Press, 1999.

Ligon, Richard. *A True and Exact History of the Island of Barbados*. London, 1657.

Liverpool, Hollis. *Kaiso and Society*. Diego Martin, Trinidad: Juba Publications, 1990.

Manuel, Peter. *Caribbean Currents: Caribbean Music from Rumba to Reggae*. With Kenneth Bilby and Michael Largey. Philadelphia: Temple University Press, 1995.

Margolis, Lynne. "Independents' Day". *Christian Science Monitor*. 11 April 2003. http://www.csmonitor.com/2003/0411/p13s02-almp.html.

Marshall, Trevor. *Notes on the History and Evolution of Calypso in Barbados*. Cave Hill, Barbados: University of the West Indies, 1986.

Marshall, Trevor, Peggy McGeary and Grace Thompson. *Folk Songs of Barbados*. Kingston, Jamaica: Ian Randle, 1996.

Martin, Geoff. *Introduction to Sound Recording*. 2002. http://www.tonmeister.ca/main/textbook/index.html.

Mason, Peter. *Bacchanal: The Carnival Culture of Trinidad*. Kingston, Jamaica: Ian Randle, 1998.

McConnell, D. R. *A Different Gospel: Biblical and Historical Insights into the Word of Faith Movement*. Peabody, Mass.: Hendrickson, 1995.

McGregor, Wade. *Sound Systems*. Milwaukee: Hal Leonard, 1998.

Miller, Daniel. "Deconstructing 'Praise and Worship': The Myth of the Sacred versus the Secular". *Next-Wave* (2001). http://www.next-wave.org/jul01/deconstructing.htm.

Moore, Suzanne. "Here's Looking at You, Kid!" In *The Female Gaze: Women as Viewers of Popular Culture*, edited by Lorraine Gamman and Margaret Marshment, 44–59. Seattle: The Real Comet Press, 1988.

Mulvey, Laura. "Visual Pleasure and Narrative Cinema". *Screen* 16, no. 3 (1975): 6–18.

Murphie, Andrew, and John Potts. *Culture and Technology*. New York: Palgrave Macmillan, 2003.

Murrell, Nathaniel, William David Spencer, and Adrian Anthony McFarlane, eds. *Chanting Down Babylon: The Rastafari Reader*. Kingston, Jamaica: Ian Randle, 1998.

Nettleford, Rex, ed. "Communication Arts". *Caribbean Quarterly* 40, no. 2 (1994). Special issue.

Nitebob. *Microphones*. Milwaukee: Hal Leonard, 1998.

Nketia, J. H. *Kwabena: The Music of Africa*. London: Gollancz, 1975.

Oldmixon, John. *The British Empire in America: Containing the History of the Discovery, Settlement, Progress and Present State of All the British*

Colonies, on the Continent and Islands of America. Vol. 2. *Being an Account of the Country, Soil, Climate, Product and Trade of Barbados, St Lucia, St Vincents . . .* London, 1708.

Orderson, J. W. *Creoleana; or, Social and Domestic Scenes and Incidents in Barbados in Days of Yore.* London, 1842.

Patterson, Orlando. *The Sociology of Slavery: An Analysis of the Origins, Development and Structure of Negro Slave Society in Jamaica.* London: MacGibbon and Kee, 1967.

Patton, John. "Communication and Cultural Identity through Calypso and Poetic Discourse". *Bulletin of Eastern Caribbean Affairs* 19, no. 3 (1994): 53–68.

Pinckard, George. *Notes on the West Indies: Written during the Expedition under the Command of the Late General Sir R. Abercrombie.* 3 vols. London, 1806.

Poster, Mark. *What's the Matter with the Internet?* Minneapolis: University of Minnesota Press, 2001.

Quevedo, Raymond [Atilla the Hun]. *Atilla's Kaiso: A Short History of the Trinidad Calypso.* St Augustine, Trinidad: Extra-Mural Department, University of the West Indies, 1983.

Regis, Louis. *The Political Calypso: True Opposition in Trinidad and Tobago, 1962–1987.* Kingston, Jamaica: University of the West Indies Press, 1999.

Roaring Lion [Raphael de Leon]. *Calypso from France to Trinidad: 800 Years of History.* Port of Spain: General Printers, 1986.

Rohlehr, Gordon. *Calypso and Society in Pre-independence Trinidad.* Port of Spain: Gordon Rohlehr, 1990.

———. "We Getting the Kaiso We Deserve: Calypso and the World Music Market". *Drama Review* 42, no. 3 (1988): 82–95.

Said, Edward. *Orientalism.* New York: Pantheon, 1978.

Schlesinger, Andrew. *Signal Processors.* Milwaukee: Hal Leonard, 1998.

Shapiro, Peter. *The Rough Guide to Hip Hop.* London: Rough Guides, 2001.

Small, Geoff. *Ruthless: The Global Rise of the Yardies.* London: Warner, 1995.

Sokol, Mike. "Mixing Board Basics: Part I". *TV Technology Magazine*, April 1997. http://www.modernrecording.com/articles/soundav/link25.html.

Southern, Eileen. *The Music of Black Americans: A History.* 2nd ed. New York: Norton, 1983.

Stolzoff, Norman. *Wake the Town and Tell the People: Dancehall Culture in Jamaica.* Durham, NC: Duke University Press, 2000.

Stone, Allucquere Roseanne. *The War of Desire and Technology at the End of the Mechanical Age.* Boston: MIT Press, 1995.

Stuempfle, Stephen. *The Steelband Movement: The Forging of a National Art in Trinidad and Tobago.* Kingston, Jamaica: University of the West Indies Press, 1995.

Théberge, Paul. *Any Sound You Can Imagine: Making Music/Consuming Technology.* Hanover, NH: Wesleyan University Press, 1997.

Trubitt, David, ed. *Concert Sound: Tours, Techniques and Technology.* Milwaukee: Hal Leonard, 1993.

———, ed. *Making Music with Your Computer.* Emeryville, Calif.: EM Books, 1993.

Tucker, Jim. *Amp Basics.* Milwaukee: Hal Leonard, 1998.

UNAIDS. "UNAIDS Fact Sheet: Latin America and the Caribbean". 11 November 2003. http://www.unaids.org/EN/other/functionalities/Search.asp.

Vail, Mark. *Vintage Synthesizers.* San Francisco: Miller Freeman, 2000.

van Koningsbruggen, Peter. *Trinidad Carnival: A Quest for National Identity.* London: Macmillan, 1997.

Walser, Robert. "Forging Masculinity: Heavy-Metal Sounds and Images of Gender". In *Sound and Vision: The Music Video Reader,* edited by Simon Frith, Andrew Goodwin and Lawrence Grossberg, 153–81. London: Routledge, 1993.

Warner, Keith Q. *On Location: Cinema and Film in the Anglophone Caribbean.* London: Macmillan, 2000.

———. *The Trinidad Calypso: A Study of the Calypso as Oral Literature.* London: Heinemann, 1982.

Weber, Tom, and Brian Jahn. *Reggae Island: Jamaican Music in the Digital Age.* Kingston, Jamaica: Kingston Publishers, 1992.

Williams, Raymond. *Problems in Materialism and Culture: Selected Essays.* London: New Life, 1980.

Discography

Track 2: Sounding Calypso's Muted Tracks, Past and Present: Barbados + St Lucia

Jaunty. *Hop*. Spice Island SI 0055, 1994.

Merrymen. *Greatest Hits*. Wirl 1047, 1994.

Ruk A Tuk International. *Traditional Tuk Band Music of Barbados*. Wirl WK 335, 1991.

Various. *Ambassadores Kalaloo*. 1995.

Various. *The Barbados Folk Singers, Vol. 1*. Wirl 1006, 1964.

Various. *Carnival Fever, Vol. 1*. EBon PD006, 1997.

Various. *Musical Traditions of St Lucia*. Smithsonian/Folkways 40416, 1993.

Various. *Soca Gold, Vol. 1*. Jetstar HVCD015, 1992.

Various. *Soca Zouk Express*. Ashwax M99519, 1997.

Track 3: Towards a Caribbean Gospel Aesthetic

Davis, Carlene. *Vessel*. VP Records 1517-2, 1999.

———. "This Island Needs Jesus". *Redeemed*. VP Records 1603, 2000.

Grace Thrillers. *Can't Even Walk*. Grace Thrillers Music GT012, 1994.

Inter School Christian Fellowship Graduate Ministries. *Mystery*. ISCF 001, 1985.

Lloyd, Jerry. *Lemme Go (Release Me)*. JL, 1996.

King Obstinate. *Praises the Lord*. Greenbay Records GS001, 1999.

———. *The Annointed*. Greenbay Records GS003, 2000.

Papa San. *Victory*. B-Rite Music 2147483647, 1999.

Project H&T. *Hallelujah Beat*. Pro sound 001, 1990.

Promise. *Safari Search*. Wirl K225, 1984.

Regis, Reverend Peter. *Confident and Strong*. Tehilla Music TM003, 1994.

Sanchez. *Who Is This Man*. VP Records 1538, 1999.

Shine the Light. *Arise Wake Up O Sleepers*. JB 14348, 1998.

———. *I'm Blessed*. STL 34207, 1999.

King Short Shirt. *Jesus Touched Me*. 2000.

Stitchie. *Real Power*. Lion of Zion LZD6513, 2000.

Various. *Reggae Gospel Mix Vol. 1*. MGM MG 006, 1999.

Wesleyan Chorale of Barbados. *The Victory Is Ours*. DWYCB, 95–1, 1995.

Track 4: Discourses on AIDS (+ Sex) in Caribbean Music

Ambassadors. "Pray AIDS and Drugs Away". *We'll Survive*. Ambassadors Gospel Group, 1995.

Arrow. "Death For Sale". *Zombie Soca*. Arrow 035.CA, 1991.

Banton, Buju. "Boom Bye Bye". On Various, *Boom Bye Bye*. VP Records 1267, 1992.

———. "Willy (Don't Be Silly)". *Voice of Jamaica*. Mercury 314518013-4, 1993.

Beckett. "Stranger Man". *10th Anniversary*. Cocoa PT 0700, 1985.

Elephant Man. "Log On". *Log On*. Greensleeves, 36012662, 2001.

Gabby. "De List". *One in the Eye*. Ice BGI 1001, 1986.

Lieutenant Stitchie. *Rude Boy*. Atlantic 7 82479-4, 1993.

Mighty Sparrow. "Ah 'Fraid the AIDS". *A Touch of Class*. B's BSR- SP 041, 1985/86.

Ram, Peter. "Dangerous Test". Wirl LP006, 1992.

Shabba Ranks. *Caan Dun: The Best of Shabba Ranks*. VP Records VPCT 1450, 1995.

T.O.K. "Chi Chi Man". *My Crew My Dawgs*. VP Records 1632, 2001.

Touch. "A Sex World". *c*.1993.

Track 5: Finding the New Hardcore in Caribbean Music

Arrow. *Heat*. Dynamic DY 3434, 1983.

———. *Soca Savage*. LONLP 9820297-1, 1984.

———. *Deadly*. Arrow 027, 1985.

Beckett. "Stranger Man". *10th Anniversary*. Cocoa PT 0700, 1985.

Black Stalin. *Rebellion*. Ice Records 931302, 1994.

Gabby. *One in the Eye*. Ice Records BGI 1001, 1986.

Grynner. *The Road March King*. Ice Records ICE-1989, 1989.

Gypsy. "Caribbean Spirit-Song of Me Land". *Life.* MRS 3588, 1988.

Jacobs, Carl, and Carol Jacobs. *We Wanna Live.* Ice Records 203, 1987.

Montano, Machel. *Too Young to Soca.* Ice Records 12021, 1986.

Natasha. "De Mass in We". *Introducing Ms Natasha Wilson.* M+M MM 0010, 1987.

Slingshot. *Jump for Carnival.* Tropical Waves 1002, 2003.

Superblue. *Flag Party.* Ice Records 931502, 1994.

Tears for Fears. "Cold". *Elemental.* Mercury 514875, 1993.

Various. *Fire in de Wave.* Ice Records 941502, 1994.

Various. *Ringbang Rebel Dance.* Ice Records 951902, 1995.

Videos

Magnificent Seven. "Under Wata Medley". Dir. Kevin Lee. VP Records/K. Licious Music, 2000.

Kindred. "Ha Da Dey". Rituals Music/New Hope Entertainment, 1999.

Montano, Machel, and Xtatic. "Torro Torro". Musicrama, 1998.

———. "Outa Space". VP Records, 1999.

Track 6: Music Video to Web Streaming: Cultural Ventriloquism @ the Leading Edge

Beenie Man. *Art and Life.* Virgin Records 2147483647, 2000.

Belafonte, Harry. *Calypso.* RCA Victor LPM 1248, 1956.

Busta Rhymes (featuring Sean Paul). "Make It Clap". J Records 76500302, 2003.

Jay-Z (featuring Sean Paul). "What They Gonna Do". *The Blueprint 2.* Def Jam 063381, 2002.

Videos

Beenie Man. "Feel It Boy". Dir. Dave Meyers. EMI, 2002. http://www.beenieman.net/jukebox/lo/index.html.

Bounty Killer. "Benz and Bimma". TVT/A+M, 1996.

Bounty Killer (featuring Barrington Levy). "Living Dangerously". Breakaway/Navarre, 1996.

Buju Banton. "Make My Day". Polygram, 1993.

Bush. "Glycerine". Dir. Kevin Kerslake. Trauma/Interscope, 1996.

Capleton. "Never Get Down". Dir. Kevin Lee/Ras Kassa. Wall Street Records, 1999.

Chaka Demas and Pliers. "Murder She Wrote". Mango/Island, 1992.

Collective Soul. "The World I Know". Dir. Guy Guillet. WEA/Atlantic, 1995.

Deep Blue Something. "Breakfast at Tiffany's". Dir. Scott Kalvert. Rainmaker Records; Interscope Records, 1995.

Elephant Man. "Pon de River". Dir. Gil Green. VP Records, 2003.

Green Day. "Brain Stew/Jaded". Dir. Kevin Kerslake. Reprise Records, 1996. http://www.greenday.com/videos.php3.

I Jah Bones. "One Love in a Jah House". Dir. Ras Asher. Builders Label, c.1999.

Lady Saw. "I Don't Need to Know". VP Records, 1997.

Lieutenant Stitchie. "Prescription". Atlantic, 1991.

Mr Vegas. "Heads High". Dir. Fatima Robinson, Joe Rey. Greensleeves, 1999.

Oasis. "Wonderwall". Dir. Nigel Dick. Creation/Epic, 1995.

Osborne, Joan. "One of Us". Dir. Mark Seliger and Fred Woodward. Mercury, 1995.

Patra. "Think (About It)". Epic/Sony, 1993

———. "Pull Up to My Bumper". Dir. David Nelson. Epic/Sony, 1995.

Paul, Sean. "Get Busy". Dir. Little X. Atlantic, 2003.

———. "Gimme the Light". Dir. Little X. Atlantic, 2003.

Presidents of the United States of America. "Lump". Dir. Roman Coppola. Columbia, 1995.

Red Hot Chilli Peppers. "My Friends". Dir. Anton Corbijn. Warner, 1995.

Shabba Ranks. *Naked and Ready* (VHS). Sony/Columbia, 1992.

———. "Ting-a-Ling". Epic/Sony, 1993.

———. "Mr Lover Man". Epic/Sony, 1995.

———. "Shine Eye Gal". Epic/Sony, 1995.

Shaggy (featuring Brian and Tony Gold). "Hey Sexy Lady". Dir. Anniti J. MCA Records, 2002.

Smashing Pumpkins. "Bullet with Butterfly Wings". Dir. Samuel Bayer. Chrysalis, 1995.

Super Cat. "Girlstown". Dir. Guy Guillet. Sony/Columbia, 1995.

Terror Fabulous. "Gangsta Anthem". East/West America, 1994.

Wonder, Wayne. "No Letting Go". Dir. Little X. Atlantic, 2003.

Yami Bolo. "Too Much Blood Stain". Dir. Wayne "Lonesome" Brown. Run Things Label, c.2000.

Track 7: The "Big Technology" Question

Beckett. "Stranger Man". *10th Anniversary*. Cocoa PT0700, 1985.

Campbell, Desmond. *Calypso Variations*. Wirl, DKC 001, 1987.

Crazy. "Nani Wine". *Nani Wine*. Trinity Records, TR001, 1989.

Dublin, Godfrey. "To Take Away". VP Records 16110, 2001

Ivory. "Print Out". *Print Out* WIRL CASS TL 002, 1984.

Lyttle, Kevin. "Turn Me On". On Various, *D'Soca Zone, 2nd Wave*. VP Records 1633, 2002.

London Beat. "I've Been Thinking about You". *In the Blood*. Universal AARARD10192, 1991.

Maddzart, "Poor People Song". Dimensions, 2001.

McDonald, Michael. "No Looking Back". *Cry Sweet Freedom*. Warner 2292410492, 1986.

Oliver, Allan. "Friends of Freedom". 1988.

———. "Pappy". 1988.

Second Avenue. "Here Comes the Rain Again". *The Time Is Right*. SA 002, 1988.

Tears for Fears. "Shout". *Songs from the Big Chair*. Polygram 824300, 1985.

Touch. "Back Off". *Back Off*. Wirl W1051, 1988.

———. "Jam Dem". *Brilliance*. Wirl W294, 1989.

Williams, Cornelius. "Hairy Bank". 2001. On Various, *D'Soca Zone, 2nd Wave*. VP Records 1633, 2002

———. "Chucking". On Various, *D'Soca Zone: 3rd Wave*. VP Records 1655, 2003.

———. "Poorsah". On Various, *D'Soca Zone: 3rd Wave*. VP Records 1655, 2003.

Winwood, Steve. "Back in the High Life". *Back in the High Life*. Island CID9844, 1986.

Index

ADAT, 203, 215
Adisa, 138, 142
AIDS. *See* HIV/AIDS
Ajamu, 149
Akai, 198, 204, 210
Akwa, 48
Alesis, 191, 198, 202, 203
Allamby, Da Costa, 28
Alleyne, Mike, 115–116
Altman, Rick, 153
Ambassadors, 47, 108, 246
Amplification, 188, 190, 192, 193, 194, 235
Amplifier, 188, 189, 190, 194, 235
Analogue, 120, 146, 185, 212
Anthems, 61
Anthony B, 106, 108
Antigua, 34, 143, 196
  dance songs, 101
  gospel, 81, 84, 86
  synthesized brass tones, 209
Arrow, 100, 118, 126, 127, 128
  application of rock aesthetics, 141
  arrangers, 129
  format for soca recordings, 130
Artists Against Aids, 113
Ashanti, 33, 37, 38
Atilla the Hun, 16, 17, 25, 26, 149
Atlantic, 196
Atlantic Records, 145, 176, 181

Bachelor, 38
Bahamas, 86, 87, 88
Bailey, Judy, 80

Baldhead, 143
Ballosingh, Nicole, 84
Ballosingh-Holder, 56
Banja, 24–31
Barbadian Popular Music, 64, 118, 119, 136, 226
Barbados, 196
  Artists Against Aids, 113
  calypso, 10, 19–31, 34, 95
    artists, 120
    early signs of, 19–21
    impact on Trinidad, 12–13
    instruments, 21–22
    tuk band, 22–23
  church music, 59
  gospel, 81, 88
  music producers, 216
  post-soca, 133
  soca, 133
  synthesized brass tones, 209
Barbados's Crop Over. *See* Crop Over
Barbuda, 81
Barlow, John Perry, 4
Baron, 99
Battle Axe, 32
Beckett, 17, 101, 125, 149, 208
Beenie Man, 106, 145, 177, 178
Belafonte, Harry, 149
Belasco band, 24, 148
Belfon, Denise, 102
Belize, 87
Bermuda, 87
BET, 83, 176
Bickler, David, 132

Birthright, 66
Black, Herb, 33, 43
Black, Peter, 143
Black Pawn, 33, 37
Black Pearl, 48
Black Stalin, 133, 246
Blacksand, 196, 214
Blue Wave Studio, 124–130, 134, 136, 141, 214
    bass-guitar patterns, 139
    early post-soca experiments, 130
Bolo, Yami, 174
Bounty Killer, 106, 112, 155, 177, 212
    music video, 168
Bouyon, 142
Brito, Phil, 30
Brown, Foxxy, 113
Brown, Jazbo, 15
Buju Banton, 105, 106, 112, 170
Bumba, 37
Burning Flames, 101, 143, 196
Bush, 161, 164

Call and response, 19
Calypso, 2, 3, 188
    Barbados, 10, 19–21
    commentary, 11
    defending, 103
    defined, 15, 17
    etymology of, 15–16
    extemporaneous performance, 18
    live vs. recorded, 34
    lyrics, 38
    picong, 18
    recorded vs. live, 34
    role of women in, 48
    satire, 18
    soca and, 35
    St Lucia, 10, 19
    technological evolution, 117
    technology and, 115
    tents, 46
    Trinidad, 3
Calypso Rose, 141

Calypsonian
    calypso singer vs., 49
    female, 50
Campbell, Desmond ("Kalabash"), 209
Capleton, 106, 174
Caribbean Christian Artistes Network, 74
Caribbean Festival of Creative Arts, 29
Caribbean Satellite Network (CSN), 167
Casio, 121, 209, 234
Catholicism, 55, 59
Ce'Cile, 178, 180
Center for Black Music Research, 55
Chaka Demus and Pliers, 155, 169
Chalkdust, 36, 144
Change, 56
Charmer, 18, 27, 28
Cheryl and Colours, 33, 36, 48
    reputation, 49
    social commitment, 50–52
    standards for material, 49
"Chi chi man", 106–107, 108
Christafiri, 86
Christian music, gospel vs., 55
Chutney, 142
Clarke, Adrian, 38
Collective Soul, 164, 248
Communication(s), 2, 48, 229, 232
    control, 89
    developments, 5
    Internet as medium of, 89
    networks, 68
    St Lucia, 48
    technology, 86
Compact disc, 2, 204, 206
    recorders, 205
Competition winners, 37–38
Compilations, 46, 112, 143
    gospel, 85
    tent, 47
Composer
    calypso, 28
    gospel, 74, 75, 76, 77, 79, 80

Composer (continued)
　　Grenadian, 209
　　male, 49
　　relationship with performer, 49
Computer, 177, 179–180, 200
　　computer music, 200–207, 209,
　　　219
Connectivity, 5, 201
Cooper, Carolyn, 3
Copyright, 74, 149
Crazy, 139, 197
Cricket, 114
Crop Over, 11, 30, 37, 95, 118, 122
Crossover, 80, 209
Crouch, Andre, 58
Crowded House, 186
Crowley, John, 3
Cutting edge
　　effect, 3
　　lack of criticism of issues at, 2
　　technology, role of, 6
Cybercriticism, 181
Cybercriticue, 181
Cyberculture, 3, 4–6, 179
Cybertheory, 5, 181

Dancehall music, 166–169
　　Jamaican, 3
　　music video, 3, 167
　　in prevention of AIDS, 110
　　reggae-style, 167
　　sex and, 101, 103
　　soca and, 135
　　technology and, 6, 7, 115
　　video, 3, 155, 157, 167, 172
Daniel, Sean, 81–82, 84, 109
Davis, Carlene, 48, 66, 81
De Controller, 37
De Professor, 37, 39, 40, 46
　　moral commentary, 104
Deep Blue Something, 161, 164, 169
Degree, 180
de Leon, Raphael. See Roaring Lion
Dempster, Sanell, 143

Destra, 102
Destroyer, 37
Devonte, 176
Dickson, William, 20
Digital technology, 5, 6, 71, 121, 130,
　　161, 215, 231, 234, 235
　　sampling, 211
Dixon, Jessie, 58
Dominica, 89
Dorsey, Thomas, 57
Dove Award, categories, 55
Downloads, 179, 216
Dragonaires, 143, 196
Dread, 143
Dread and the Baldhead, 117
Drug(s)
　　culture, 47
　　HIV and, 93, 94, 95
　　intravenous use, 94
　　pushers, 51
　　songs against, 44, 75, 108, 246
　　traffickers, 137
Drum(s), 124, 125–133, 195–199
　　acoustic, 196
　　electronic, 196
　　machines, 199, 198
　　ringbang, 125
Dynamic force, 87

Educator, 37, 38, 44–45
Elephant Man, 107, 178, 212
Engineers (sound), 6, 73, 122, 140,
　　215
Ensoniq, 71, 204, 206, 210, 211, 234
Entertainment
　　artist control by industry, 175
　　computer as source of, 6, 152
　　developments, 5, 150
　　frontier, 175
　　global culture, 174
　　institutions, 22
　　international industry, 107, 150
　　live packages, 223
　　major companies, 157

as social messenger, 110
  via Internet, 152
Equalizers, 205
Evangelicals, 55, 56, 59, 60, 62, 64, 75
Exploitation, 3
Explosion Band, 143
Ezi, 18

Fanon, Frantz, 156–157
Faulty camera, 163–164
Female artists, 33, 102
Fireman Hooper, 117, 143, 146
  energy and innovation, 147
Flames, 56, 67
Folk songs, 15, 17, 23, 24, 96, 148,
  184
4de People, 174
Franklin, Chevelle, 84
Franklin, Kurt, 81, 83

Gabby, 18, 24, 37, 38, 120, 149
  AIDS commentary, 95, 98–99
  use of drums, 125
  use of piano, 132
  use of technology, 125, 130
Gardner, Sherwin, 56, 66, 82, 84
Garlin, Bunji, 143
Gay. See Homosexuality
George, Iwer, 41, 143
Globalization, 74, 76, 220, 232
Goddard, Pelham, 129
Golden Star Band, 24
Goodwin, Harella, 56
Gospel, composers, 74, 75, 76, 77,
  79, 80
Gospel Comforters, 66
Gospel Motion, 86
Gospel music, 2, 3
  American vs. Caribbean, 55
  anti-drug songs, 75, 108, 246
  audience, 54
  Caribbean, 3, 54–90
    features of, 63–64
  chorales, 56, 69
  Christian music vs., 56

culture, 3
  defined, 54, 55–56, 61–62
  Dove Awards, 55
  evolution, 55
  Grammy Awards, 55
  increasing sophistication of, 58
  lyrics, 74–80
  popularity, 63
  post-soca and -dancehall beats, 84
  radio programmes, 88
  secular music vs., 54
Gospel Pearls, 57
Gospelypso, 82
Grace Thrillers, 56, 66, 86
Grammy Award, 181
  for gospel, 55
Grant, Darron, 216
Grant, Eddy, 118, 119, 126, 129, 134,
  216
Greaves, Vasco, 77
Green, Al, 58
Green Day, 161
Grenada, 102, 143
  calypso, 34
  church music, 59
  gospel, 82, 87, 88, 89
  synthesized brass tones, 209
Gros Jean, 16
Grynner, 13, 37, 120, 121, 122, 134
  application of rock aesthetics, 141
  use of technology, 125, 133
Guitar, 141, 191–195
Guyana, 110, 114
  music producers, 217
Gypsy, 95, 125

Hammond, Beres, 155, 174, 176
Hardcore, 9, 69
  gospel presentation, 81
  soca, 7, 72, 82, 115–147
  social commentary, 30
Hardware, 5, 123, 130, 190, 200,
  216, 218
  upgrades, 204

Highest Praise, 80
Hinds, Alison, 102
Hinkson, Boo. *See* Hinkson, Ronald "Boo"
Hinkson, Ronald "Boo", 33, 34–35, 49, 216
Hip Hop, 106, 107
Hippolyte, Kendel, 12
HIV/AIDS, 91–114
    high risk groups, 93, 94
    homosexuality and, 97, 100
    impact, 91
    pan-Caribbean partnership against, 92
    prevention, 110–114
    shifting attitudes regarding, 94
Homophobia, 3, 103–110
Homosexuality, 93, 94
    AIDS and, 97, 100
    dancehall artists abhorrence of, 104–105
    GLAAD, 105
Houdini, 24, 25
Hybrid forms, 12, 31, 44
    calypso, 12, 31, 35, 44
    gadgetry, 176
    legitimizing, 39

I Jah Bones, 174
Ice records, 120, 121, 122, 124, 132, 133, 134, 135, 138, 144, 231
Identity, 14, 67, 64, 172, 213
Image(s), 49, 75, 81, 113
    biblical, 57, 77, 78, 85
    creation of, 52
    interaction with sound, 154
    macho heterosexual, 106
    in music videos, 104
    in packaged performance, 151
    rebuilding, 65
    sound loops and, 124
    television, 147
Independence, 37
Inferior, 37

Instrument(s). *See also* Drum(s); Synthesizers
    band, 23
    brass, 34
    "dry," 140
    early, 21
    electronic musical, 188
    in folk churches, 57
    in gospel ensembles, 62
    linking sound instruments through MIDI, 166
    multi-timbral, 8
    precussion, 31
    range of, balance in, 128
    in ringbang, 119, 132
    soca, 141
    state-of-the-art, 21–22, 183
    synthesized, 34, 35
    technological, 117
    users, 183
Internet, 2, 4–6, 146, 175, 180
    entertainment via, 152
    impact of, 4
    as medium of communication, 86
    Underground Music Archive, 87
    World Wide Web *vs.*, 5
Invader, 18, 32, 33, 37, 38, 117, 143, 149. *See* Lord Invader
Iscf ministries, 74
Ivory, 208

Jackson, Mahalia, 58
Jackson, Michael, 42, 102
Jacobs, Carl, 124–125, 133, 139
Jacobs, Carol, 125, 133
Jah Pinckney, 87
Jahrusalem, 218
Jamaica, 196
    church music, 59
    gospel, 81
    music producers, 216
    synthesized brass tones, 209
Jaunty, 42–44, 120, 143, 146

Jazz, 15, 33, 73
Joel, Billy, 138
Johnny ma Boy, 37
Joseph, Clarence, 33
Joseph, Emmanuel, 64
Judah Development, 56, 84, 85, 86
Jump-and-wave party syndrome, 41
Junior C, 87

Kalinda, 26
Kid Site, 37
Kindred, 144
King, John, 24, 37
King Ellie Matt, 143, 146, 149
Kirton, Jiggs, 24
Kitchener, 27, 36
Korg, 194, 208, 212, 218
Kurzweil, 34–35, 219

Lady Leen, 36, 48
Lady Saw, 102, 176, 178, 181
Lady Spice, 36, 38
Lady Strong, 50
Landship, 15
Lee, Byron, 117, 196
Lewis, Charles D., 24
Liar, 37
Licorish, Lionel, 24
Lieutenant Stitchie. See Stitchie
Ligon, Richard, 20
Lil Man, 81
Lion of Zion Entertainment, 86
Little Baron, 37
Lloyd, Jerry, 56, 82
Lord Carro, 33, 37
Lord Invader, 26
Lord Jackson, 33, 37
Lord Kitchener, 27, 36
Lord Melody, 26, 29
Lord Radio, 18
Lord Shorty, 118
Lord Zandolie, 37
L.T. Stitchie. See Stitchie

Lyons, Faye-Ann, 102
Lyrics, 2, 74–80
Lyttle, Kevin, 178, 215, 216

Mad Anju, 178
Madam Sequin, 33
Maddzart, 212, 215
Manuel, Peter, 3
Marshall, Trevor, 19
Mary G, 33, 36
    as artist, 48
    reputation, 49
    as social commentator, 48
Matt, Ellie, 32
McIntosh, Frankie, 33, 41, 129
Merrymen, 28
MIDI, 166, 199–200, 218
Mighty Bake, 32
Mighty Barrie, 37
Mighty Cobra, 32
Mighty Desper, 37
Mighty Dragon, 37
Mighty Killer, 28
Mighty Pelay, 37, 38
Mighty Pep, 33, 37, 38, 40–42
Mighty Prince, 37
Mighty Sparrow. See Sparrow
Mighty Terra, 28, 29, 32, 33, 37
Monophony, 207, 208, 223
Montano, Machel, 117, 120, 132, 139, 143, 144, 212
Montserrat, 68, 100
    synthesized brass tones, 209
Monty G, 84, 86
Morgan Heritage, 174
MPEG, 178
MP3, 86, 87, 176
Mr Vegas, 145, 173–174
MTV, 152, 168, 176, 180
Multi-track layering, 7
Multi-track reading, 6, 7
Multi-track recording, 121, 123
Multitimbrality, 209, 223
    polyphony vs., 8

Music
  alternatives, 14
  dissemination, 3
  live *vs.* recorded, 2
  lyrics and, 2
  production, 3
  religious *vs.* secular, 3
  sound *vs.* video, 2–3
  traditional *vs.* innovative, 3
Music-swapping, 179
Music video, 2–3, 152, 154
  images in, 104
  Internet transmitted, 152
  lack of autonomy, 159
  potential of, 174
  sex and, 167
  stark realism of, 157
  weakness of, 167

Nadiege, 48
Napster, 179
Narrative, 28, 156, 157
Niles, Joseph, 64– 65

Oasis, 164, 165, 187
Obstinate, 81, 139, 149
Opel, Jackie, 14, 24
Organization for Economic
  Cooperation and Development,
  220

Pace, Adger, 61
Papa San, 56, 66, 81, 84, 85
Patra, 84, 103, 104, 169, 170, 171, 177
Paul, Leston, 126, 129
Paul, Sean, 176, 177, 179
Pelay, 19, 33, 36, 149
Pentecostalism, 15, 60, 66
Pep, 33, 37, 38, 40–42
Performance
  calypso, 16, 18–19, 26, 27
  composition and, 49
  dancehall, 176
  folk, 192
  gospel, 82, 84, 87

  packaged, 151
  post-soca, 101, 145, 147
  reggae, 193
  soca, 41, 101, 102, 103, 104, 105
  video, 113
Peter Ram, 110
Phillips, Kenny, 216
Physical modelling synthesizers, 219
Picong, 18
Pinckard, George, 21, 23
Planet sound, 126, 128
Policy
  culture, 30, 212
Politics, 134, 138, 142, 156, 160, 175,
  181, 182, 220, 223
Polyphony, 7
  multitimbrality *vs.*, 8
Poorsah, 146, 147, 215
Popular culture, 2
  studies, 10
Popular music, 1
Post-dancehall, 84, 220
Post-hip hop, 178
Post-soca, 84, 101, 115, 118, 220
  band, 103
  defending, 103
  drums in, 120
  early experiments, 130
  in gospel, 84
  mix, 131
  producers, 127
  support for, 207
Power, 3, 4, 5, 53, 117, 130, 150
  of calypso singer, 19
  of drums, 134
  gender and, 156
  of homosexuals, 105
  of multitrack recording, 3, 4, 5, 53,
    117, 121
  surrendering, 159
  of technology, 34, 123, 130, 159
Praise and worship, 87
Presidents of the United States of
  America, 161

Primus, Kelisha, 87
Prodigal Son, 82, 84, 85
Producer, 37
Project Band, 78
Promise, 68, 211
Prophet Haggai, 37

Quantization, 214, 217
Quevedo, Raymond. *See* Atilla the Hun

Radio, 2, 150
    call-in programmes, 103
Radio stations, 88, 89
Ragamuffin, 6, 116
Ragga, 7, 135
    technology and, 7
Raggasoca, 2, 135, 136, 142
    technology, 6
Rapso, 142, 144
Ras Shorty, 118
Reasons, 196
Reaves, Karen, 77
Rebel, 149
Reconciled, 87
Recording
    analogue, 202, 210, 212
    digital, 202
    hard-disk, 203–204
Recording industry, 148
Red Hot Chili Peppers, 161, 166
Red Plastic Bag, 19, 24, 37, 38, 122
Red Rat, 112
Regenerated Singers, 56, 66
Reggae, 2, 14, 189
    interface with other styles, 116
    technological evolution, 116
Religious song, 59
Representation, 211
    music video as artistic, 172
    popular music as cultural, 157
    symbolic, 171
Reverend Peter Regis, 74, 76
Reverend V. B., 56, 67

Rhythm Express, 167, 174
Richards, Noel ("Professor"), 82
Ringbang, 2, 133, 142
    defined, 119
    emergence of, 120
    soca *vs.*, 134
    soft, 136
    songs, 120
    technology and, 6
Rita, 37
Roaring Lion, 16, 149
Robbie, 33, 41
    as social commentator, 48
Rock
    music video, 3
Rockwell, 102
Rohlehr, Gordon, 3, 17, 35
Roland, 74, 194, 195, 217, 218, 219
Romeo, 37
Roots to Popular Culture, 75, 226, 230
Royal Priesthood, 82
Rudder, David, 17–18, 103
Rupee, 146

Sampling, 31, 187, 210–211
Samplers, 7, 210–211
Satellite, 82, 83, 150, 180
Satire, 18, 99
Scott, Cleve, 214–216
Scripture, 63, 64, 66, 80, 97
Scrubb, 32
SCSI, 199–200
Secular artists, conversion to Christianity, 81
Secular music, 54, 67, 70, 83
Seon, Rowan, 40
Sequencers, 7
Serenaders, 37
Sex, 96
    abstinence *vs.*, 85
    dancehall music and, 101
    music video and, 155, 167
    soca and, 100
Sexuality. *See* Sex

Shabba Ranks, 84, 105, 107, 169, 170, 177
Shaggy, 144, 178
Shakademus and Pliers, 155, 169
Shilling, 27
Shine the Light, 56, 77
Short Shirt, 81, 139, 149
Signal processors, 206, 235
Silvertones, 68, 86
Simpson, A. G., 36
Simulation, 160, 172, 182, 198, 215
Singing Francine, 102
Sir Don, 30, 37
Sister Margreta Marshall, 56, 66
Sizzla, 106, 180
Slackness, 85, 103. 104, 155, 168
Slaves, 23
Small Island Pride, 27, 28
Smashing Pumpkin, 161, 164, 165
Smith, Wayne, 121
Soca, 2, 17, 126, 129
    boundaries, 147
    calypso and, 35
    conventional mix, 131
    dancehall and, 135
    defending, 103
    divas, 101–102
    drum pattern, 127
    format for recordings, 130
    hardcore, 7, 72
    ringbang vs., 134
    sex and, 100
    stereophonic soundscape, 130
    technology and, 7, 115, 119
    Trinidadian, 41
    video, 155
Socretes, 111
Software, 5, 130, 200, 204, 215, 216, 218
Sound loop, 124, 210
Soundscape, 130
Southern, Eileen, 57
Southern, National Baptist Convention, 57
Sparrow, 95, 149

Spice, 196
Spouge, 14, 68
Spragga Benz, 180
Square One, 117, 133, 136
    application of rock aesthetics, 141
St Kitts and Nevis, 89, 111, 143
    calypso, 32, 34
St Lucia, 110, 111, 143, 189, 196
    calypso, 10, 19, 31–47, 104
        history of, 12
        hybrid form, 31, 35–47
    commentary calypso, 11
    communications, 48
    music producers, 216
    play songs, 20
    post-soca, 46
    soca, 46
    synthesized brass tones, 209
St Maarten, 143
St Vincent, 101, 109, 117, 129, 196, 214
    church music, 34
    gospel music, radio programmes featuring, 88
    music producers, 216
State-of-the-art, 183
    instruments and gadgetry, 183
    sound-mixing console, 6, 222
    technology, 185, 187, 200
Steelpan, 198, 208, 213
Stellar Award, 84
Stick-fighting bands, 26
Stitchie, 81, 84, 85, 170
    conversion to Christianity, 104
Studio, 6, 34. See also Blue Wave Studio
    home-recording, 73
Sumfest, 103
Super Cat, 172–173, 176
Super P, 102, 143
Super Sweet, 111
Superblue, 41, 120, 133, 134, 139
Survivor, 132
Sutherland, Elaine, 87
Synclavier, 121–122

Synthesizers, 7, 121–122, 146, 193, 207–212

Tallpree, 143
Tanto Metro, 176
Tascam, 201, 202–203, 214, 215
TC Brown, 38
Tears for Fears, 141, 196, 213
Technology, 7, 115–119
    sound-loop, 124
Telescriptions, 152
Televangelism, 82–83, 137
Television, 2, 10, 150, 175
culture, 3
    as means of projecting Caribbean images, 147
Television stations, 83, 176
Terra Fabulous, 169
The Cure, 187
The Man C.P., 117
Theory, 91, 151–154
Third Exodus Singers, 87
Tiko and Gitta, 82, 86, 183
T.O.K., 106, 107, 176
Touch, 109, 117
Track recording, 121, 189, 203
Tricky, 18, 33, 44–45
    as social commentator, 48
Trinidad/Tobago, 12–15, 117, 134, 196
    Barbadian calypsonians in, 24
    calypso, 24, 95
    church music, 59
    gospel, 81, 88
    music producers, 216
    post-emancipation, 17
    radio talk show, 108
    soca, 41
    social commentary, 99
    synthesized brass tones, 209
Trinity Broadcasting Network (TBN), 83
Tru Tones, 33
True-true reality, 160, 163, 164, 166, 167, 169

Tuk band, 22–23, 32
Tweaking, 185

Van Koningsbruggen, Peter, 3
Vaughn, J. W. and J. D., 61
Ventriloquism, 154–158
Video, 147
    clips, 147, 152, 157, 180–181
    games, 160
    networks, 167
    on-demand,175
Viking Thunder, 133, 134–135, 137, 138
Viper, 95, 96–97, 98, 109
Virtual analogue, 120, 146, 185, 216, 219
    technology, 160
Voice of Life, 89
VP Records, 176, 177

Walker, Albertina, 58
Ward Sisters, 58
Watson, Ed, 129
Web streaming, 180, 182, 231, 247
Wesleyan chorale, 71, 246
Wilkinson, Mike, 29, 37
Wilson, Natasha, 125
Women, 3, 47–52
Wonder, Wayne, 176, 181, 248
Word of faith, 83, 227, 242
Workstation, 34, 77, 190, 204, 211–212
World music, 35, 74, 120, 143, 176, 186, 226, 231, 243
World Trade Organization, 184, 220
World Wide Web, 2, 4, 5
    Internet vs., 5

X-rated, 169–175
Xtatik, 103, 146

Yamaha, 194, 218, 219
Yearwood, Edwin, 37

Zouk, 188